Shakespeare and Textual Theory

RELATED TITLES

ARDEN SHAKESPEARE AND THEORY

Series Editor: Evelyn Gajowski

AVAILABLE TITLES

FORTHCOMING TITLES

Shakespeare and Textual Theory

Suzanne Gossett

THE ARDEN SHAKESPEARE
LONDON • NEW YORK • OXFORD • NEW DELHI • SYDNEY

THE ARDEN SHAKESPEARE
Bloomsbury Publishing Plc
50 Bedford Square, London, WC1B 3DP, UK
1385 Broadway, New York, NY 10018, USA
29 Earlsfort Terrace, Dublin 2, Ireland

BLOOMSBURY, THE ARDEN SHAKESPEARE and the Arden Shakespeare logo are
trademarks of Bloomsbury Publishing Plc

First published in Great Britain 2022

Copyright © Suzanne Gossett, 2022

Suzanne Gossett has asserted her right under the Copyright, Designs and Patents
Act, 1988, to be identified as the author of this work.

For legal purposes the Acknowledgements on p. xi constitute an extension
of this copyright page.

Series design by Sutchinda Rangsi Thompson
Cover image: Green tea plant, X-ray © Getty Images

A catalogue record for this book is available from the British Library.

A catalog record for this book is available from the Library of Congress.

ISBN: HB: 978-1-3501-2124-9
        PB: 978-1-3501-2123-2
        ePDF: 978-1-3501-2126-3
        eBook: 978-1-3501-2125-6

Series: Shakespeare and Theory

Typeset by RefineCatch Limited, Bungay, Suffolk
Printed and bound in Great Britain

To find out more about our authors and books visit www.bloomsbury.com
and sign up for our newsletters.

CONTENTS

Part Three: Current Debates

Coda: The Immaterial Text

SERIES EDITOR'S PREFACE

'Asking questions about literary texts – that's literary criticism. Asking "Which questions shall we ask about literary texts?" – that's literary theory'. So goes my explanation of the current state of English studies, and Shakespeare studies, in my never-ending attempt to demystify, and simplify, theory for students in my classrooms. Another way to put it is that theory is a systematic account of the nature of literature, the act of writing and the act of reading.

One of the primary responsibilities of any academic discipline – whether in the natural sciences, the social sciences or the humanities – is to examine its methodologies and tools of analysis. Particularly at a time of great theoretical ferment, such as that which has characterized English studies, and Shakespeare studies, in recent years, it is incumbent upon scholars in a given discipline to provide such reflection and analysis.

We all construct meanings in Shakespeare's texts and culture. Shouldering responsibility for our active role in constructing meanings in literary texts, moreover, constitutes a theoretical stance. To the extent that we examine our own critical premises and operations, that theoretical stance requires reflection on our part. It requires honesty, as well. It is thereby a fundamentally radical act. All critical analysis puts into practice a particular set of theoretical premises. Theory occurs from a particular standpoint. There is no critical practice that is somehow devoid of theory. There is no critical practice that is not implicated in theory. A common-sense, transparent encounter with any text is thereby impossible.

Indeed, to the extent that theory requires us to question anew that with which we thought we were familiar, that which we thought we understood, theory constitutes a critique of common sense.

Since the advent of postmodernism, the discipline of English studies has undergone a seismic shift. The discipline of Shakespeare studies has been at the epicentre of this shift. Indeed, it has been Shakespeare scholars who have played a major role in several of the theoretical and critical developments (e.g. new historicism, cultural materialism, presentism) that have shaped the discipline of English studies in recent years. Yet a comprehensive scholarly analysis of these crucial developments has yet to be done, and is long overdue. As the first series to foreground analysis of contemporary theoretical developments in the discipline of Shakespeare studies, *Arden Shakespeare and Theory* aims to fill a yawning gap.

To the delight of some and the chagrin of others, since 1980 or so, theory has dominated Shakespeare studies. *Arden Shakespeare and Theory* focuses on the state of the art at the outset of the twenty-first century. For the first time, it provides a comprehensive analysis of the theoretical developments that are emerging at the present moment, as well as those that are dominant or residual in Shakespeare studies.

Each volume in the series aims to offer the reader the following components: to provide a clear definition of a particular theory; to explain its key concepts; to trace its major developments, theorists and critics; to perform a reading of a Shakespeare text; to elucidate a specific theory's intersection with or relationship to other theories; to situate it in the context of contemporary political, social and economic developments; to analyse its significance in Shakespeare studies; and to suggest resources for further investigation. Authors of individual volumes thereby attempt to strike a balance, bringing their unique expertise, experience and perspectives to bear upon particular theories while simultaneously fulfilling the common purpose of the series. Individual volumes in the Series are devoted to elucidating particular theoretical perspectives, such as adaptation, close reading, critical race theory, cultural materialism, ecocriticism, ecofeminism, economic theory, feminism, film theory, legal theory, new historicism, performance, political theology, postcoloniality, posthumanism, presentism, psychoanalysis, queer theory, reception theory, textual theory, and transgender theory.

Arden Shakespeare and Theory aims to enable scholars, teachers and students alike to define their own theoretical strategies and refine their own critical practices. And students have as much at stake in these theoretical and critical enterprises – in the reading and the writing practices that characterize our discipline – as do scholars and teachers. Janus-like, the series looks forward as well as backward, serving as an inspiration and a guide for new work in Shakespeare studies at the outset of the twenty-first century, on the one hand, and providing a retrospective analysis of the intellectual labour that has been accomplished in recent years, on the other.

To return to the beginning: what is at stake in our reading of literary texts? Once we come to understand the various ways in which theory resonates with not only Shakespeare's texts, and literary texts, but the so-called 'real' world – the world outside the world of the mind, the world outside the world of academia – then we come to understand that theory is capable of powerfully enriching not only our reading of Shakespeare's texts, and literary texts, but our lives.

*   *   *

I am indebted to David Avital, publisher at Bloomsbury Academic, who was instrumental in developing the idea of the *Arden Shakespeare and Theory* series. I am also grateful to Margaret Bartley and Mark Dudgeon, publishers for the Arden Shakespeare, for their guidance and support throughout the development of this series.

Evelyn Gajowski
Series Editor
University of Nevada, Las Vegas

ACKNOWLEDGEMENTS

Many people have helped me write this book. I would like to thank first Evelyn Gajowski, who surprised me with the commission one summer afternoon at an International Shakespeare Conference in Stratford-upon-Avon. My support system while writing has felt robust, despite all the limitations posed by the Covid epidemic. During a dark and lonely pandemic winter, Margaret Bartley at The Arden Shakespeare found time while working from home to read a penultimate draft and convince me that the book was ready. Margaret has been present in so many of my projects – The Arden Shakespeare, Arden Early Modern Drama, *Shakespeare and Textual Theory*, *Shakespeare in Our Time* – that she has become a warm and wonderful friend. I was also encouraged and assisted by Mark Dudgeon and Lara Bateman at The Arden Shakespeare and assisted by my able copyeditor, Mark Fisher. My early readers, whom I cannot thank enough, were my ever-stalwart friends Gordon McMullan, who urged me at all points to think theoretically, and Tiffany Stern, who made suggestions about performance and about the book's potential readers. Both have improved not only this book but my life.

Writing a scholarly book without access to libraries has proved a challenge. Fortunately, when I started this project, pre-Covid, I could still visit the Folger Shakespeare Library as well as Chicago libraries. And as described in the final chapter, contemporary scholars have many digital resources available even during lockdowns. Interlibrary Loan at Loyola University Chicago has diligently supplied materials. But as I look at my own text I find that I am indebted not only to printed and electronic sources but to the many scholars I have encountered and worked with in the course of an active career as a

Shakespearean and an editor. These include people from every stage of my life: G.E. Bentley, Peter Blayney, Martin Butler, Dympna Callaghan, Gabriel Egan, Alan Galey, Adam Hooks, Janelle Jenstad, John Jowett, David Kastan, David Kay, Leah Marcus, Carol Neely, Gail Paster, Gary Taylor, Valerie Wayne, Henry Woudhuysen, and all the editors of the *Norton Shakespeare 3*. Here I will single out only two scholars for special mention: first, Richard Proudfoot, who as editor of the Malone Society long ago encouraged me to send him an edition of a manuscript play I had found in the archives of the Venerable English College in Rome and thirty years later led me through the editing of *Pericles* for the Arden Shakespeare, and second, the late David Bevington, my friend and neighbor, who gave me opportunities to edit Shakespeare's contemporaries, lent me books, invited me on to panels, and in retirement accepted an invitation to write for the SAA collection *Shakespeare in Our Time*. I have been fortunate in my friends and colleagues.

Suzanne Gossett
Loyola University Chicago

Introduction

There is no Shakespeare without text. Other than a few surviving signatures, a number of legal documents, some warm words of praise from fellow dramatists such as Ben Jonson, and bits of gossip from contemporary Stratford and London, 'Shakespeare' means simply the plays and poems that have come down to us. Because this seems self-evident, readers often do not think about the decisions behind the words in the book they hold or the dialogue they hear from the stage. Yet these words, read and heard, have been adjusted, changed, and challenged at least since 1598, when a quarto of *Love's Labour's Lost* was printed with a title page claiming it had been 'Newly corrected and augmented by W. Shakespere', and the following year when a second quarto of *Romeo and Juliet* named no responsible party but similarly announced it was 'Newly corrected, augmented, and amended'. *Shakespeare and Textual Theory* will trace the explanatory underpinnings of these changes through the centuries, with a major focus on twentieth- and twenty-first-century debates.

These theoretical debates have concerned three major topics: 1) the nature (and sometimes the number) of the surviving texts we call Shakespeare's; 2) the relationship of the author 'Shakespeare' to any of these texts; 3) the best or most desirable way to present the texts, i.e. in editions or performances. Many of the issues raised in a study of Shakespeare and textual theory are no different from those raised in a study of Virginia Woolf or Chaucer and textual theory – textual theory is a form of scholarship that can be applied to any author or language – but because of the singular place of Shakespeare in the English-language canon, and because successive textual theories have been developed through and applied first to Shakespeare's works, the relationship of textual theory to this author's works is unparalleled. In English, theoretical work on text, though derived historically from analysis of Biblical and classical texts, has usually focused intently on the works of Shakespeare.

A word about 'theory'. Readers of a book in this series, *Arden Shakespeare and Theory*, are most accustomed to the literary/critical use of the term 'theory' to mean a broad philosophical premise explaining the underpinnings of a swath of literature. For example, a reading of *Romeo and Juliet* based on feminist theory may attempt to demonstrate that the action, although externally concentrated on the moving love story, implicitly supports the power of the patriarchal system in which a young girl who resists her father's desire 'to have her matched' to the man he has chosen will inevitably be led to her death. A cultural materialist reading of the same play might instead concentrate on how the resistance of the two feuding families to the imperative to gain power by uniting their respective heirs leads to an increase in the centralized power of the state as represented by the Duke. Textual theory is different. It is a form of scholarship that focuses most often on developing an informed inference about the nature and history of a surviving text, or, as in the case of *Romeo and Juliet*, two texts that differ and occasionally conflict. The feminist critic may concentrate on the powerlessness of Lady Capulet that leads her to abandon Juliet: 'Talk not to me, for I'll not speak a word'; the textual critic hypothesizes how it came about that in speech prefixes and stage directions this cold parent is identified sometimes as 'Lady', sometimes as 'Old Lady', sometimes as 'Wife', sometimes as 'Mother'.

As we shall see, philosophical premises are often implicit in textual work, and alterations in broad philosophical attitudes, such as happened with the arrival of poststructuralism, have had profound effects on fundamental concepts of textual theory. Nevertheless, much textual theory is primarily concerned with methodology and procedure. In other words, theory, for textual scholars, most often refers to the structured conjectures that book and theatre historians make as they try to understand the implications of printed or manuscript materials. Textual theorists are deeply concerned with evidence in all its forms, whether to argue that an error may have arisen in the printshop or to trace it to an author's manuscript, or to propose that some words in a 'Shakespeare' text were written by another individual or derive from performance. Similarly, book historians examine actual volumes to develop theories about the popularity of genres or the gender of readership.

Many textual theorists, such as the present writer, spend most of their time as editors, where the line between theory and practice is often permeable. For editors, theory becomes a *theory of practice*, that is, a series of propositions and premises based on knowledge and inference, about what writers and printers and sometimes actors are most likely to have done to create the document(s) in front of them. Editors may also have an implicit theory, often embodied in guidelines, about how to change and adjust the surviving documents into an edition. For many readers the idea that the edition of a Shakespeare play is based on a theory will seem strange: isn't *Hamlet* just *Hamlet*? One of the major aims of *Shakespeare and Textual Theory* is to demonstrate that this simple tautology is not true – after all, as we shall see, there are three early texts of *Hamlet* that differ in numerous and significant ways, – and to introduce the unfamiliar idea that an editor is a theorist and all texts but the author's original manuscript(s) are editions. Furthermore, textual and editorial theory is prior to and frequently underlies other, more familiar, theoretical approaches, such as feminist or Marxist theory.

Shakespeare and Textual Theory is, accordingly, divided into three Parts. The first, 'Textual Studies Before "Theory"', traces the treatment of Shakespeare's texts from the late sixteenth to the early twentieth century. It describes the nature of Shakespeare's surviving texts and the ways in which they were originally produced, introducing key technical terms. In order to clarify later debates about the surviving texts, it traces the two paths a holograph – a manuscript in the author's handwriting, sometimes called an autograph – could take, explaining the physical processes by which the manuscripts were transitioned into print, as well as what might happen to a text in the theatre. It then describes the 'editing' of Shakespeare from the first four Folios to the Globe Shakespeare edition of 1864, arguing that the lack of explicitly formulated theories of the text did not mean a lack of editorial rationales, as can be seen both in the varying methods used in these books and in frequent debates between early editors.

The second Part, 'Twentieth-Century Theories', begins with a chapter on the 'New Bibliography'. This was a combination of new technical methods of analysis that had the specific goal of determining the manuscript(s) that underlie a surviving printed text, especially one by Shakespeare. The New Bibliographers advanced theories (or hypotheses) about everything from the provenance of variant texts to printing house practices, and used them to issue instructions for the 'proper' editorial treatment of Shakespeare's texts. These theories dominated Shakespearean textual analysis in the first half of the twentieth century. The following chapter, 'The Advent of Poststructuralism', traces the unsettling effects of poststructuralism on the New Bibliography and on textual theory more generally. Under the influence of French theory, fundamental concepts – especially 'author', 'text' and 'intention' – were re-examined and contested. Poststructuralism challenged the exclusive role of the author, and introduced the model of the socialized, collaborative text that might never be definitive. Poststructuralist textual theory, sometimes called the 'New Textualism', intersected with and often formed the basis of other new readings, which might be feminist, post-colonial, new historicist or queer. The relation between 'Textual and Other Theories' is discussed in the last chapter of this Part.

The third and longest Part of *Shakespeare and Textual Theory* presents 'Current Debates' in the field. These include duelling conceptions of authorship, agency, and intentionality; arguments about attribution and collaboration; challenges to the New Bibliographers' conclusions about the nature of the surviving texts; debates between interventionist and hands-off editors; claims for Shakespeare as a 'literary dramatist' or exclusively a man of the theatre. Current work in performance history has led to debates about whether or how to incorporate theatrical elements into a text. Throughout we will see that no, *Hamlet* is not 'just' *Hamlet*, and even many of the plays that survive in only one version, whether found only in the 1623 First Folio or in a unique quarto, do not present stable texts. Through these debates, theories of the text multiply: as twenty-first-century scholars turn to new electronic tools for analysis and presentation, fundamental questions about which plays are Shakespeare's, how the texts that survive were created, what words belong in those texts, and the best way to present the texts, are being re-explored with fresh excitement. A 'Coda' considers what has happened to 'Textual Studies After the Digital Turn'.

Inevitably my introduction to these debates will be subjective, presenting my own understanding and knowledge, coloured by my values and my experience as a scholar and editor. Readers may learn more than they expect not only about *Hamlet* but about *Pericles* and *All's Well That Ends Well* because those less familiar plays are ones I have edited, but I have also General Edited the text of the entire canon for the *Norton Shakespeare 3*. I will do my best to present all sides of an argument, distinguishing between fact and interpretation and giving ample acknowledgement to those who disagree with my conclusions. Still, part of the fun of textual studies is that some of it is detective work, and readers are invited to become detectives themselves. There is always more to discover and a newer view. With what you will learn in this volume, you may be the one who solves some of the remaining riddles.

PART ONE

Textual Studies Before 'Theory'

1

Shakespeare's Texts from the Sixteenth to the Nineteenth Century

The key moment in the creation of any Shakespeare text is invisible to us. We can assert definitively that there once was a time when William Shakespeare, aged about 30, picked up his quill and began to write *King Richard II*. This may have occurred during the plague closure of the theatres in 1592–3 or shortly after, in 1594, by which time he had joined a theatrical company, the Lord Chamberlain's Men (after 1603 renamed the King's Men), that he would remain with for the rest of his working life. His draft might have been 'foul', a term which meant not simply messy but that it was to be copied over, as when the dramatist Robert Daborne wrote to the theatrical entrepreneur Philip Henslowe to show that he had finished a scene: 'I send you the foul sheet and the fair I was writing' (Werstine 2013: 31, 98).[1] Hence when Shakespeare had finished his draft, he may have copied it 'fair' before presenting it to his company, possibly in 1595, Martin Wiggins

---

[1]All quotations are in modern spelling unless the original spelling affects the meaning.

and Catherine Richardson's best guess for its date.[2] Or he or the company may have paid a scribe to copy that draft. In that case the scribe may have formatted such matters as stage directions to suit his own preferred style. We know the name of one scribe – Ralph Crane – who later worked for the company helping to prepare the First Folio in 1623, and he is recognizable through his heavy punctuation and fondness for parentheses. It is, however, likely that a scribe copying Shakespeare's draft for his company early in his career would have been in a hurry and possibly not so careful. In any case, given a Shakespeare draft and perhaps a scribal copy, there would have been only one or two exemplars of the whole. From that point on the play belonged to the company, not to Shakespeare. The company, in turn, needed a copy – one of the originals or hypothetically an additional one – to submit to the Master of the Revels for approval. They would also have created parts with cues for each actor.

There are no surviving manuscripts for any of the printed plays or poems in the Shakespeare canon, though a few of the sonnets were copied into commonplace books (see Chapter 9). We only know *Richard II* because in 1597 the company chose to have it printed. They engaged the stationer Andrew Wise – a stationer was a publisher, but often also a bookseller (the copies were 'to be sold at his shop in Paul's churchyard at the sign of the Angel') and sometimes a printer. To publish, Wise needed to see that the manuscript had been properly authorized for printing. Until 1606 the relevant authority for the publication of plays, as for all books, was the Bishop of London or his delegates; after 1606 the Master of the Revels, who authorized plays for performance, was also granted the right to allow plays for the press. Once armed with authorization, Wise next needed to ask the Wardens of the Stationers'

---

[2] Wiggins and Richardson (2013–15), *British Drama* 3.291 (*Richard II* is play number 1002). All further dates are taken from Wiggins and Richardson unless otherwise noted.

Company for 'licence'. No book could be published without the Company's licence or permission, and printers who defied Company rules risked having their presses confiscated. The licence, which gave exclusive right to the text in question, would be written into the manuscript that the stationer presented. Finally, for further assurance of his ownership, Wise paid an optional additional fee for 'entrance', that is, an entry written in the Stationers' Register, the official catalogue of publishers' books. With these permissions Wise was able to publish a small format book, a 'quarto', of *Richard II*, with a title page explaining that the play had been 'publicly acted by the right honourable Lord Chamberlain his servants'. No author was named. Because Wise had fulfilled all of the requirements, in June of 1603 he was able to sell his rights to *Richard II* to Matthew Law, who in 1608 brought out a later edition with a different printer.

Despite the apparently smooth sequence just described, Law's later edition, the fourth printing of *Richard II* (commonly referred to by textual scholars as Q4) contains a scene not present in the preceding three. This is the so-called deposition scene, in which Richard II hands his crown to his cousin Henry Bolingbroke. In the *Arden 3* edition, the relevant lines are 4.1.155–318.[3] Yet the version of the additional scene found in that and other modern editions is not based on the one in Law's edition, but follows the better form found in the Shakespeare First Folio of 1623. And here we enter the realm of textual scholarship. Some of the questions that arise are profoundly tied to our conception of Shakespeare: How can we, or even more simply, *can* we, know what Shakespeare wrote? How is it possible that the texts vary? What is meant by better and worse texts, and how did they come about? Some are more technical: What does 'Q4' mean? What is the difference between a quarto and a folio? What is the

---

[3] All quotations from Shakespeare's plays and all act, scene and line numbers are taken from the *Arden 3* editions unless otherwise noted.

responsibility of stationers, printers or actors for the texts we have? And on what basis do the explanations of scholars vary? The debates that arise about Shakespeare's texts will be the subject of the majority of this book, but to understand and evaluate them, it is helpful to become familiar with the vocabulary used to describe the construction of early modern books and to understand the process of early modern printing by which Shakespeare's manuscripts became those books. We will also consider what may have occurred when manuscripts to be printed had been previously used in the theatre. Only then will we return, briefly, to *Richard II*.

The progress of an early modern play

Most early modern books were quartos. A quarto is so-called because it is a small book made up of full-size sheets of paper folded into four quarters. Each sheet was folded once lengthwise and once across. With the top cut open, this yields a set of four leaves or eight pages. Each group of eight little pages constituted one 'signature', so called because the right-hand pages or 'rectos' were marked or 'signed' on the bottom of the page. Markings in the first or A signature of a quarto were A1, A2, A3, and A4, although frequently this final signature mark was omitted. The left-hand or 'verso' pages were not marked, but the page identification for an early book made by a scholar may read, for example, 'B4v' (the verso of the fourth leaf in the B signature). The last signature marked in Q1 *Richard II* is K1; the final page, which would be K2, has no signature marking but instead has *Finis* followed by a printer's ornament. Because the letters I and J were used interchangeably in early modern texts, J was not used in signature markings.

For a printer, the signatures indicated how to put a book together. Signatures were more important than page numbers, which do not appear in Shakespeare's quartos before the 1622 quarto of *Othello* and in any case frequently go wrong in early modern books. The nature of the quarto folding for a signature also directed the printing, as you can see if you take a sheet of paper, fold it in four but do not cut it, insert the signature indications from A1r to A4v and now open it. As you see, each side of the sheet carries four pages, but these are not continuous. Textual analysts refer to the side that begins with A1r and includes A2v, A3r and A4v as 'A outer'; the side that begins with A1v and includes A2r, A3v and A4r is 'A inner'. Most quartos were printed by 'formes', that is, by the sheet holding four non-consecutive pages.

Consequently, the first step in printing was to 'cast off' the text or 'copy', that is, to calculate the number of pages the text would occupy and to do a careful estimation of where the text would divide into pages. Paper for *Richard II* would be easy to estimate, as it is one of Shakespeare's few plays that is entirely in verse. For Q1, having decided how many lines would fit on a page, the printer Simmes realized that the play would occupy signatures from A–K and hence he needed 10 sheets to print it. In contrast, *Richard III*, which Simmes also printed for Wise the same year, is one of Shakespeare's longest plays. Its quarto signatures run up to M3v and hence Wise had to supply 12 sheets of paper for each copy. Casting off of pages was necessary because if it was not correct, the printer might find he had too much or too little text left when he arrived at, for example, A4r on the inner forme. Errors in casting off may explain places where verse text is printed as if it were prose to take up less room – as on D2 (recto and verso) of the 1608 quarto of *King Lear* – or, alternatively, where there is unexpectedly large white space and the prose is broken up into lines as if it were verse to occupy more space, as on F2r of the 1600 quarto of *Henry V*.

It is likely that a new manuscript would be prepared – 'read through, corrected, and annotated' (Gaskell 1972: 40), before it was handed over to the compositor (or typesetter). Some printshops employed 'correctors'; at other times it seems to have been the owner of the shop who undertook the task. Ultimately, however, at least some correction was incumbent upon compositors. Joseph Moxon, later in the seventeenth century, spells out the compositor's duties: 'a compositor is strictly to follow his copy ... but the carelessness of some good authors, and the ignorance of other authors, has forced printers to introduce a custom, which among them is looked upon as a task and duty incumbent on the compositor, viz., to discern and amend the bad spelling and pointing [punctuation] of his copy, if it be English' (1677: 2.197–8).

Once the material had been prepared and cast off, a compositor would stand before an upright wooden 'case' with separate compartments or boxes, each holding the metal types of one letter or printing symbol. The majuscule or capital letters were in the boxes at the upper end of the case (hence we still say 'upper case' letters) and the minuscule or small letters were in boxes beneath (hence 'lower case' letters). One by one he would choose from the case the metal 'types' that would print what he believed he had read in the manuscript tacked up in front of him. That manuscript might be a clean scribal or authorial copy, or it might be one that well deserved the title of 'foul' papers. Either way the compositor had to decipher the handwriting in the manuscript. The most common handwriting style was known as 'secretary hand', sometimes intermixed with italic script, usually used for names and foreign words. In secretary hand certain letters, such as c and t, or d and e, may appear very similar. Another problem was distinguishing what are called 'minims', the small downstrokes that make up the letters m, n, and u. Minim errors are very common, for example turning 'smiles' into 'soules' (*Richard II*, 1.4.28). Further complicating the compositor's work, a long form of the letter s – ſ –, used everywhere except at the end of words, was very similar to f without the cross-stroke. In Chapter 4, I will discuss some possible consequences of this confusion.

To some extent the compositor might be like a modern 'touch typist', working letter-by-letter rather mechanically, but inevitably his work also involved memory. Because one of a compositor's duties was to add punctuation, it is likely that he read at least a line at a time. Of course some punctuation may have been added in the printshop before he started. Nevertheless, in the interval between his reading a bit of the manuscript and picking up the required types, there was always the possibility of his misremembering and introducing errors. Then, once type from previous sheets had been 'distributed', that is, the pages broken up and all the individual types returned to their boxes, there was another possible occasion for error, 'foul case', the term used to describe a letter placed in the wrong box of the case, which the compositor might pick up without inspection, assuming it was correct.

As the compositor pulled the selected types, he placed them in a composing stick – a rack or frame that held the types (upside down so they would be correct when printed), adjusted to the length of the line desired. Once the stick held six or eight lines of type, he transferred the type into a galley or tray until he gradually had a complete page. In a prose passage the compositor had to justify each line, that is, adjust the spacing of words so that the page would have even margins. Your computer will do this for you automatically, but the compositor had to find ways to do it himself. His methods included adding or substituting spaces of different widths or using abbreviations or contractions like y^e and y^t for 'the' and 'that'. Most significantly, because English spelling was permissive in Shakespeare's era, the compositor could alter spellings to take up less or more room. For example, he could add or remove a final 'e' (bold/ bolde), he could choose between scene or scaene and drum or drumme. For this reason it is problematic to assume that a printed page gives us an author's preferred spelling, although some unusual forms, for example the c in 'scilens' for 'silence' and a few other words found in some quartos, have been thought to indicate Shakespeare's preference.

Once prepared, each page was tied up with string and set aside until there were enough completed to print a sheet, at which point the pages were placed or 'imposed' on a flat table or 'stone' and surrounded with a 'chase' or iron frame to create a 'forme' ready for printing– a forme is 'a body of type, secured in a chase, for printing in one impression' (OED). When printed the sheets were hung up until the ink was dry, and later they were reinserted in the press and the other side would be printed. Yet another reason for casting off was efficiency: once the compositor had prepared the pages of one forme, it could be machined by the press while the next forme was being prepared, even though the pages were not sequential.

Unlike a quarto, the First Folio is put together in 'quires', with three large sheets ('Folio sheets') of paper folded in half around each other, forming 6 leaves or 12 pages. If you take three sheets, fold them and mark them with signature numbers, you will see that except for the central pair (A3v/A4r), the inner and outer forme for each printed Folio sheet carries two non-contiguous pages. For instance the outer forme A contains page A1r and A6v (or pages 1 and 12). Most of the Folio was printed by formes, so that only two pages needed to be set at a time. Had the Folio text been set 'seriatim', or in the order of the pages we read, the press could not have started printing before that central pair of pages, A3v and A4r (an inner forme), had been set, and the printshop would have needed enough pieces of type to set seven pages before any could be redistributed into the type case and reused. Nevertheless, although setting by formes was the norm, occasionally those who study the fine points of printing conclude that certain books, or sections of books, were set seriatim. This was more likely to happen in a Folio, where a sheet was only folded once and hence each side of the printed sheet held only two pages.

After a forme was set, a 'foul proof' would be pulled and given to a corrector, who looked it over for errors and indicated needed adjustments. (Although some dramatists, like John Webster and Ben Jonson, are known to have visited the printshop and to have occasionally served as correctors, there is no indication that Shakespeare ever worked in this way on any of his quartos.) The forme would be 'unlocked' so the type could be altered and corrections made. The foul proofsheets were usually discarded, and consequently this first proofing was ignored by Charlton Hinman when he studied the First Folio. But, as Peter Blayney writes, 'it has always been customary to proofread all pages before beginning to print them . . . pages of text in Jaggard's printing house (as in all others) were routinely proofread and corrected before the presswork began' (1996: xxxi). Next, the corrected forme was set for printing. A new proofsheet was pulled, that is, printed and handed to the corrector for further checking, primarily to be sure that the errors found in the foul proof had been fixed. Meanwhile, printing continued. When the corrector finished his work, the press might be stopped again for further correction.

To understand what happened next it helps to know that paper, largely imported from France in this period, was a printer's greatest expense. Consequently, although Blayney found that for the First Folio 'on more than 100 occasions, the press was stopped so that corrections could be made' (1991: 14), the sheets already printed were not discarded but bound into the volumes, mixed with other corrected or uncorrected sheets. Picture picking up pages from piles of sheets, some printed before and some after correction, and you will understand why no two copies of the Folio have exactly the same mixture of corrected and uncorrected pages. Even a few pages marked for correction survive, bound into various volumes. When Hinman created the Norton Facsimile of the Folio, he chose for each page 'the best' in his view from among the many copies at the Folger Shakespeare Library, creating, thus, a facsimile of no single copy that actually exists. At the back of the Norton volume are facsimiles of some variant pages, showing corrections that range from moving the position of a comma to the substitution of 'grievously' for 'heavily' (*TGV* 3.2.14) and the change of 'cop of sack' to 'cup of sack' (*1H4* 2.4.111). The facsimile also includes examples of pages marked for correction by the proofreader.

In the quarto we have been following, the printed pages would now be folded into signatures and stabbed through in the margin for a rough stitching together. (These stab-stitch holes turn out to provide important evidence about the history of a group of quartos printed in 1619; see Chapter 9). Having a book bound was a separate expense, and consequently most quartos (like cheap modern paperbacks) were not bound. Often only a few copies from a printing survive. In an extreme case, there is only one known copy of the first quarto of *Titus Andronicus*, now housed as a 'unique' at the Folger Shakespeare Library. More survive of the first quarto of *Richard II*, which is now ready for sale in the bookshop of Andrew Wise. But meanwhile, to understand more about the text included in our quarto, we need to return to the other progress of an early modern play: progress on to the stage. Not every manuscript that came to the printshop came directly from the author or his scribe. Most plays came from the companies.

As mentioned, plays were normally sold to acting companies, and they, not the authors, became their owners. Before 1594 we do not know precisely to which company Shakespeare belonged. The 1594 quarto of *Titus Andronicus*, one of Shakespeare's early plays, advertises on the title page that 'it was played by the right honourable the Earl of Derby, Earl of Pembroke, and Earl of Sussex their servants'. This is a list of a series of companies – the Earl of Derby later became Lord Strange, who sponsored Strange's Men – one or more of which may have included Shakespeare in his early years. Several of the actors who formed the Lord Chamberlain's Men in 1594 had belonged to one or other of these companies, which had formed or failed at various times in the early 1590s. Indeed, the second quarto in 1600 adds to the list of companies who had played *Titus* 'the Lord Chamberlain their servants'. Andrew Gurr (2008: 228) would like to suppose that '*Titus* travelled through its succession of companies along with its author, who, uniquely as an author but not uniquely as a player, may have kept the allowed playbook in his possession throughout'. But James Marino refutes this pleasant fantasy because there is no evidence 'to suggest that Shakespeare kept control of any play he had written, or had collaborated in writing, before joining the Chamberlain's Men. Such control over a script was for the buyer, not the seller' (2011: 30).

However a company obtained a dramatic manuscript, it needed to be prepared for performance. Such preparation falls into two general categories. Pre-performance preparation concerned such matters as entering timely stage directions, for instance for entrances and exits, and assigning roles; the second possibility was revision. The first was the concern of a company employee conventionally known as the bookkeeper.[4] It used to be believed (see Chapter 2 on the New Bibliography) that theatres would not or could not tolerate inconsistencies, like irregularities in the naming of a character, or permissive directions like calling for the entrance of 'four or five' or 'others', or missing entrances or exits. Consequently textual scholars assumed that the presence of such irregularities in a Shakespeare text indicated that it was based on authorial papers rather than on a 'promptbook', that is, on a manuscript used in the theatre. However, research on the surviving theatrical manuscripts has revealed just such inconsistency. Bookkeepers were irregular in naming characters when they supplied warning directions (those alerting an actor that he is to enter a few lines later); they sometimes moved or removed a passage without removing a consequently irrelevant character's name from stage directions; they wrote stage directions with indefinite numbers. The one sure sign that the printer's copy was based on a playhouse manuscript is the presence of actors' names (Werstine 2013: 194).

Revision, the other possible cause for changes to a manuscript in the theatre, might occur in many different ways. The simplest was alteration by the original author. Recent scholarship has argued that the Folio text of *King Lear* is based on a revision by Shakespeare of the text found in the 1608 quarto (see Chapters 5 and 7). This was probably the rarest kind of alteration, and assuming that it did occur in the case of *King Lear*, it is even more rare that both authorial versions

---

[4]Tiffany Stern argues that the responsible person was the 'prompter' or 'bookholder'. The 'bookkeeper', as this person is called in most of the scholarship, may have had a different job from the prompter/bookholder (2020: personal communication).

survive. Ben Jonson tells us that he rewrote *Sejanus* to remove the parts written by 'another hand', but all that survives is that final version. Of course a play also might be revised by another dramatist, sometimes someone identifiable, sometimes not. Marston's *Malcontent* was printed in 1604 'with the additions played by the King's Majesty's servants written by John Webster'. As we shall see, there are reasons for presuming that the text we have of *Macbeth* was revised after Shakespeare's death by Thomas Middleton, and recent proposals allege that Middleton or Fletcher had a hand in other surviving texts (see Chapter 6). But theatrical revision was not necessarily a single act with all changes made at a single moment. Tracing the history of plays like *Henry V* and *Taming of the Shrew*, known to exist in other versions before they came to the Lord Chamberlain's Men in 1594, James Marino argues for a pattern of continual revision that worked to confirm the company's possession. In these cases, the company's strategy was to use revision to distinguish their versions from those of their 'forerunners' and to weaken potential claims by any rival company. The Chamberlain's Men also 'increasingly used Shakespeare's authorship as a signifier of possession' (Marino 2011: 41–2). In a later article expanding on Tiffany Stern's discussion of the separate cue-scripts given to actors to learn their parts, Marino demonstrates that some revisions (e.g., those that required changing cues already learned by several members of the company) were difficult, requiring simultaneous changes in several scripts, while others (e.g., cuts in the middle of a soliloquy or changes when a new boy took on a part) might be made at any time (2020: 60). Marino's claim that 'the actors never ceased revising' and consequently that the surviving texts of the Shakespeare plays, for example the two plays about shrews, 'are not the production of any discrete historical moment . . . . not written at one time' has radical implications for understanding these texts (2011: 73).

Textual scholars are interested in what happened to Shakespeare's manuscripts in the theatre because the printed texts may bear signs of that history. For the better part of three centuries scholars have tried to separate the words Shakespeare put on paper from those added or altered by scribes, revisers, actors and printers. The texts may also contain extraneous material introduced in the playhouse by clowns (see Preiss 2020). Hence, in arguing that dramatic texts were 'potentially open until the moment of publication', Marino flirts with 'one of the last great taboos of Shakespeare scholarship: the ... hypothesis that Shakespeare's works might have been substantially improved by his collaborators' (2011: 70). More on this in Chapter 6. Let's return now to the progress of *Richard II*.

Richard II was popular enough to be immediately reprinted, twice in 1598 (Q2, Q3, both now with Shakespeare's name on the title page) and then again in 1608 (Q4) and 1615 (Q5). As mentioned, there is a notable difference between the earlier quartos and the later ones. The fourth quarto, printed after the death of Queen Elizabeth, is largely based on Q1 but includes what is referred to either as the 'abdication' or as the 'deposition' scene, that is, 4.1.155–318, in which Richard is brought on the stage and yields the crown to his cousin Henry Bolingbroke. Here theatrical text intersects with historical events and cultural norms in a way always implicitly present but seldom so overt and visible.

An Elizabethan playtext could undergo two levels of approval. The first was obligatory: all plays to be performed had to be submitted for inspection to a court official called the Master of the Revels, who in 1595 was Sir Edmund Tilney. As we know from the surviving manuscript of *Sir Thomas More*, an unfinished, much revised play in which Shakespeare's hand is thought to be present, Tilney could be peremptory in his orders. For *Sir Thomas More* he ordered the entire first scene cut and its action summarized in a brief 'report' (see Chapter 6 for detailed discussion). There could be serious penalties if a play was presented without the approval of the Master of the Revels. Second, as we have already seen, if the company also desired to have the play printed, until 1606 a second level of approval would have to be sought from the ecclesiastical censors appointed by the Bishop of London. After 1606 the Master of the Revels also took responsibility for approving publication.

Theoretically, the major difference in the *Richard II* texts could have arisen either from addition, Shakespeare writing a new scene sometime between 1595 and 1608, or from restoration – the reintroduction of a scene missing from the original text. As we will see repeatedly in this book, conclusions about a surviving text are based on a combination of various kinds of evidence, physical, historical, theatrical and literary. *Richard II* is a good example. The most likely scenario in this case is that the scene was performed before 1608, but not printed until then. We gain a sense of the scene's cogency for the period through an extraordinary event that points to earlier performance. On 7 February 1601, the night before an uprising against Queen Elizabeth led by Robert Devereux, Earl of Essex (the 'Essex Rebellion'), the Lord Chamberlain's Men put on a special performance of what was almost certainly Shakespeare's play. When questioned as to why by the authorities, the actor Augustine Phillipps, representing the company, explained that they only performed this 'old' play because they were offered a substantial fee, 40 shillings, to do so by some of the aristocratic young men who surrounded Essex. As the company was excused without penalty, it seems that they were not thought to have known or understood the intentions of Essex's supporters. Nonetheless, not long afterwards Queen Elizabeth is reported to have said to the antiquary William Lambard, 'I am King Richard II know ye not that?' Thus it is likely that the scene was too dangerous to print in Elizabeth's lifetime, but was familiar from regular performances to the group of Essex's followers who commissioned the special production. Supporting this conclusion, the style of the scene, with its elaborate metaphors, rhymes, and wordplay, is similar to that of the rest of the play, and others of the same period, not to the style of Shakespeare's plays around 1608.

The First Folio

King Richard II appeared again in the 1623 First Folio (F). Exactly half, eighteen, of the plays included had not been printed before. As the volume was overseen by John Heminges and Henry Condell, senior members of the King's Men, and as all of the plays had passed from the author to the company, it is most likely that the new plays were printed on the basis of manuscripts held in the company archive. These could have been Shakespeare's original papers, if that is all that remained, or transcripts (scribal or authorial), or promptbooks with theatrical notations. The promptbook normally carried the licence of the Master of the Revels. For the other eighteen, previously published, plays, the Folio editors had a choice of using an earlier quarto or a transcript as the base text. The Folio compositors 'clearly preferred [working from] transcripts (seventeen) or existing editions (eleven)', either of which would have been easier to read than an authorial draft. Moreover, when they did consult earlier quartos, with some exceptions the Folio editors 'favoured recent reprints over earlier first editions' (*TxC* 1987: 39).

The history of Folio *Richard II* follows most though not all of this pattern. Most of the text was set from the 1598 third quarto rather than from either the earliest, Q1, or the latest, Q5 from 1615, although some scholars have suggested that the copy of Q3 used may have had pages interpolated from Q5. Nevertheless the text of F varies from that in the quartos, suggesting that the compositors of F also consulted a manuscript promptbook, the working performance text. First, F includes more frequent and more precise stage directions than Q1 and its successors. These directions point to the playhouse, while those in Q1 are the kind that suggest an author thinking while he writes. For example, an author is more likely to call for the entrance of the King's 'nobles' or even 'King, Queen, &c.' without specifying which characters are to enter. A bookholder or prompter needs to know precisely which actors are to enter at any time. Another important difference between the Q and F texts that again suggests consultation of a theatrical manuscript is the substitution of 'heaven' for 'God' throughout. Such an alteration was presumably caused by the 1606 Act to Restrain Abuses of Players, which forbade the use of profanity on stage but not in printed texts. Obviously, at some time after 1606 the performance text of *Richard II* was brought into conformity with the new requirement. Possibly the manuscript consulted for the printing of F, while it ultimately derives from the same source as that behind Q1 and its successor quartos, had been revised, or perhaps the copy of Q3 consulted had served previously as a promptbook and had had manuscript additions or changes made in it (Stern 2020: personal communication). In other words, all of the quartos and any manuscripts ultimately derive from Shakespeare's original holograph, but the materials consulted in the making of the Folio included substitutions made over time or onstage by the author (active in the company until he retired in 1612), the company bookkeeper, or the actors.

The Folio also includes the deposition scene in a better literary form than that found in quartos 4 and 5. Here again the history of *Richard II* leads us to the uncertainties with which textual scholarship contends. In their preface to the Folio, Heminges and Condell explain – boast, really – that they have replaced earlier 'maimed and deformed' copies with texts 'cured, and perfect of their limbs'. It appears most likely that the imperfect copies Heminges and Condell refer to are those which have become known as the 'bad' quartos, versions not only much abbreviated from the familiar texts but which reorder events and include striking differences in famous lines. Among explanations for these versions, one recurrent proposal is that they were 'memorial reconstructions', that is, texts put together surreptitiously by actors (see Chapters 2 and 7 for discussion). This much-debated theory has also been proposed as explanation for the imperfect text of the deposition scene of *Richard II* found in Q4, as that has some of the hallmarks of a text put together from memory. On the other hand, some scholars have argued that the Q4 version of the scene was merely a hasty transcript by a copyist (Forker 2002: 506, n1). In any case, the Folio, in this instance, lived up to its promise to offer the scene 'cured' and presumably 'perfect in [its] limbs'.

In retrospect, the most surprising aspect of the First Folio is what it omits. Shakespeare's first great successes had been the two long narrative poems, *Venus and Adonis* (1593) and *The Rape of Lucrece* (1594). These appear to be the only texts he oversaw for publication, and they were elegantly printed by Richard Field, a fellow Stratfordian who produced 'books which looked good and made claims to high literary status' (Burrow 2002: 6). Each poem bore a dedication to Henry Wriothesley, Earl of Southampton, signed 'Your Honour's' [or, in *Lucrece*, 'Your Lordship's'] 'in all duty, William Shakespeare'. The poems' success as publications is confirmed by their repeated reprintings – for the sexy *Venus and Adonis*, there were at least 16 editions by 1640 (Burrow 2002: 7) – and the Cambridge play, *Return to Parnassus*, jokes about young men sleeping with *Venus and Adonis* under their pillows. Then, in 1609, the 'sugered sonnets', which according to Francis Meres previously had circulated among Shakespeare's 'private friends', appeared under the unambiguous title, *Shakespeare's Sonnets*. Yet the Folio printed only Mr William Shakespeare's 'Comedies, Histories, & Tragedies'. This is even more unexpected given the involvement in the production of the Folio by Ben Jonson, who some scholars suggest may have acted as the editor of the volume and whose poem 'In memory of my beloved, the Author Mr William Shakespeare and what he has left us' appears immediately after Heminges and Condell's address 'To the great variety of readers.' Jonson's own 1616 Folio, usually seen to be the model for Shakespeare's, included plays, poetry collections, pageantry, entertainments and masques. True, Jonson's volume had been mocked for its pretensions – *The Works of Benjamin Jonson* suggests the title, *Opera Omnia* [complete works], normally reserved for classical authors – and because, some said, a play was not a work. But this would not explain why Shakespeare's poems were not included in the Folio, among 'what he has left us'.

In all likelihood the reasons were practical and commercial. As Colin Burrow writes, 'many of those responsible for putting the volume [i.e., the Folio] together were men of the theatre' (2002: 2). It was Shakespeare's plays that Heminges and Condell knew and had performed in; it was plays, not poems, that the archive of the King's Men contained. Perhaps most important, because the two long poems remained popular, 'it would have been difficult and expensive to obtain the right to print them' (Burrow 2002: 7–8). Then, given the many uncertainties about the 1609 printing of the Sonnets – did Shakespeare authorize the collection? Or did the printer, Thomas Thorpe, obtain a copy in some underhanded way? Were the published sonnets the same as the 'sugared' ones circulating? Is the order within the collection that intended by the author? Why is the dedication the printer's, rather than the author's? – it seems unsurprising that once the longer poems were excluded, the sonnets would be too. In the event the sonnets were not reprinted until 1640, and then in a collection whose oddities will be discussed in Chapter 9.

The omission of the poems continued through the seventeenth-century Folios, and probably as a consequence, in the eighteenth-century multi-volume Shakespeare editions the poems were either omitted entirely or banished to a final volume. Sometimes these volumes, like Gildon's supplement to the 1709 Rowe edition or Edmond Malone's supplementary volumes to the edition of George Steevens, were undertaken by someone other than the primary editor. Consequently, most of the textual analysis of Shakespeare's works and most of the theoretical debates about his text have concerned the plays. They will, in general, be the subject of this book.

Successive Folios

Although there were occasional quartos published in the seventeenth century after the First Folio, most notably a quarto text of *The Two Noble Kinsmen* in 1634 that acknowledged on its title page that the play was 'Written by the memorable Worthies of their time; Mr *John Fletcher*, and Mr *William Shakspeare*, Gent.', the significant volumes of the seventeenth century were the succession of Folios. The Second Folio appeared in 1632, the Third after the interregnum in 1663 and the Fourth in 1685. The important thing to recognize about these volumes is that while none of the later Folios has any *textual* authority, if what we are looking for is getting closer to Shakespeare's original text or his 'original intentions' (to be discussed further), each was, effectively, an edition. The Second Folio, though essentially a line-by-line reprint of the first, made almost 1700 changes, nearly 700 of which are regularly accepted still. These changes were basically 'a form of modernization not much different from that which twentieth-century editors have characteristically undertaken' (Kastan 2001: 80), although some, like modifying out-of-date grammatical forms, such as a plural subject with a singular verb, would not be attempted by modern editors. Errors of spelling were rectified, and occasional misreadings or misprints, which could be recognized by an attentive reading of the text for meaning, such as 'smiles' for 'similes', were corrected. In general there was an easy slippage from changing the text because the meaning of the original words on the page seemed not to represent what the author must have written to changing the text because a grammatical or spelling form did not seem comfortable or familiar to the reader. The Second Folio, in the words of David Kastan, 'initiates the procedures by which Shakespeare becomes the contemporary of his readers' and 'the plays escape their moment of creation and appear as contemporaneous with their moment of reception' (2001: 82).

The Third Folio continued in the line of the Second, further 'correcting' to the taste of the post-Restoration reader rather than returning to the earliest witnesses. The most interesting thing about this edition was that in 1664 it was reissued. (A new issue is a republication with a few changes rather than a full re-editing). In this case the second issue added seven more plays, all but one (*Pericles*) now viewed as apocryphal. With the theatres reopened there seems to have been a desire for 'more' Shakespeare, and the stationers behind F3 were determined to supply whatever they could find. Unlike modern editors who, especially in recent years, have argued for Shakespeare's hand in all or part of a growing number of plays (see Chapter 6), the publishers of F3 offered no justification for their choices. The additional plays are separately and sequentially paginated, with no preface or other paratext (i.e. material outside the main body) to explain their presence. *Pericles*, the first of the additions and the only one subsequently accepted, has as a heading "Written by W. Shakespeare, and published in his life time' – which is true, the only quarto having appeared with the attribution in 1609 – and the *London Prodigal* is marked 'Written by W. Shakespeare' as it had been in the 1605 quarto. Otherwise even the plays that had earlier been published in quarto as 'by William Shakespeare' (*A Yorkshire Tragedy* 1608, *Sir John Oldcastle* in a 1619 quarto falsely dated 1600) or as 'by W. S.' (*The Life and Death of Lord Cromwell* 1602, *The Puritan* 1607, *Locrine* 1595), have no attribution. They are simply there, and they remain so through the 1685 printing of the Fourth Folio.

Sonia Massai has performed a close analysis of F4, arguing that although the book was produced in three different print shops, the text had first been 'corrected' by what she calls 'an annotating reader' who supplied the copy from which the compositors set the text (2007: 182). The corrections of the annotating reader were often astute, as Massai shows in a close analysis of the changes in *Coriolanus*, but the purpose was still 'to "improve" the text, not to "restore" authorial or theatrical intentions' (2007: 189).

Massai considers several possible annotators for F4. These include Henry Herringman, the main publisher of the volume, and the poet John Dryden, who at times worked for and possibly even lived with Herringman, but she concludes that the most likely candidate was Nahum Tate, 'the main editorial agent regularly employed by Herringman in the mid-1680s' (2007: 187). Tate has become infamous for creating a version of *King Lear* with a happy ending, but in his lifetime he was a serious dramatist (his version of *Lear* was very successful), and his work forms a transition from the earlier 'improving' correctors to the series of dramatists who were hired by the publishing house of successive Tonsons to create editions of Shakespeare in the eighteenth century. The first of these was the dramatist Nicholas Rowe; several of the other eighteenth-century editors, including Alexander Pope and Lewis Theobald, were notable poets or dramatists in their own right. While this chapter will give only a brief account of their contributions, the main things to remember are the two major changes that occurred in the approximately 100 years from the Fourth Folio to the 1790 edition of Edmond Malone. First, the editors or annotators do not remain nameless but eventually lay claim to their rights to emendations as intellectual property. In this they were assisted by the 'Statute of Anne' of 1709, commonly thought of as the first copyright law (see below) Even more important, by the time of Malone, a fundamental change of purpose had occurred. The search ceased to be simply for the best possible reading and came instead to be for the text as originally created by its author.

Early editions

In 1709 the publishing house of Jacob Tonson put out the first of what may be regarded as the modern editions of Shakespeare's works. In his six volumes Nicholas Rowe included the first biography of Shakespeare and regularized the plays by introducing act and scene numbers. For the tragedies he also supplied lists of dramatis personae and scene locations. Ostensibly modest about his accomplishment, in his dedication to the Duke of Somerset Rowe complains of the fundamental problem that frustrates editors to this day: 'I must not pretend to have restored this work to the exactness of the author's original manuscripts: Those are lost, or, at least, are gone beyond any Inquiry I could make'. Lacking manuscripts, Rowe claims to have compared 'the several editions, and give the true reading as well as I could from thence' (A2r–v). However, he did not know which were the earliest editions, and seems mainly to have compared the Folios.

The history of the successive eighteenth-century editions of Shakespeare – those of Rowe (1709), Alexander Pope (1723–5), Lewis Theobald (1733), Thomas Hanmer (1744), William Warburton (1747), Samuel Johnson (1765), Edward Capell (1768), George Steevens (1773) and finally Malone (1790) – is partially explained by the growing interest in Shakespeare but also by legal changes to the publishing industry. The copyright law of 1709 came into effect on 10 April 1710 and gave the owners of copyrights in old books 'the sole right to publish these works for the next twenty-one years' (Seary 1990: 133). Between 1707 and 1709 Jacob Tonson purchased the copyright of twenty-three Shakespeare plays from descendants of those with rights in the text of the Fourth Folio; subsequently he acquired rights to the rest. Once Rowe's edition was published, the Tonson publishing house effectively controlled the rights to Shakespeare's text. Furthermore, the copyright act further 'provided for the protection of new material for a period of fourteen years', and Tonson, a clever businessman, 'maintained that the emendations and other textual matter of his editors came under this head'. Thus he 'attempted to reinforce his claims to perpetual copyright in the original material by claiming successively the fourteen-year copyrights in the work of each of his editors', arranging for successive editions to appear at fourteen-year intervals. Consequently, each editor hired by Tonson, whatever his understanding of the relation between his edition and earlier texts, was compelled to base his work on the preceding Tonson edition. As an example, 'Theobald's *Shakespeare* is based on Pope's second edition (1728), which was based on Rowe's third edition (1714)', even though an indignant Theobald had described both of these earlier editions as 'of no authority' (Seary 1990: 132–4). The editions listed above, with the exception of Hanmer's, were published by Tonson up to and including the Steevens edition.

When Hanmer attempted to break Tonson's control by publishing with Oxford, Tonson retaliated by denouncing Hanmer's appropriation of notes from Tonson editions and by publishing a competing octavo edition (De Grazia 1991: 192).

In her study of the sequence of eighteenth-century editions, Margreta de Grazia has argued that until the 1790 edition of Malone, who introduced the editorial criteria of 'authenticity', none of the eighteenth-century editors understood what a modern reader would consider the proper goal of the editor of an early modern text. Malone's work thus constituted a 'sharp break' from that of his predecessors. Their continuing purpose had been to correct and 'perfect' the text of Shakespeare. Consequently it seemed to them logical that the most recent, and thus, they assumed, the most nearly perfected, rather than the oldest, original source, should serve as the basis for further work. Only towards the end of the century did Samuel Johnson recognize that the First Folio alone had any authority, all the others merely deriving from it. It was left to Malone to announce what De Grazia calls the 'basic and simple principle behind modern collation', namely that 'An edition is more or less correct as it approaches nearer to or is more distant from the first' (1991: 57).

There were nevertheless some striking differences between Malone's predecessors. Several of them had grasped, in general, the concept of collating (systematically comparing, word by word or letter by letter) the surviving texts. Even Rowe had consulted the Second Folio and several quartos and had claimed to compare them; Pope catalogued twenty-eight quartos; Theobald announced he had consulted 'the oldest copies'; Steevens in 1766 published twenty quartos; and Capell spent fifteen years transcribing quartos (De Grazia 1991: 54–5). Johnson had proposed to create a new text by returning to the earliest sources and collating them afresh, but due to his inability to obtain materials, particularly the quartos owned by the actor David Garrick, with whom he had quarrelled (Stern: 2007), he once again based an edition on earlier Tonson editions, first Warburton's, then Theobald's (Seary 1990: 7).

Yet in most cases these editions used their sources only to supply possible emendations when the text seemed corrupt to the editor of the moment. It was the editor's job to choose the best, not the earliest or most authentic, emendation, whether this came from a variant text or from his own invention. A rather extreme example is supplied by Pope. The poet's familiarity with the early quartos seems only to have bred contempt. He disliked 'trifling and bombast passages', which he blamed on the actors, and based on his preference, was 'liable to prefer a bad quarto [these tended to be short] to a good quarto or the folio' (Seary 1990: 60–1). Knowledge of early texts did not keep Pope from regularizing Shakespeare's metre to an eighteenth-century standard, from extirpating 'passages he deemed defective', or from degrading whole passages to the bottom of the page (De Grazia 1991: 114). As Andrew Murphy summarizes, Pope, refashioning Shakespeare to 'the norms and aesthetic expectations of the early eighteenth century . . . . acted as Shakespeare's artistic partner, rather than his textual servant' (2007b: 96).

On the other hand Theobald, although constrained by Tonson to base his edition on Pope's, 'marks the beginning of a consistently historical approach to English texts' (Seary 1990: 131). Theobald was for a long time disregarded because his negative review of Pope's edition, *Shakespeare Restored*, led the poet to mock him as 'piddling Tibbald' in *The Dunciad*. But Pope was best as a poet; Theobald was better as an editor of Shakespeare, partly because as a popular playwright he understood the theatre, but even more because of his 'desire to reproduce what Shakespeare had written'. To do so he initiated many of the techniques that modern editors would employ but did so without the convenience of such reference tools as the *Oxford English Dictionary* (*OED*) or *Early English Books Online* (*EEBO-TCP*), which now offers searchable digital images of the pages of almost all books published in the British Isles before 1700. For instance, to understand unfamiliar Elizabethan and Jacobean words or usages, Theobald (with his friend Warburton) searched for parallels in the works of

Shakespeare and his contemporaries. He collated the variant texts and developed theories about their sequence and about the nature of the underlying manuscripts. He collected old manuscripts, was familiar with secretary hand, and could imagine how a compositor might misread certain of its letter forms. As someone who had published plays himself, he also was familiar 'with the possible kinds of manuscript associated with the evolution of a play' (Seary 1990: 176, 145).

Among editors and readers of Shakespeare, Theobald is famous for a particularly brilliant emendation that shows him using a combination of these methods. In the Folio text of *Henry V*, Mistress Quickly reports that as Falstaff lay dying 'his Nose was as sharpe as a pen, and a Table of greene fields'. Theobald, drawing on his ability to visualize the manuscript tacked up before the compositor, on his 'knowledge of secretary script and Elizabethan orthography', but also on his deep familiarity with Shakespeare's habits of mind and composition, surmised that the second part of the phrase should be emended to 'and a' [he] babled of green fields'. One can see here how the error, simple when deciphered, arose: a', a common Shakespearean contraction of 'he', becomes simply a; the b is misread as t; Elizabethan spelling allows for 'babled' where we would expect 'babbled'. But Theobald was also led to the correction by recognizing context and development of character: on his deathbed the previously cynical Falstaff is attempting to recite the twenty-third psalm, where the Lord 'maketh me to lie down in green pastures'. Many of Theobald's emendations, the result of his skills as a critic/editor, are found in Shakespeare texts to this day.

By the end of the eighteenth century, Malone's edition – with its commitment to authenticity, its biography constructed around facts rather than legends, its essay on 'the linguistic and poetic particulars of Shakespeare's period', its inclusion of the sonnets, and its repeated attempts to determine the chronology of the plays – had created a textual schema that has remained at the centre of Shakespeare textual studies for over two hundred years (De Grazia 1991: 2). Rowe had included a biography, but only with Malone does the relationship between the author's life and the order of his writing become a matter of textual interest, permitting, for example, analysis of changing prosody. Furthermore, although the 'author' had always been an essential element of a 'work', the relation to his actual life – to a possible connection (or not) between the death of eleven-year-old Hamnet Shakespeare and the speech on young Arthur's death in *King John* – could only occur once the timing of the plays was established. Everything from Edward Dowden's 1875 division of Shakespeare's plays into four periods reflecting his personal emotions (i.e. tragedies written when he was 'in the depths' and tragicomedies once he returned to 'the heights') to convincing descriptions of the development of verse style, was tied back to 'the author' as he was envisioned in the Romantic period.

The last of the three successive Jacob Tonsons died in 1767 and the publishing house, closed, lost its exclusive control of Shakespeare's texts. However, the sequence of editions that the Tonsons had initiated continued into the mid-nineteenth century. George Steevens's edition, which began with Johnson's and was revised by Isaac Reed, was reprinted in 1778, 1785, and 1793, with Malone's two-volume Supplement added in 1780. Malone's own edition was published in 1790. Externally the most visible change began with Johnson's 1765 edition, which 'initiated a whole series of variorum editions (1773, 1778, 1790, 1803, and 1813), culminating in Malone's variorum', itself completed after Malone's death by James Boswell the younger in 1821 (De Grazia 1991: 209). These editions became more and more voluminous. Shakespeare's text was crowded into a few lines while the rest of the page was occupied by extensive notes and disagreements attributed to a variety of editors and commentators.

Change finally came in the 1860s, when J. Glover, W.G. Clark, and W.A. Wright, all of Trinity College Cambridge, undertook what became known as the 'Cambridge Shakespeare'. These academics concentrated on the text, which whenever possible they based on a first quarto or the First

Folio. In the prospectus for the edition they explained that when they thought that text faulty, they altered it 'from the subsequent editions, the reading which has the greatest weight of authority being chosen. When none of the early editions give a reading that can stand, recourse has been had to the later ones; conjectural emendations have been rarely mentioned, and never admitted into the text except when they appeared in our judgment to carry certain conviction of their truth with them' (Murphy 2007b: 108). The Cambridge editors presented not a variorum of commentary but of text, with notes limited to 'all the readings of the early printings and selected readings from the intervening editorial tradition' (Werstine 2007: 110). This limitation became even greater in the so-called 'Globe Shakespeare' (1864), which was, for the next half-century, widely adopted. In the Cambridge edition, as the editors explained, when the 'text of the earliest editions is manifestly faulty but it is impossible to decide which, if any, of several suggested emendations is right', they retained the original reading and listed 'all the proposed alterations' in notes. However, in the one-volume Globe complete works, the editors substitute 'in the text the emendation which seemed most probable, or in cases of absolute equality, the earliest suggested'. Thus the Globe Shakespeare, carrying the authority of the scholars of Cambridge behind it, gave the unsuspecting reader the impression that the text of Shakespeare had, finally, been settled. As this book will show, that is anything but true, and yet in the twenty-first century the Globe text does live on, freely available and widely downloaded from the internet, as the Moby Shakespeare (see Chapter 12). Paradoxically, even as our texts appear brand new in their digital guise, they may be taking the reader back to an earlier moment in textual history.

PART TWO

Twentieth-Century Theories

2

The New Bibliography

The apparent certainty of the Cambridge/Globe editors slowly dissolved as the next generation of scholars began a new analysis of Shakespeare's texts. Recall that no authorial manuscripts for the printed plays and poems in the Shakespeare canon survive. In all likelihood the company archive went up in the fire that burned down the first Globe in 1613. Seeking to come as close as possible to what Heminges and Condell in their address to the readers call the author's 'own writings', much of the new scholarship searched for answers to three questions about the lost originals of the printed texts: 1) what kind(s) of manuscripts – authorial, scribal, theatrical – might these have been; 2) what do printing-house processes imply about the manuscripts; 3) is it possible to 'strip the veil of print' and, working backwards by inference, effectively recreate the content of the manuscripts. The ultimate goal was the authorial text. Two of the New Bibliographers, W.W. Greg and A.W. Pollard, did important work on the only surviving manuscript that may in part be Shakespeare's, that of *Sir Thomas More*. Unfortunately this is a play that was, as far as we know, never produced and never printed; hence it could not offer what textual scholars most longed for, an opportunity to compare a Shakespeare manuscript with its eventual printed version. Greg prepared a transcript of the manuscript for the Malone Society Editions, and Pollard published a collection of essays whose title encapsulates its argument: *Shakespeare's*

Hand in the Play of Sir Thomas More (1923). The surviving manuscript was in several different hands, which were given alphabetical letters to identify them. Evidence gradually accumulated that the three pages of the manuscript in 'Hand D' were Shakespeare's, and probably in his own handwriting. Certain idiosyncratic spellings (e.g., 'scilens' for silence) and some letter forms could perhaps be matched in the signatures. Nevertheless the complexity of the manuscript, with its several authors, scribal interventions and multiple stages of revision, described more fully in Chapter 6, might have stood as a warning as these scholars set out to work backwards from printed pages to Shakespeare's original.

Most of the work of the so-called New Bibliographers – in England primarily Pollard, Greg, and R.B. McKerrow and in America Fredson Bowers at the University of Virginia and Charlton Hinman working at the Folger Library – concerned the origins of the Shakespeare printed texts. These scholars made important advances in the technical analysis of the early publications that had implications for understanding the ways in which the content of the original manuscripts might have been altered in the printshop. For instance, they identified the various compositors who worked on the Folio through their individual spelling habits, and they analysed methods used to deal with errors in casting off, that is, miscalculating the space available on a page, which could lead to the omission of a line or the misplacement of a stage direction. Although not all the conclusions they drew have been sustained, their methods have proved permanently useful. Next, the New Bibliographers put forward a number of textual theories that dominated the field in their period but which, as we shall see, have been contested more recently. Finally, they argued that their conclusions indicated how early modern texts, especially drama of the period of Shakespeare, should be edited.

The goal of lifting 'the veil of print', in Fredson Bowers's phrase, was advanced by Charlton Hinman. Both men had worked in cryptography during the Second World War, and one might think of them as becoming spies into the past. Just as they had sought the truth beneath coded language, their desire to get 'under' the print suggests a theory of language in which words sit on top of hidden meaning, which is extractable from beneath the obfuscation caused by successive covering layers, first of manuscript and then of print. Some of their work was methodological. For instance, Hinman invented a mechanical collator that employs lenses and mirrors to allow a user to compare two pages from copies of the same book by superimposing images of the pages, one on top of another. Points where the resulting single image appears smudged expose instances where, for example, a letter varies. Hinman's work on the many Folios collected in the Folger Shakespeare Library thus revealed the presence of variants in pages where, accustomed as we are to modern machine printing, we would have assumed no differences. In fact, Hinman showed, no two copies of the Shakespeare Folio are identical, because, as we saw, corrected and uncorrected pages were bound into each copy indifferently. Hinman's view of how these variants came about has been refined by contemporary bibliographer Peter Blayney, and newer machinery for comparing pages has been introduced, but the usefulness of the conceptual method has remained.

Using their understanding of early modern printing methods and its exigencies, the New Bibliographers described the process by which the Folio was printed. For instance, they noticed that one of the compositors ('E', dubbed the 'apprentice compositor') was more likely to make errors, and that his sheets were more frequently corrected than others. They understood that there were pauses in the printing, and by identifying specific types and their gradual damage they demonstrated sequences in the volume's production. They showed, for example, that the compositors setting the comedies had 'suddenly jumped ahead to the Histories, and set the first 24 pages of *King John* before finishing *All's Well*' (Blayney 1991: 6). They reconstructed the complex history that brought *Troilus and Cressida* to the Folio late, so that it is not included in the 'Catalog' or table of contents but is silently inserted between the histories and tragedies, with an unusual first page that has no heading but simply prints 'The Prologue' surrounded by a great deal of white space. A few surviving copies of the Folio still include the sheet in which the first page of *Troilus* follows *Romeo and Juliet*, as must have been the original plan. Much of the technical work of the New Bibliographers has served as the basis for more recent analytical bibliography, and their major publications, such as W.W. Greg's *Bibliography of the English Printed Drama* (1939) and his *Dramatic Documents from the Elizabethan Playhouses* (1931), have proven invaluable to later scholars.

However, after a long period in which they dominated textual criticism, several working premises of the New Bibliographers have been challenged and in some cases overturned. Particularly important were their developing explanations for the presence of 'good' and 'bad' texts and their associated proposals for the progress from authorial papers to print. The good and bad division was partially based on the already mentioned promise of Heminges and Condell, who assured buyers of the First Folio that:

As where (before) you were abused with diverse stolen, and surreptitious copies, maimed, and deformed by the frauds and stealths of injurious imposters, that exposed them: even those are now offered to your view cured, and perfect of their limbs, and all the rest, absolute in their numbers, as he conceived them.

Debates about the precise meaning of this promise, its implication that some texts were made with corrupt intent ('frauds and stealths'), its dismissal of certain texts as 'deformed' and its implications for the possibility of finding Shakespeare's 'perfect' originals 'as he conceived them', have continued to exercise scholars.

The first question the new Bibliographers addressed was what Heminges and Condell meant by describing some copies as 'maimed' and others as 'absolute in their numbers'. Before the New Bibliography, it had been assumed that the distinction meant that all the early quartos were defective and only the Folio could be trusted. However, collation by the eighteenth- and nineteenth-century editors had revealed that a number of the Folio texts were printed from quartos. Pollard, in *Shakespeare's Folios and Quartos* (1909), consequently argued that only certain of the quartos – the first editions of *Romeo and Juliet* (1597), *Richard III* (1597) *Henry V* (1600), *Merry Wives of Windsor* (1603), *Hamlet* (1603), and the unique quarto of *Pericles* (1609) – were defective or 'bad'.

The question, then, was the derivation of these quartos. Perhaps influenced by the claim that the quartos were 'stolen and surreptitious', Pollard argued that they were 'pirated' or reproduced without authority. None, he pointed out, had been entered in the Stationers' Register. Pollard did not know that, as already explained, entrance was not required for printing, but merely served as an additional safeguard against someone else reprinting a text. He concluded that the quartos in question had been printed by unscrupulous stationers, and he further suggested that their defective texts might have been taken down by shorthand.

In Pollard's view the good quartos had been made from Shakespeare's holographs, which had been submitted to the state censor and subsequently served as promptbooks for performance. This view came to be called 'continuous copy', because it imagined a single or continuing draft or 'copy' in Shakespeare's hand going from the writer to the Master of the Revels for approval and finally serving as the promptbook in the theatre. However, W.W. Greg modified Pollard's theory. Noting a playhouse scribe's explanation for the text he is copying, 'the book whereby it was first acted from is lost: and this hath been transcribed from the foul papers of the author' (Egan 2010: 25), Greg argued that there had to be at least two copies of a play, the author's draft ('foul papers') and a fair copy made into a promptbook, that is, the book a play was 'acted from'. As time passed, other suggestions were made and abandoned as explanations for the 'bad quartos', but a general recognition of the inferior nature of these texts and arguments about their history and about how editors should handle them have continued. These will be further discussed in Chapter 7.

When the New Bibliographers began publishing, the most widely disseminated text of Shakespeare was still the Globe edition. In 1929 R.B. McKerrow was asked by Oxford University Press to undertake a new edition in original spelling. In the event, he published an account of his goals and methods in a *Prolegamena* (1939), but he died the next year. McKerrow's contributions were nevertheless important for textual theory. He proposed that the goal of an edition was to present the author's text as he had completed it, a formulation that became known as the rule of 'final intentions'. Further, McKerrow insisted that if various substantive printings survived, only the edition that came first should have any authority. He argued that one clue to the source of an early printing of a playtext could be found in the speech prefixes, which, he thought, if erratic (as in *Romeo and Juliet*, where Lady Capulet is identified at various points as 'Lady' 'Mother' 'Lady Capulet', etc.) were likely to indicate an authorial manuscript because, he believed, a theatrical manuscript would have regularized them.

Partly based on McKerrow's work, partly based on disagreeing with him, Greg spelled out editorial theories that were to dominate Shakespeare editing for the next half-century. Greg had already disagreed with Pollard's view of continuous copy by dividing the imagined theatrical manuscripts between foul papers (which he thought an author would give to the company) and promptbooks used in the playhouse for production. Crucially, one but not both of these would contain the censor's stamp of approval, which was required to authorize performance. This authorized copy, he maintained, the company would never part with to a printer, thus necessitating the existence of at least two copies. Next, Greg considered how an editor was to choose the 'copy-text', sometimes called the 'base text', that was to be the edition's default source. It might appear that, if there were more than one text, the obvious choice would be the one that seemed 'better'. This is more or less what earlier editors had believed and opted for, often preferring Folio over quarto texts when both existed. In a seminal article called 'The Rationale of Copy-Text' (1950–51), however, Greg overturned this apparent common sense. Partly based on the New Bibliographers' persistent desire to get as near as possible to the author's text, he introduced a critical distinction between what he called the 'substantives' and the 'accidentals' of a text. In his view, the accidentals (primarily punctuation and spelling, as well as capitalization) of the earliest text would likely be closest to those of the author (or 'his own writing'). Thus this earliest text should be chosen as the copy-text and its accidentals respected. Nevertheless, substantive readings, the words which affect meaning or the essence of 'the author's expression', might in some cases be found in another, later text, the one based, for example, on a corrected manuscript. So, he argued, these readings could be introduced into the edition. Thus Greg proposed what has been called the 'eclectic text'. Such a text is based as far as possible on the copy-text, with the author's accidentals and probably most of his substantives, but it is eclectic in that it borrows from diverse sources and might be emended from another text.

Greg also discussed many major issues that confront an editor, such as how to distinguish between promptbooks and foul (or fair) papers. Some of the criteria he proposed, such as the presence of actors' names alongside characters' names as a sign of use in the theatre, may seem persuasive – examining the theatrical manuscripts, Werstine has found 'not one instance of an actor's name written in an authorial hand' (2012: 194) – but others, like the search for surviving authorial spellings, are more dubious. Although Greg himself had divided Pollard's imaginary continuous copy into two, he had a strong objection to theories which further multiplied hypothesized manuscripts. For instance, he objected to the suggestion made by Alice Walker, a prominent textual scholar commissioned to complete McKerrow's edition, that quartos used as copy for the Folio were 'improved by comparison with authoritative manuscripts', an idea widely accepted later.

Much modern textual analysis still depends on the scholarship of the New Bibliographers and the questions they raised, even when they could not answer them or their answers have subsequently been rejected. They attempted to create a scientific method for the textual study of Shakespeare. Much of their work was ultimately limited by binary thinking (e.g., a text was based either on a promptbook or on foul papers); by a failure fully to consider the textual implications of Shakespeare's relationship to the theatres he wrote for (he may have had specific actors in mind and put their names in a manuscript or the additions of actors may have been recorded in various manuscripts); by a desire for uniform, global explanations for diverse phenomena; and by a reluctance to engage with other forms of literary criticism. Nevertheless, the topics they argued about – the explanation for good and bad texts, the role of actors, audience members, stationers and compositors in the construction of surviving texts, the difference between texts written for different venues (London or the provinces, the court or the public theatres), the relationship between the surviving printed texts and Shakespeare's manuscripts, the effects of the printing process on the resultant texts, and finally, how an editor of Shakespeare is to treat the surviving texts – all continue to be prominent issues for textual scholars today. The technical work of the New Bibliographers led to a material understanding of texts, where earlier editors had often used aesthetic criteria in their analysis. Nevertheless, the conclusions of the New Bibliographers, such as the greater authority of the earliest texts, had been partially anticipated by the scholarship of Theobald, Malone, and the Cambridge editors. Most important, like their predecessors, the New Bibliographers continued to be focused on the author as the ultimate source of authority, and they accepted as the goal of a modern editor the elimination of all other sources of interference with a text. All of this changed with the advent of poststructuralist theory.

3

The Advent of Poststructuralism

Imagine that in 1623 you are a purchaser of the first collected works of William Shakespeare, a playwright whose plays you have seen on the Globe or Blackfriars stage, or at court. Perhaps you own a quarto or two of his plays, say of *Richard III* and *Hamlet*. You decide to buy the Folio, although it is very expensive, normally costing 15 shillings Blayney 1991: 26, (and more if you have it bound), because you have heard that it includes eighteen plays that have never been printed before. Some you have seen, others not.

Because you like its title, you start reading *All's Well That Ends Well*. This comedy concerns a young aristocrat, Bertram, who is forced into a marriage with a young woman, Helen, who deeply loves him but whom he considers unsuitable for a person of his status. Once Helen, having cured the King of a terrible illness, is allowed to choose her husband, and picks him, Bertram decides that his only choice is to flee. He tells his follower, Paroles (in the Folio spelling) that 'Warres is no strife / To the darke house, and the detected wife'. This strikes you as strange, and it occurs to you that there must be an error: Bertram is running away from his 'detested wife'. To you it appears that this is a necessary correction, requiring the change of only one letter, and you tell yourself that of course 'detested' is what Shakespeare intended. You may even correct the letter on the page or in the margin of your volume, as many readers did in the course of 'perfecting' and correcting the books they owned (Mayer 2018).

In this sequence of events you depend on what seems to you obvious – that the play has an author, Shakespeare (after all his name is given on the title page of the volume), and that his intentions are determinable in two ways. First of all, he had what Peter Shillingsburg refers to as an intention 'to do', that is, in this case an 'intention to record on paper, or in some other medium, a specific sequence of words and punctuation according to an acceptable or feasible grammar or relevant linguistic convention' (1996: 33). 'Detected' just might work grammatically, but still may not have been what Shakespeare 'did', that is, put on paper. The mistake could have been made by a scribe misreading or a compositor picking up a wrong type. But it is what Shillingsburg refers to as an intention 'to mean' that has alerted you to the error. At no time does Bertram 'detect' Helen, even when she tricks him into sleeping with her by pretending to be another woman. He does, however, mightily detest her.

You accept, then, that the author 'meant' something. But as you look at the play, you realize that it isn't always so clear what the author meant. As Shillingsburg says, 'the intention to *mean* is inconclusively recoverable through critical interpretation; the intention to *do* is . . . more immediately recoverable from the signs written' (34–5). You have grasped the error using one of several 'guides' that Shillingsburg identifies to help the reader find the intention to 'do', in this case 'the implications of context' or, in a different formulation, what John Jowett argues justifies emendation, the recognition that Shakespeare meant to make sense (2017c: lvi). That usually, but not always, works to give a definitive and certain correction. For example, earlier in the play (1.3.156) the Countess, Bertram's mother, has realized what is making Helen so sad; she tells Helen, as the original spelling has it, that she has found 'the mistrie of your louelinesse'. The Countess does love Helen, but, except to Bertram, there seems to be no mystery about the young woman's loveliness. In this case, in the opinion of most textual critics, this is a simple compositorial error of a 'turned letter', rendering 'n' as 'u': the word should be 'lonelinesse'. The Countess is not simply praising Helen but noting that since Bertram's departure for court Helen has kept to herself. Here, using critical interpretation strengthened by an understanding of the procedures of the printshop, you think that you have found Shakespeare's intended word.

The assumption that the author was an identifiable person of a particular historical period, with a style, a cultural context, and often interconnected and repeated thematic interests, and that recognition of these identifiers will assist the careful reader or the textual editor to determine his or her intentions, seems obvious and was taken for granted for centuries. The New Bibliographers, like the eighteenth-century scholars who preceded them, had disagreed about specifics but not about such fundamentals. Without precisely saying so, these earlier textual critics imagined that the texts before them were written, usually, by one man, William Shakespeare, the 'author', who had full control or 'authority' over the text, which therefore reflected his intentions at the moment of writing. If he later reworked his material, the resulting text would embody his 'final intentions'. Although the text or texts that survive may contain errors or may have been damaged in transmission, the New Bibliographers, using their spatial metaphors, assumed that lying 'behind' – or 'beneath' – the veil, whatever has come down to us was originally a single, perfect work as Shakespeare intended it to be. Occasionally they conceded that dramatic texts could have been cut or adjusted for specific performances, but the task of the editor was obvious. It was to determine, restore and if necessary recreate the original text as an expression of the author's intentions. Using methods that aspired to be scientific, the editor expected to find firm and persuasive solutions for any uncertainties and to establish a definitive text.

The challenge to this concept of the unitary author with singular responsibility for the desired object of textual criticism, the definitive text, came in the late twentieth century. It was sparked by essays by Roland Barthes and Michel Foucault that were not focused particularly on Shakespeare but went directly to the heart of canonical Shakespeare criticism. The first assault was on the idea of the author. Barthes' very title, 'The Death of the Author' (1967), was an attack on the central focus of all textual analysis, the author, who (or which) he viewed as a 'modern figure', the product of a post-medieval society which 'discovered the prestige of the individual' and hence 'attached the greatest importance to the "person" of the author'. For Barthes, on the contrary, in a text 'it is language which speaks, not the author'. Barthes' further objection was to the idea of a unique, stable text, created at one moment in the past by that individual author (rather as, in various religions, the Bible or the Torah is said to have come directly from God). Instead, Barthes argues, 'the text is not a line of words releasing a single "theological" meaning (the "message" of the Author-God) but a multi-dimensional space in which a variety of writings, none of them original, blend and clash. The text is a tissue of quotations drawn from the innumerable centres of culture'. For this multiple text it is not the writer (the absent and omnipotent deity or 'Author-God') but ultimately the reader who creates cohesion and meaning: 'a text's unity lies not in its original but in its destination' (Barthes 2006: 277–80).

The issue was then taken up and somewhat modified by Michel Foucault, in an essay called 'What is an Author?' (1969). Using as an introduction the playwright Samuel Beckett's provocative question, 'What does it matter who is speaking?', Foucault challenges the idea that the author is simply the 'person to whom the production of a text, a book, or a work can be legitimately attributed'. Instead, the 'author-function' is that which is 'characteristic of the mode of existence, circulation, and functioning of certain discourses within a society'. Deprived of a 'role as an originator', the writer becomes 'a variable and complex function of the discourse'. Most pointedly, Foucault writes, 'The author is the principle of thrift in the proliferation of meaning' (2006: 284, 290). In other words, in the face of all the different things that a text might mean to different readers, the figure of the author is deployed to restrict its signification. Historically 'authorship' has been chosen as the primary, even the only, way to make the possible proliferation of meaning manageable. But history might have chosen genre (all books of sonnets regardless of who wrote them) or even size (the difference between disposable quartos or expensive Folios) as the ordering principle of a text's meaning or significance. Instead it chose the author's name and developed an entire analytic system on that basis.

Foucault also began discussion of another concept important to textual criticism, the 'work'. To some extent his concern is with the 'works' of an author, asking whether, say, a laundry list in a writer's notebook is a 'work' of his or part of his 'works'. He brings in Shakespeare as he considers the way 'the proper name and the author's name are situated between two roles of description and designation', giving the specific example that 'if we proved that Shakespeare did not write those sonnets which pass for his, that would constitute a significant change and affect the manner in which the author's name functions' (Foucault 2006: 282–4). In fact, Patrick Cheney's insistence that 'Shakespeare' signifies a 'poet-playwright' (rather than exclusively a dramatist) seems precisely an attempt to affect the way the author's name functions (2004).

The effect of these essays and others that followed was to challenge the stability and even the fundamental meaning of three apparently established concepts, the author, the work, and the text. The issues were debated both among scholars concerned with textual theory in general, and by those who would apply them, directly or indirectly, to Shakespeare. They formed part of a poststructural cultural moment in which the stability of many concepts previously viewed as immutable, up to and including truth, were challenged. Arguments ranged over general claims, such as Foucault's assertion that the 'author' did not emerge until he was subject to repression, and more specifically over the implications of these claims for textual analysis.

Two critical publications of the early 1980s had a direct effect on Shakespeare studies. The first was a brief article by Stephen Orgel, 'What is a Text?' (1981), clearly titled to parallel Foucault's notorious essay. Here Orgel, partly tracing out the implications of E.A.J. Honigmann's earlier *The Stability of Shakespeare's Text* (1965), argued against a series of central New Bibliographical assumptions: first, that 'by developing rules of evidence and refining techniques of description . . . the relation of editions of a work to each other and to the author's manuscript could be understood, and an accurate text could thereby be produced', and further, that 'the correct text is the author's final manuscript' and 'the authority of a text derives from the author' (1981: 3). Instead, Orgel pointed out, Shakespeare's plays were the result of a collaborative process. The authority controlling and represented by the performance text was that of the company, while the authority controlling and represented by the published text was that of the stationer. Most important of all, Orgel asserted, the goal of the New Bibliographers was inherently futile. There is no way we can get back to the author's original text. Texts were always unstable, likely to have been altered and rewritten repeatedly both by the poet and by his collaborators, the company. Thus Honigmann's book would have been more accurately titled 'the instability of Shakespeare's text', an idea discussed further in Chapter 7.

Orgel was concerned specifically with Shakespeare, but two years later, in *A Critique of Modern Textual Criticism*, Jerome McGann introduced the general concept of the 'socialized text', whose author was always collaborative and whose 'mode of existence . . . is fundamentally social rather than personal' (1983: 8). McGann insisted that 'Authoritative texts are arrived at by an exhaustive reconstruction not of an author and his intentions so much as of an author and his context of work'; in fact, 'a definitive text, like the author's final intentions, may not exist, may never have existed' (1983: 84, 89–90). McGann was a scholar of romantic poetry, well aware that there are differences   between   the   textual   problems   posed   by

Shakespeare's works, for which no manuscripts survive, and those posed by the writings of poets such as Byron, whose poems exist in many manuscripts in different forms, materially demonstrating the instability of his text. But because so much textual criticism in English had been devoted to Shakespeare, McGann addressed a considerable part of his book to arguments about how to prepare Shakespeare's texts.

McGann's *Critique* took on fundamental elements of traditional textual criticism, with special attention to the theories of the New Bibliographers W.W. Greg and Fredson Bowers. He objected in particular to the idealized concept of 'final intentions.' The concept had been especially significant as a tool for textual work, because it assisted an editor in choosing the copy-text for a critical edition. Greg and his followers Bowers and G. Thomas Tanselle had assumed that the author's final intentions would be found in the manuscript the author submitted for printing, and therefore (as Greg argued) a manuscript or, if that was absent, the earliest printed version, should be chosen as copy-text because that would come closest to the author's 'accidentals'. Such a theory implicitly accorded all 'authority' to the 'author'. Other textual scholars, like Philip Gaskell, instead thought that even when manuscripts existed, the first printed version, incorporating normalized punctuation and spelling, might embody what the author intended. Indeed directions to compositors of the early modern period clearly show that they had responsibility for spelling and punctuation, as authors no doubt knew. (The three pages in the hand D section of *Sir Thomas More*, whether or not they are by Shakespeare, reveal that writers might hardly punctuate at all, leaving that task to the actors on the stage and the compositors in the printshop.) After showing that the fundamental concept of final intentions did not function for the romantic period – when, for example, manuscripts exhibiting Byron's repeated rewriting as well as Mary Shelley's intervention in his work vividly complicate such a claim – McGann went on to challenge it for the early modern period. The problem, as he identified it, is that the concept of final intentions 'hypothesizes two related phenomena which do not and cannot exist: an autonomous author, and an ideal ("finally intended") text' (1983: 56). The error is the assignment of all authority to the author, where really, as is easily understood in the case of a dramatist like Shakespeare, the poet, the company, the publisher, the censor, all had different kinds of authority over the text that would finally emerge.

McGann also addressed two other concepts. He helpfully defined the 'work' as 'a series of specific "texts", a series of specific acts of production, and the entire process which both of these series constitute' (1983: 52). (In a similar vein Paul Eggert more recently calls the work a 'regulative concept that comprehends all acts of editing as well as writing, copying and reading'; each of the successive texts that emerges is a 're-presentation' of the work (2019: 174).) When one starts to imagine what is meant by 'King Lear', such broad definitions become especially useful. Clearly King Lear is not just the quarto of 1608, or the somewhat different Folio text, or the Restoration version with a happy ending, or a particular modern edition conflating quarto and Folio, or a different edition with certain emendations, or even the cut version used in a theatrical performance or a film. Those are the 'texts'; the work, 'King Lear', is something larger, not confined to or revealed in a single text or document. McGann, in his discussion of authority over a text, also acknowledged the role of the editor. All in all, in the case of Shakespeare a socialized textual view means understanding literary creation as the result of collaboration not only with other authors and with the writers of source materials, but with the demands of the repertory company, with the necessities and quirks of early modern theatres whether open-air or 'private', with the historical and social environment, and eventually with the constraints of book production from the width of columns to the habits of compositors.

In contrast to literary critics, theatre historians found it easy to understand theories limiting the authority of the original author. For example, T.H. Howard-Hill asserted that 'playwrights' intentions can be fulfilled only in performance' (Tanselle 2005: 194). Therefore a revision – for example, the Folio text of *King Lear*, now generally thought to be Shakespeare's own reworking a few years after the quarto text had been staged – might reflect a playwright's intentions better than a pre-production text. Even if a surviving text incorporated theatrical changes and revisions made by someone other than the original writer, it might still represent the play as he or she had intended it. To support this theory scholars often point out that Shakespeare, as a member of his company, probably approved many changes large and small made before or during performances. Yet whether he enjoyed yielding some of his authorial control in this way or whether these changes matched his intentions is unknowable. In any case, the impact of Foucault, Orgel, McGann and other poststructuralists has been to underline the fact that the playwright is only one source of meaning in an early modern theatrical text, and that his traditional status as all-knowing, all-controlling 'author' is no longer intellectually sustainable.

Poststructuralism and its implied rejection of certainty affected textual studies on all fronts, not only authorship and intentionality. Eventually almost every element of the New Bibliography was reconsidered: apparently definite conclusions about the procedures of the printshop, the methodology for determining collaboration, and the most desirable ways of editing were all challenged. As we will see, lively and sometimes heated debate on these questions is still continuing.

4

Textual and Other Theories

The challenge to the New Bibliography occurred at the same time as critical theorists of all kinds were being challenged by poststructuralism and its questioning of traditional ideas of authorship and intention. For Shakespeareans, as Barbara Mowat put it, 'the setting aside of Shakespeare-as-Author' allowed the plays to be read freed of 'the father's signature' but instead 'as woven from a stereographic plurality of signifiers' (1998: 137–8). The new approaches varied – they were new historicist, feminist, post-colonialist, queer – but all were facilitated by the explosion of poststructuralist reconsiderations of text, work and author. Although the new readings focused primarily on reinterpretation, some of these analyses revealed the limitations of traditionally constructed texts and, more particularly, the ways they had been affected by textual theories and editorial methods.

Among the New Historicists, Stephen Greenblatt concluded that 'there has probably never been a time since the early eighteenth century when there was less confidence in the "text"'. In his view, not only had the new textual historians undermined the belief that skilled editing can 'give us an authentic record of Shakespeare's original intentions, but theater historians have challenged the whole notion of the text as the central, stable locale of theatrical meaning'. Greenblatt recognized that the 'textual traces' that interest scholars are not 'sources of numinous authority' (i.e. emanations of the author-god) but 'signs of contingent social practices ... products of extended borrowings, collective exchanges, and mutual enchantments' (1998: 3–5, 7). In such an understanding of the text, the author and his intentions are sidelined, and the singularity of the plays and poems is reduced as they are placed on a level with police reports and exorcisms. Like Barthes, Greenblatt accepts that 'a text's unity lies not in its origin but in its destination', and just as Barthes transfers authority from the author to the reader, so Shakespeare's 'magical power and princely authority', like Prospero's, 'pass . . . from the performer onstage to the crowd of spectators' (1998: 157). Translating these beliefs into concrete terms, the third edition of the *Norton Shakespeare* that Greenblatt oversaw accepted as its stated mission to 'edit the text, not the work', addressing the surviving texts without assuming that the editor could recreate the author's original intentions and taking advantage of being 'born digital' to yield some power over text and paratext to the destination reader (McMullan and Gossett 2015: 84–5). (See Chapter 8 for further discussion.)

Another poststructural approach, queer textual work, was exemplified by Jeffrey Masten's *Textual Intercourse: Collaboration, Authorship, and Sexualities in Renaissance Drama*. Masten's study situates itself 'at the intersection of the textual and the sexual' and relates 'the material conditions and cultural representations of sex/gender and of textual production' (1997: 5). Masten accepts Foucault's description of the author as an ideological construct whose function is to limit 'the proliferation of meaning' (1997: 10) – the 'author' is thus distinct from the 'writer', who lacks an author's total control – and he examines the 'historical and theoretical challenges', both in life and composition, that collaboration poses to the ideology of authorship. Collaboration, Masten argues, must be understood as a 'dispersal of author/ity, rather than a simple doubling of it' (1997: 19) Contending that 'late sixteenth- and early seventeenth-century dramatic writing

occurs within [a] context of collaborative homoerotics',
Masten analyses both male friendship and joint writing in the
period, examining such plays as *Two Gentlemen of Verona* to
show how collaboration is 'implicated in and enabled by
Renaissance discourses of eroticism, gender, and power'.
Masten's focus at this point was interpretive. For instance, he
re-read the controversial conclusion of *Two Gentlemen*, in
which one young man 'apparently offers his beloved to the
friend who has just attempted to rape her' as a 'conflation of
Petrarchan love within male friendship' (1997: 37, 45–7).

Criticizing editorial work that remains 'at the level of the
word, the crux, the lemma, the line, the gloss', Masten then
further developed what he named 'queer philology', which
examines 'the ramifications of research into the history of
sexuality' for editing 'the text itself' (2016: 582, 570–1). For
example, he analyses the consequences of editorial decisions
about a word –or possibly two words – in *Othello*. In 1.1, in
both Folio and quarto, the villain Iago warns Desdemona's
father, Brabantio, a Venetian senator, that his daughter has
eloped with the Moor Othello: 'Even now, now, very now, an
old black ram / Is tupping your white ewe'. In 3.3 Iago asks
Othello if he would 'grossly gape on? Behold her topped'. The
verb here is spelled 'topt' in Q and top'd' in F; Theobald
changed it to 'tupp'd'. Similarly, when in the final scene Othello
justifies killing his wife because 'Cassio did top her', Pope
emended the word to 'tup'. A modern editor, Michael Neill,
accepted both emendations to tupped, arguing that 'the word,
with its powerfully animalistic suggestions, is clearly a favourite
of Iago's, and it seems important to preserve the echo of 1.1'
(cited in Masten 2016: 573).

The words 'top' and 'tup' are phonetically very similar and
are likely to sound almost identical in the theatre. But they
have different implications, 'tupping' suggesting animal-like
sexual contact, 'topping' suggesting gendered dominance.
Masten cites the objection of the late seventeenth-century
classical critic, Thomas Rymer, to reversing 'tupped' to 'topped'
in the opening scene, as it would remove the bestiality at

the – to Rymer, unacceptable – cost of having a Moor on top. On the other hand, Masten points out that in emending the line in 3.3, 'choosing "tupped" puts the bestial back in Desdemona' and gives the ruling discursive hand to 'the racist Iago'. In either case, 'what is persistent in these lines is the centrality of hierarchy as inseparable from sexual acts' (2016: 574–5). Citing but rejecting Greenblatt's warning against the 'diminishing returns [of] too much explanatory whispering at the margins' (2016: 570), Masten uses this example to demand a 'broader, deeper, more polymorphous attention to matters of gender, sex, affect, sexual identity . . . and their relation to race as a more global background' to the text. Hence his proposed solution to the editorial conundrum in *Othello* is to print t*pping (and presumably also t*pped and t*p), thus sending 'the reader, hailed now as a queer philologist, into the glossarial notes . . . to produce the meaning of the text him- or herself' (582–3). Such a method embodies the poststructuralist sense that final textual authority lies not with the author but with the reader; the sense could be even stronger if the edition were on a modern electronic platform that would allow words like 'top' and 'tup' to flicker or permit the reader to enter her choice into the text 'itself' (see Chapter 12).

Feminist theory has also affected textual work in a variety of forms, not all of it poststructuralist. In general, as Kate Ozment writes, feminist textual editors have critiqued the notion of an 'objective' editorial apparatus. Arguing that traditional editorial practice 'is based on the ideology of both editor and reader', feminist practice considers 'the "messy" facts of authorship, production, and reception: race, class, gender and sexuality' (2020: 163). Usually editors have found the most scope for change in their annotations. Refocused commentary notes were among the earliest feminist contributions: Ann Thompson, editing *The Taming of the Shrew* in the early 1980s, explicitly worked against traditional interpretations of that play. For instance, in commentary to the first scene between Petruccio and Katherina, she points out how Petruccio 'seems to relish her performance as much as his own' (1984:

87) and wryly notes that 'he is not the only Shakespearean hero to assume that a woman with spirit must be unchaste' (92). Such attempts to disturb usual readings of the play have continued: a performance comment in the *Norton 3* warns that although 'Katherina's final speech may suggest she has been tamed, many actors have delivered it in ways that undercut or ironize its meaning' (Greenblatt et al 2015: 414).

Different attitudes towards gender have also affected 'the text itself'. For example, in the final lines of *As You Like It*, which exists only in a Folio text, Hymen tells the Duke that he has brought '*thy daughter . . . . That thou mightst ioine his hand with his, / Whose heart within his bosome is*' (5.4.109–13). Editors since F3 have changed the first 'his' – which refers to the Duke's daughter Rosalind – to 'her', arguing that here, as in an earlier line of the play, 'Helen's cheek but not his heart' (3.2.142), 'his' is a misreading of what was presumably written in the manuscript, 'hir', a frequent spelling for 'her' at the time. Laurie Maguire, however, shows that the change is tied to an editorial intervention by Rowe, who added a stage direction for the previously cross-dressed Rosalind to enter 'in Woman's Cloths'. Although Rowe was himself a dramatist, he ignored the short time available between Rosalind's exit and her reappearance, a theatrical constraint that makes a costume change unlikely. Thus the stage image intended, Maguire maintains, is more probably one of a male–male marriage. In a comedy that has consistently teased about the sex and gender(s) of Rosalind and the boy actor who embodies her, this is just 'one more exuberant coup' for the heroine, 'adding to the play's multiple perspectives on gender'. In fact, Maguire concludes, 'Analyzing this crux in the context of a reading of gender removes the crux' (2000: 62–3).

A minor war among textual critics over one word in *The Tempest*, another play for which we have only a Folio text, instructively reveals continuing tensions about the roles of technical analysis, philosophical belief and political commitment in editing texts. In the midst of the betrothal masque, Ferdinand expresses his delight: 'Let me live here ever!

/ So rare a wondered father and a wise / Makes this place paradise' (4.1.122–4). Or does he say this? Rowe substituted 'wife' for 'wise' 'on the tacit assumptions that it made better sense for Ferdinand to acknowledge Miranda's importance and that F's compositor had misread a long "s"' (Vaughan and Vaughan, 1999: 136). Many subsequent editors accepted Rowe's emendation. Nevertheless, by the middle of the twentieth century, 'wise' had returned as 'the reading of choice'. Then, in 1978, at a high moment of feminist scholarship and reinterpretation, Jeanne Addison Roberts had an 'aha!' moment in the Folger Shakespeare Library. Re-examining the library's multiple copies of the Shakespeare Folio, she claimed that in two she found 'wife' clearly visible, and in two more 'the crossbar of the *f* was in the process of breaking', thus giving the appearance of the long s – ſ – described earlier (Wayne 1998: 184–5). Consequently, 'Feminists took comfort in the text's reference to Miranda's importance in a play so male-oriented' and the emendation was accepted into various editions (Vaughan and Vaughan 1999: 136). But the argument refused to die. One male critic complained that 'wife' gave 'trite sense'; a feminist critic retorted that such objections were 'interpretive and partial', the product of 'gender bias' (Jowett in *TxC* 1987: 616; Wayne 1998: 186). Even then the argument did not rest. In 1996 Peter Blayney, an expert on early modern printing techniques, writing 'as a typographer' and using electronic magnification of the lines, announced that 'I cannot agree that what resembles a crossbar in Folger copies 6 and 73 is in fact part of the type at all' (Blayney 1996, Intro: xxxi). Blayney concluded that the letter in contention was, in fact, always a long s. Valerie Wayne, while acknowledging the difficulty of refuting such claims 'in a culture so dependent upon the scientific discourse of technology', responded that 'such discourse is usually gendered as male' (1996: 187), and fell back upon the suggestion that technology can only offer information about the printed Folio, not about the underlying manuscript. Reviewing the entire conflict, Ronald Tumelson found flaws in both the 'masculinist' bibliographical evidence and the 'gynocritic system that insists on its own ideological control over and dissemination of Shakespeare's texts' (2006: 88). He concluded that 'The time for appeals to a singular First Folio *Tempest*, or for claims that it *reads* a certain way, has come and gone. Our editions of Shakespeare continue to choose multi-lexicality over univocality' (2006: 90). The 'aha' moment vanishes and once again, the poststructuralist reader has the last word.

Undeterred, after almost two decades of feminist editing, Wayne returned to confront how, in her view, Shakespeare's texts are 'gendered by those who edit, annotate, and introduce them' (2018: 549). Many of Wayne's examples come from *Cymbeline*, where 'editorial discretion' has masked the play's attention 'to the slander of women under the sign of propriety'. For Wayne, such choices 'disrupt the long-standing binary between editing and criticism as they make meaning through text, introductions and commentary notes' (2018: 551). She also points out a selective absence of notes, like the traditional failure to explain the erotic meaning of 'pudency' as the banished husband Posthumus Leonatus recounts how his new wife, the princess Innogen, restrained him from his 'lawful pleasure ... with / A pudency so rosy' (2.5.8–10). Earlier editors were likely to gloss 'pudency' discreetly in French, as a '*double entendre*' (double meaning), just hinting at a sexual significance, or else to fall back on the *OED* definition, modesty or bashfulness. Unabashed, in her Arden edition Wayne instead proposes that the reference is to 'genitalia *rosy* from sexual arousal, since *pudency* is associated through Latin with 'pudendum', meaning 'the external genitals, *esp.* the vulva'. Within the editorial history of 'the text itself' Wayne also rejects common emendations that alter the relationship between the central figures, Innogen and Posthumus. The first occurs in a letter from Posthumus introducing the villain Iachimo. Where in the Folio Posthumus urges Innogen to '*Reflect upon him accordingly, as you value your trust*', signing 'Leonatus' on a separate line, Hanmer and many subsequent editors changed 'trust' to 'truest' and relineated, so that the letter closed with a statement about her 'truest Leonatus'. As Wayne notes, the emendation and relineation 'emphasize Posthumus' truth rather than, as in F, conveying the conditional character of his trust' (2017: 181). Posthumus's second letter (3.2.40–7) concludes with a similarly ambiguous phrase, once again presented in a modern edition (New Cambridge) in a way that occludes 'the contingent nature of Posthumus's affection'. 'As a woman and a feminist' Wayne objects to changes that 'transpose comparative and ambiguous statements about a woman's trust into plainer assertions of a man's truth' (2018: 564–5). Her commitments also lead her to 'unediting', a movement we will discuss in Chapter 8.

A different form of textual work influenced by feminism is seen in works of book history (see Chapter 9). Foundational research is presented by Helen Smith in *Grossly Material Things: Women and Book Production in Early Modern England* (2012), which traces the contributions women made to early printed books 'at each stage of their production, dissemination, and appropriation' (4). A 2020 collection of essays on *Women's Labour and the History of the Book in Early Modern England* further explores the roles of women as everything from rag-pickers and paper makers, to widows who continued printing businesses after their husbands' deaths, to book owners, readers, annotators and finally editors (Wayne 2020). Women's attitudes towards Shakespeare's works specifically have been gleaned from the history of early modern women who purchased and owned quartos or the Folio. Some of these women annotated their books or signed their names, appropriating the volumes to themselves (Mayer 2018: 50–1). Particularly notable as a female collector of books was Frances Wolfreston. About 400 of her pre-1677 books were included in a later auction catalogue, including 'about 100 playbooks' (Newcomb 2020: 259). Her volumes of Shakespeare's plays and poems included not only first editions, among them the only surviving copy of the first edition of *Venus and Adonis*, but volumes that appeared between 1632–1659, which suggests that she continued to seek out freshly published editions. For Newcomb, Wolfreston's interest and her collection confirm 'that female readership helped to sustain Shakespeare's reputation through this tumultuous century' (2020: 260). Even later, women kept Shakespeare alive through editorial work; Molly Yarn identifies 'at least seventy women who edited Shakespeare prior to 1950'. One of these, Katherine Lee Bates, seems to have been a poststructuralist *avant la lettre*, inviting student 'engagement with the text's material history by deflecting the assumption of a single, authoritative reading'. Each of her textual notes presents variant possibilities and leaves it up to the reader to decide 'Which is better?' (Yarn 2020: 194–6).

Yet a different intersection of textual and critical analysis is found in Leah Marcus's *How Shakespeare Became Colonial* (2017). Marcus, who earlier set out suggestions for 'editing Shakespeare in a postmodern age' (2007), objects that 'the editing of Shakespeare remains imbued with significant traces of a colonial mindset even as the literary study of Shakespeare works to critique that very mindset' (2017: 14). Like the feminist critics, Marcus offers close readings of the ways in which editors have shaped interpretation through glosses, but the heart of her argument is a general description of 'Editing Shakespeare for the Raj'. Here she analyses how editions of Shakespeare's works were used to spread and confirm colonial values in the long period of British dominance in Asia. Relating her project to Critical Race Theory, Marcus attacks the English New Bibliographers, arguing that 'advances made a century ago in perfecting Shakespeare's texts so that he could serve as the best possible exemplar of English to the world are very much at odds with our present goal of reducing the colonial accretions that remain in those texts' (2017: 18).

Striking illustrations for Marcus's argument come from *The Taming of the Shrew* and *The Merchant of Venice*. In both plays much editorial intervention has taken the form of added stage directions rather than emendations to the text. To *Taming*, eighteenth- and nineteenth-century editors added many directions for the tamer Petruccio to use physical violence, thus deflecting attention from his 'more sophisticated' verbal tactics. Marcus surmises that such stage violence 'resonated with audiences .... because it mimicked elements of "necessary" British colonial violence against subject populations'. Pope's isolation of the first scenes as a separate 'Induction' she believes had a similar purpose: according to Marcus it protected the play's 'miniature portrait of Warwickshire from contamination by the main plot, which takes place at a safe distance in Italy'. Equally important, Marcus notes, while no asides are marked in the Folio, those added by editors are given exclusively to the male characters, setting up a hierarchy between those characters (Petruccio, Lucentio) with direct access to the audience and those characters (Kate, Bianca) without, who, consequently, 'lose in depth and sophistication' (Marcus 2017: 60–7).

Marcus finds a similarly unequal assignment of asides in *The Merchant of Venice*. An editorial 'aside' is standardly added to the Jewish merchant Shylock's line, 'I hate him for he is a Christian' (1.3.38), while usually none is added to the Christian Venetian Antonio's comment that 'The devil can cite Scripture for his purpose' (1.3.94). Editors thus construct 'a Jew who is at least outwardly fair-minded towards the Christians, but inwardly seething with a hatred born of ancestral persecution .... In most modern editions, the Christians are allowed to openly articulate their anti-Semitism, but Shylock's parallel sentiment with regard to Christians is constructed as something hidden, more venomous because of its secrecy' (2017: 114, 116).

Turning to 'the text itself', Marcus analyses editorial emendations of the Folio's 'Mistris' to 'Masters' or 'Master' in *Taming of the Shrew*. The persuasiveness of these emendations is variable. When Vincentio says to his servant Biondello, 'What, you notorious villaine, didst thou neuer / see thy Mistris father, *Vincentio*?' (5.1.47–8), the second Folio emends to 'thy Master's father' because Vincentio is the father of (the male) Lucentio. Yet Marcus argues for retaining 'Mistris' nevertheless because the line 'can be understood as contributing to a subtext of female authority in the folio text ... Rather than being emended out of existence, the theme could help compromise Petruchio's much flaunted masculine dominance' (2017: 66). Here Marcus's willingness to retain 'mistress' may strike some readers as a case of textual work being used for contemporary political purposes.

How such purposes vary over time and between editors is well exemplified as different editors of *The Merchant of Venice* determine speech prefixes for a central character. Throughout the first quarto, those for the Jewish moneylender switch between *Shy(l)* and *Iew(e)*. Early in the twentieth century Dover Wilson proposed that the compositors were short of upper-case *S* types and hence when necessary substituted *Jew* (*Iew*) or *Jewe* (*Iewe*) for *Shylock*. For Wilson, this was a 'plausible explanation for the otherwise apparently meaningless variation' (cited in Marcus 2017: 122). However, Marcus argues, after the Holocaust these variations no longer appear so meaningless. Indeed, she points out, 'the speech prefix "Jew" is especially prevalent at points in the play in which the action resonates with traditional anti-Semitic stereotypes', such as 1.3, where Shylock's character begins to mesh with 'stereotypes about the Jewish usurer'; 3.3, where Shylock repeatedly stifles Antonio's attempts to speak; and 4.1, the trial scene (2017: 122). Consequently, in Marcus's *Norton Critical Edition* she maintains the original variation. When the guidelines for the *Norton Shakespeare 3* instead required the use of a personal name, her edition used Shylock for all the speech prefixes, reifying what Dover Wilson had assumed was the original intention all along.

However, the debate among editors continued. In his 2010 *Arden 3* edition of *Merchant*, John Drakakis again reveals how theoretical commitments may affect textual methodology. Persuaded by Richard Kennedy's argument that the compositors' shortage was not of *S* but of *I* (roman and italic), Drakakis concludes that the compositor started by 'following his copy and setting the speech prefix "*Iew(e)*"'. He only 'departed from that practice whenever his supply became depleted. In so far as we can speculate upon Shakespeare's intentions from these details, they point inescapably towards the conclusion that the dramatic character . . . was designated throughout the manuscript by the speech prefix ' "Jew" ' (Drakakis 2010: 422). On the basis of these inferred intentions, Drakakis makes 'Jew' the speech prefix throughout his edition. Marcus objects vigorously, on two grounds. The first is based on the technology of textual production: Kennedy's work assumes a regularity in the printing house procedures that has been refuted by McKenzie and others (see Chapter 7). We now know that printers did not work on signatures seriatim and that they often set type for more than one book at a time, so it is unclear how to judge their need for individual types (or letters). Furthermore, Drakakis does not explain lines where the compositor uses '*Shy*' as a speech prefix but the dialogue includes italic upper-case 'I', nor why the other Jews in the play (Jessica, Tubal) are identified by their names, rather than, for example, as '2 Jew'. Yet clearly Marcus's most profound objection arises from her political commitments: 'Drakakis constructs a text of *Merchant* that takes away Shylock's most obvious connection with Englishness – his thoroughly English name – and forces him back into the age-old anti-Semitic, alien stereotype of the Jew'. In her view, Drakakis implies a Shakespeare who thinks of 'the Jew as a type but is feeling his way to a more individuated view of character, as indicated in the name Shylock, which in Drakakis' text is only visible to readers when it is conferred on the Jew by Christians'. This does reduce the possibility that some of the play's anti-Semitism derives from Shakespeare, but, Marcus concludes, for Drakakis 'the cost of saving Shakespeare . . .was the creation of a text of *Merchant* more deeply immersed than any previous edition in stereotypes about the Jew through its substitution of 53 speech prefixes of "Jew" for Shylock's name' (125–6). Once again, what is meant by 'Shakespeare' is established by the action of textual editors.

The various theoretical stances described in this chapter intersect unevenly with new textual work, though all were stimulated and supported by the general ferment that overturned apparent certainties about what Shakespeare had written and how to determine its meaning. Meanwhile textual theorists argued among themselves in a number of debates not ended yet. The most heated went back to such fundamental issues as authorship, authority, and intention, the stability of a text, or the identification of collaboration. It is to those debates we turn in the remainder of this book.

PART THREE

Current Debates

5

Authorship, Agency, and Intentionality

Two decades after the first explosion of poststructural textual theory, in an essay first published in 1986, G. Thomas Tanselle described the editorial implications of different views on authorship and intentionality, identifying the two fundamentally opposed positions that continue to underlie recent debates. First:

> [T]he view that literature is social and collaborative in nature and therefore that the historical forms in which a work is presented to the public are of primary significance; and [instead] ... the view that literary works are the products of discrete private acts of creation and therefore that their essential forms do not include alterations by others nor even later revisions by the authors themselves.
>
> Tanselle 2005: 111–12

Tanselle proposed that 'the issue turns on whether one is willing to admit the legitimacy of being interested in the artistic intentions of authors as private individuals rather than as social beings accommodating their intentions to various pressures emerging from the publishing process' (2005: 123). In the end, Tanselle defended as a legitimate intellectual pursuit an interest in 'the minds of particular persons from the past' and 'just what the initiating mind contributed' (129).

A Foucauldian might object that in this binary Tanselle creates a false choice between a real living, breathing Shakespeare – an 'initiating mind' with 'artistic intentions' – and a Shakespearean social being whose 'acts of creation' almost certainly were altered and distorted by social and historical forces. Tanselle thus rejects the fundamental poststructural premise, that the author is a construct, not a particular person, whereas the playwright, who is a person, lacks the author's controlling status. Indeed, Tanselle was not alone. In the world of Shakespeare scholarship, as Margreta de Grazia and Peter Stallybrass note regretfully, 'it is the category of solitary and unitary authorship that Shakespeareans have been most loathe to forgo' (1993: 276).

De Grazia and Stallybrass take as an example the treatment of the differences between Q and F *King Lear*. Traditionally these texts had been regarded as two imperfect versions of a single original, and consequently editors from the seventeenth to the late twentieth century saw it as their task to conflate the two into a single text – *King Lear* – as close as possible to what the editor divined had been Shakespeare's intentions. However, in the 1970s and 1980s scholars including Michael Warren, Gary Taylor, and Steven Urkowitz upset this belief. They argued that each of the early texts was self-consistent, with the Folio text a revision by Shakespeare himself of the quarto text. Essays in Warren and Taylor's 1983 collection *The Division of the Kingdoms*, and the printing of the two texts separately in the 1986 *Oxford Shakespeare*, sustained and embodied the theory, which was widely accepted. However, what troubles De Grazia and Stallybrass is the conclusion that the Folio revision was made by Shakespeare himself. Apparently radical new scholarship thus returns to conventional belief. Both Q and F retain the authority of the author, even as they demonstrate that there can be more than one authoritative text of a given work. Once all the variants 'are claimed in the name of a revising Shakespeare', the traditional understanding of 'the author' remains in place. Instead, De Grazia and Stallybrass urge rethinking Shakespeare 'in relation to our new knowledge of collaborative writing, collaborative printing, and the historical contingencies of textual production' (1993: 279).

Like De Grazia and Stallybrass, Graham Holderness, Brian Loughrey and Andrew Murphy attacked the new theories of revision because they remain tied to the author function (1995: 110–11). However, for these Marxist critics, De Grazia and Stallybrass do not go far enough in their objections: their insufficiently materialist bibliography is 'subsumed into an extremely general history of early modern cultural process'. Indeed, Holderness et al find a surprising parallel between the New Bibliography and the poststructuralist wing of New Textualism: 'both regard any individual text . . . as a signpost pointing towards something greater and more complete than itself . . . . (for New Bibliography) the authorial manuscript or the author's intentions, or (for poststructuralist "New Textualism") the continuum of language, the process of history, or the system of cultural production'. For both methods, 'The meaning and value of a text always lie outside and beyond it' (1995: 107).

Despite these caveats, many textual critics accepted at least some of the poststructuralist line of thought and acknowledged a dispersal of authority in the creation of texts. Alongside the rejection, or at least the slighting, of the author and his intentions, the controlling hand of the editor was denigrated as unnecessarily authoritarian. The new theories are often grouped as the 'New Textualism', an approach in which, rather than looking for the text beneath the veil of print, the analyst looks *at* each text, considering its place in history, its existence as a book, or its role in performance. For several decades such views appeared to prevail, but occasionally disagreements became confrontational. Perhaps the most stunning example was the response to Jeffrey Masten's *Textual Intercourse* (1997) by Brian Vickers, author of *Shakespeare, Co-Author* (2002). As we saw in Chapter 4, Masten's study connects 'the material conditions and cultural representations of sex/gender and of textual production', accepts Foucault's reduction of the author to an 'ideological figure', and argues that collaboration is 'a dispersal of author/ity, rather than a simple doubling of it' (1997: 5, 19).

Vickers used Masten's book as his target for a wide-ranging attack on disruptive poststructuralist conceptions of the author. In an appendix entitled 'Abolishing the Author? Theory *versus* History', Vickers's true antagonist was Foucault's claim that the 'author' only emerged towards the beginning of the nineteenth century, when 'strict rules concerning author's rights' such as copyright, and the legal consequences for transgressions of these rules, arose. To demonstrate that 'Foucault took away power and identity from the author', Vickers traced evidence for the historical recognition of authorship back to antiquity (2002: 507–8). As proof that Shakespeare's contemporaries believed that 'a writer owned his own work', he described episodes when Elizabethan and Jacobean writers were distressed that their work had appeared without permission or was plagiarized (2002: 515–18). But his particular fury was apparently aroused by the 'politicizing strand' in literary criticism, leading him to characterize 'theory driven work' as 'a new form of locomotion owing nothing to historical scholarship' (2002: 539). Vickers's coinage, 'co-author', was intended to confirm that even in the case of collaborated work, authorship as traditionally understood was not lost or dispersed but merely multiplied.

For editors, even those less hostile than Vickers to the advent of 'theory' in literary and textual studies, neither the author nor his intentions has proven easy to eliminate. Without an author, intention becomes a 'problematic concept' (Jowett 2017c: l), and 'error', a fundamental concern in preparing text, becomes more difficult to describe or identify. In a telling example, James Purkis traces the editorial problem caused by 'openness of character designation' and consequent uncertainty of authorial intention found in the *Sir Thomas More* manuscript. In the Hand D section thought to be Shakespeare's, four speech headings are merely 'other' or 'oth' or 'o', place holders for further identification. Both the writer of the original text, Anthony Munday, and another reviser, Hand B, possibly the dramatist Thomas Heywood, also leave some speakers indeterminate (2015: 42–9). What should be done in these cases, when the author's 'intention' is not visible? Greg thought the bookkeeper was required 'to assign the speech to whom he pleases' (Purkis 2015: 42), and indeed the bookkeeper, labelled 'C' in the scholarship, did add speakers' names. Perhaps he could ask Shakespeare or Heywood his intention, or perhaps Shakespeare, who was brought in as a late collaborator, didn't have clear intentions about the minor characters. For Purkis, the absence of 'determinate, or definite, authorial intention' in D and B's writing shows that at least sometimes 'the notion of non-authorial intentions as corruptions that stand in the way of the author's text' may be inappropriate (2015: 51).

Without what can be inferred as an author's intention as a guideline, the editor's critical judgement of 'corruption' becomes the deciding factor. Certainly Greg considered that 'C' was improving or completing, rather than corrupting, the text. Jowett, editing *Sir Thomas More* for *Arden 3* and having worked out the complex sequence of events, including original composition, censorship, revisions and additions, that he believes exists behind the manuscript, concludes that 'there is perhaps no such thing as a uniform stage of completion in the revised text' (2011: 122). In other words, we cannot be certain what the various authors' final intentions were or, consequently, the corruption of those intentions. Any assignment of speakers is guesswork in which the assigner, whether Greg's bookkeeper or Jowett the editor, effectively becomes one of the authors.

In an appendix on 'Shakespeare, *Sir Thomas More* and the ideology of authorship', Jowett places arguments about Shakespeare's claimed presence in the manuscript within the larger debate about authorship. He notes that 'the act of ascribing something to Shakespeare draws attention to the figure of the author' and feeds what David Kastan has called 'our obvious yearning for the "real presence" of Shakespeare', while on the other hand 'the anti-authorial critique of this yearning leads unerringly to a predisposition against the evidence' for Shakespeare as Hand D. That is, an unwavering poststructural theoretical position may trump evidence-based research finding that we do have one Shakespeare holograph. Yet accepting Hand D as Shakespeare's will, conversely, also affect the meaning of the author: 'redefining Shakespeare in such a way as to see him more clearly as a dramatist working alongside others . . . . What is meant by Shakespeare as the signifier of a body of writing, and what that writing itself means, are different when part of Shakespeare is *Sir Thomas More*' (Jowett 2011: 459–60).

Bit by bit, recent critics, not only those engaged in editing texts, have attempted to reinstate the author and, sometimes directly, sometimes by implication, his or her intentions. For instance, Adam Smyth, a book historian, argues that the presence of errata lists in seventeenth-century books, as well as descriptions of correction in the printshop by dramatists contemporary with Shakespeare, indicate that the author was at the very least an active agent, if only one among many: 'The figure who is conjured most frequently in errata lists is the author: the absent author . . . . In a blend of authorial centrality and absence, errata addresses frequently stress the importance of the author by invoking his nonattendance as the cause of mistakes'. But here again 'the author' is redefined: 'errata discourse makes texts more authorial than we expect – although the version of the author they promote is not the lone genius of post-Romantic criticism, but the author always in collaboration with others, the author as one agent among several'. Similarly, intention is no longer singular: Smyth concludes that 'the shift is not from intention to anti-intention, but rather from intention as author-centric and singular, to intention as spread across several agents' (Smyth 2018: 91–2).

Gabriel Egan, writing in defence of the New Bibliography, accepts this claim only partially. For Egan, the author remains at the top of the 'hierarchy of agencies', and his purpose in *The Struggle for Shakespeare's Text* is 'to help push the pendulum back from a currently fashionable dispersal of agency and

insist upon authors as the main determinants of what we read'
(2010: 3). Most recently, discussing attribution studies (see
Chapter 6) in the *Authorship Companion* to the *New Oxford
Shakespeare*, Gary Taylor, 'reconceptualizing authorship as
artisanal labour' has justified reinstating the author on the
'fundamental ethical principle of giving people credit for work
they have done'(2017b: 22, 20).

A somewhat different approach to restoring the centrality
of the singular author has been to pay attention to indications
of Shakespeare as a recognized literary figure, as shown by the
appearance of his name on quartos beginning in 1598 and by
the frequent (re)publication of such quartos (Farmer 2015;
Farmer and Lesser 2013). That naming Shakespeare as author
gained commercial utility in his lifetime is revealed by the
numerous play quartos that, like *Locrine*, put either
Shakespeare's full name or his initials on the title page. Thomas
Heywood – complaining because poems of his were included
in an expanded 1612 edition of *The Passionate Pilgrim*, which
was published under Shakespeare's name alone – acknowledges
both Shakespeare's stature and his value to a publisher: 'my
lines not worthy his [Shakespeare's] patronage, under whom
he [the stationer William Jaggard] hath published them, so the
Author [Shakespeare] I know much offended with Mr. Jaggard
(that altogether unknown to him [Shakespeare]) presumed to
make bold with his name'. Heywood, who asserted that he had
had a 'hand or a main finger' in over 200 plays, was well aware
that authors were not always credited with their work, but for
him in this case Shakespeare was 'the Author' and Jaggard was
using the Author's prestige for his own benefit.

A clear manifestation of recent changes in attitude towards
authorship and intentionality can be seen by comparing
statements about these matters, and the consequent textual
decisions, in the *Oxford Shakespeare* of 1986–7 and the *New
Oxford Shakespeare* of 2016–17. The changes are even more
revealing about developments in textual theory because Gary
Taylor was a General Editor of both editions. In the earlier
Oxford Shakespeare the General Introduction posed an editor's

choice thus: 'should readers be offered a text which is as close as possible to what Shakespeare originally wrote, or should the editor aim to formulate a text presenting the play as it appeared when performed by the company of which Shakespeare was a principal shareholder in the theatres that he helped to control and on whose success his livelihood depended?' Taking a then radically new approach that pointed away from the singular author, the Oxford editors of the 1980s, led by Stanley Wells, opted, 'when possible, to print the more theatrical version of each play' (Wells and Taylor 1986: xxxviii–xxxix). This meant not only choosing between surviving texts and presenting whichever the editors believed had been the theatrical version, but going further, taking action to recreate the performance text, for example inserting oaths that the editors thought had been removed by the censor when a play was published, and presenting 'A Reconstructed Text' of *Pericles*. Even so, Holderness, Loughrey and Murphy complained that in dealing with multiple texts the editors were still tied to the author function: 'the final explanation of a text's mobility is located not in theatre or history or cultural context, but in the controlling mastery of authorial intention' (1995: 111). From a different point of view, the edition disturbed some readers because, in presenting the theatrical version as *the* text, the *Oxford Shakespeare* necessarily omitted some well-known lines that may have been within the author's intention at one time. For example, most of *Hamlet* 4.4, including the soliloquy 'How all occasions do inform against me', appears in the second quarto but is not present in the 'more theatrical' Folio text that the *Oxford Shakepeare* chose as their copy-text; hence the lines were omitted. The problem was avoided in *King Lear* where both texts were printed, so a reader of that play's 'more theatrical' Folio text could turn to the quarto for such missing but familiar elements as the mock trial of Goneril (3.7) or the entire scene (quarto 4.4) in which a Gentleman describes Cordelia's grief to Kent. The first and second *Norton Shakespeare*, using the Oxford text, facilitated comparison by printing the two *King Lear* texts on facing pages.

Thirty years later the *New Oxford* General Editors, Taylor, Jowett, Terri Bourus and Egan, reversed some of these decisions. Most significantly, the editors announced that in choosing copy-texts for the single-volume *Modern Critical Edition*, they would use 'a criterion that, though related to the qualities of the underlying manuscripts, is directly observable and even measurable in the printed texts themselves. It is the criterion of length' (Jowett 2017b: xli). Length, the editors happily note, 'does not depend on debatable editorial theories about what kind of manuscript lies behind a particular printed edition ... [or] on fiercely contested aesthetic preferences about which version is the more satisfying work of art' (Taylor and Bourus 2016: 52).

In practice, the *New Oxford* principle sometimes caused a reversal of the earlier *Oxford*'s choice of base text for a play. For example, rather than the Folio text of *Hamlet*, the *Modern Critical Edition* uses the second quarto as copy-text 'because it is a significantly longer text than the first quarto or the Folio'. Consequently 4.4 and 'How all occasions do inform against me' return. Similarly, the text of *King Lear* is based on 'the first quarto of 1608, which gives the longest early text'; the text of the Folio is due to be published in an Alternative Versions volume. Yet this apparently objective criterion implicitly reinstates the author. Although, as Jowett points out, length 'shifts the editorial emphasis away from the textual minutiae that reflect proximity or distance from Shakespeare's hand and onto the literally larger issues of structure and content', the *New Oxford* editors nevertheless believe that 'an authorial text, as it is transmitted away from the immediate engagement of the author, will tend to shrink rather than grow. The text might be subject to censorship, theatrical cutting, accidental omission, or loss of leaves, all of which will make it shorter.' Hence the longer quarto texts 'are typically less altered from the author's draft than the later playbooks that influence the Folio texts' (Jowett 2017b: xli–xlii). In effect, the *New Oxford* editors admit that 'Our basic principle was to choose the version of the work that contains the most Shakespeare', thus giving implicit deference to readers' desire for an authorial text (Taylor and Bourus 2016: 51).

The full consequences of these decisions can be seen in the treatment of *Richard III*. The play, one of Shakespeare's most popular, exists in a series of early quartos and in the Folio. There are significant differences between the texts, although both the quartos and the Folio present clear and coherent texts and are thus what textual critics call 'good'. Although Q1 was printed in 1597, scholarship has generally agreed that F, 1623, is based on an earlier manuscript, and that the shorter Q1, although still very long, shows signs of streamlining for the theatre. In 1986 the Oxford editors accepted a then-common view, that the Q1 text was the result of a 'communal reconstruction'. As a result, the *Oxford Shakespeare*, committed to printing the theatrical text, based its text on Q1. In a separate Oxford Shakespeare volume (2000), Jowett followed suit, basing his text on Q1 because of its 'high theatrical authority'. Even so, he admitted to uneasiness, recognizing that a consequence of following the theatrical text is that the editorial process becomes unstable. 'If the author cannot be invoked as sole arbiter, the cut-off point between what is treated as acceptable variation and what is treated as corruption or error becomes harder to define' (2000: 130–1). In practice this meant that Jowett incorporated both lines and words from F into his edition, creating an eclectic text.

In the *New Oxford* the editors once again reversed an earlier *Oxford Shakespeare* decision. Based on the criterion of greater length, the base text for *Richard III* is now the Folio. But despite the *New Oxford* commitment to 'the most Shakespeare', the 'clock passage', which was identified by the earlier editors as 'a dramatic gem' (*TxC* 1987: 228), but which is found only in the quarto version, is not present. The 'most' Shakespeare is therefore actually presented in James Siemon's *Arden 3* conflated edition, where the copy-text is F but the text 'incorporates substantive variants from both Q and F', including the clock passage (2009: 421). These variants are marked with superscripts to show their source. Siemon's justification parallels the *New Oxford* as it once again takes us back to the author: 'This edition attempts to provide as much as it can of the "raw material" from which actors and readers have constructed . . . *Richard III*' (2009: 460).

When looking for the most Shakespeare, the *New Oxford* was forced to confront the larger problem: how to determine authorial intentions and consequently recognize the distortion of those intentions, i.e. error. Given an unwillingness to seek an author's intended meaning in a confusing passage, it becomes difficult to identify or, consequently, to emend, error, usually regarded as an editor's chief task. Returning to the kind of common sense that allowed our imaginary reader to correct 'detect' to 'detest' (see Chapter 3), Jowett objects that for an editor to retain an obvious error is to idealize the early printed texts, treating them as 'untouchable objects'. Correction, instead, assumes that Shakespeare intended to make sense and the text can be emended accordingly: 'If authors themselves make errors, it is logically no less than necessary to refer to their intentions . . . . intentions are real, and intentions are effectual' (2017c, lvi). Furthermore, some texts of Shakespeare's plays were 'censored on political and religious grounds'. The *New Oxford* tries to undo such censorship, which again amounts to an attempt to restore Shakespeare's original intentions. For example, they re-insert 'his regular invocation' of the Christian 'God' rather than retain the surviving texts' 'vague euphemism "Heaven"' (Taylor and Bourus 2016: 56). Such emendation is frequently supported, if not confirmed, by the metre, which may be more regular with the one-syllable deity. Yet not everyone would agree that modern editors can determine the intentions of a man writing over 400 years ago. There can never be proof that any individual correction restores Shakespeare's intention.

In the end, Jowett attempts to encompass both older and newer attitudes, proposing as a model 'Shakespeare the intending but socialized author' (2017c: lvii), that is, an author who wrote with deliberate meanings but expected his words and lines to go through production processes on stage and in the print shop, processes that would in unforeseeable ways affect the outcome. Much the same conclusion is articulated in the *Norton Shakespeare 3*, which, like the *New Oxford*, uses 'a pragmatic and flexible measure' to determine which version of a play to include in its print volume. Rather than claiming the power 'to determine and present the text that was Shakespeare's "original" version – or his "final" version, or the one that the company probably performed' the Norton prints 'the text that is most complete and apparently finished' (McMullan and Gossett 2015: 85). In a case like *Richard III*, the *Norton 3* uses the affordances of its electronic platform to avoid 'determining which of the two texts is more definitively "Shakespearean", an impossible task' (Greenblatt et al 2015: 565). As a result, the editors again present an author both individual and socialized: 'The general understanding of the processes of writing . . . remains firmly bound up with ideas of intention, of textual "ownership," of the creative artist as "author" . . . the sole source of "authority" in respect of the form and meaning of a given text'. But the editors suggest that

> [T]he meanings of Shakespeare's plays and poems . . . emerge from a more complex, varied, and fascinating creative base, than simply what the poet himself "meant" . . . . Shakespearean "authenticity" is a multivalent concept, one that includes . . . what the author meant but also a range of other, contiguous collaborations, negotiations, and origins for meaning.
>
> McMullan and Gossett 2015: 91–2

It is to those 'contiguous collaborations' that we turn in Chapter 6.

6

Attribution and Collaboration

HAMLET
  We'll hear a play tomorrow. [*aside to* FIRST PLAYER]
  Dost thou hear me, old friend? Can you play *The*
  Murder of Gonzago?
I PLAYER
  Ay, my lord.
HAMLET
  We'll ha't tomorrow night. You could for need study a
  speech of some dozen lines, or sixteen lines, which I
  would set down and insert in't, could you not?
I PLAYER
  Ay, my lord.

Hamlet 2.2.472–9

Imagine that you have just been commissioned to create a
'complete works' of Shakespeare. The project is exciting, but
as you sit down to draw up a table of contents, you are
suddenly struck by uncertainty. What exactly should be in the
volume(s)? There are thirty-six plays in the Folio and they will
all go in, but some other early modern quartos have either
Shakespeare's name or his initials on the title page – are those
to be included? The second issue of the Third Folio (1664)
added seven plays to those in the First Folio. What about

those? You know that the first, *Pericles*, is now usually admitted to the Shakespeare canon, but then, many scholars have argued that it is a collaboration. Does that matter? Recent scholarship has in fact increased the number of First Folio plays that some analysts claim were written in part by other authors (e.g., *1 Henry VI*, *Titus Andronicus*, *All's Well That Ends Well*). Furthermore, what should be done about non-Folio plays – say, *Edward III* – in which scholars claim to have found Shakespeare's hand? How much Shakespeare in a play merits treating the whole as Shakespeare's?

You find yourself facing one of the longest, and often most heated, debates about the text(s) of Shakespeare's works. Collaboration poses the greatest challenge to the concept of the single author, as strikingly demonstrated by the presence of *Macbeth* in both the *Collected Middleton* (2007) and the *New Oxford Shakespeare*, both under the general editorship of Gary Taylor. The kinds of evidence, the procedural methodologies, and the intensity of the argument vary, but the fundamental positions fall into two camps: inclusiveness and purity. Are you going to include everything that may be, or has been alleged to be, by Shakespeare, as a whole or in part? Or are you going to build as tight a wall as possible around whatever is definitely Shakespeare's, allowing, in the case of collaborations, only those plays that were endorsed by Heminges and Condell when they promised that in the Folio they had 'collected & published' his 'writings ... absolute in their numbers, as he conceived them'. You realize that a Folio-only collection means excluding *Pericles* as well as *The Two Noble Kinsmen*, the only play originally published as by Shakespeare and another author, but it turns out that that would align you with many earlier editors of complete works. You wonder if you should perhaps use a different typeface or some other distinguishing mark for those parts of the Folio plays no longer attributed to Shakespeare – say, the first act of *Titus*, which recent research has persuaded you (but not everyone) is by George Peele.

Arguments about what plays Shakespeare wrote, and of those, which ones include work by another hand, whether contemporaneous or as later revision, can be traced from eighteenth-century editions, through debates about 'disintegration' in the late nineteenth and early twentieth centuries, to arguments about the use and reliability of electronic programs and databases in the twenty-first. These arguments are influenced by explicit or unconscious preferences for aesthetic versus scientific evidence (that is, 'style' versus measurable data), and, for those working in the age of computers, by adherence to one or another statistical method. For an editor, speculative theories about authorship pose unavoidable practical problems. For any reader they pose the largest of all questions: what do we mean when we say 'Shakespeare'?

External evidence

Shakespeare's long poems, *Venus and Adonis* and *The Rape of Lucrece*, were published in 1593 and 1594. Both bore dedications to Henry Wriothesley, Earl of Southampton, and both were signed 'in all duty, William Shakespeare'. His plays, however, became properties of the companies for which they were written. Some scripts may have gone with him into the Lord Chamberlain's company when his previous company collapsed, but we know neither exactly which company that had been nor the precise financial arrangement with which he entered the Lord Chamberlain's Men. None of his plays was published with an authorial dedication, and the earliest quartos did not bear an authorial attribution. The 1594 quarto of *Titus* is paradigmatic of early 1590s' attitudes towards playwrights: as we saw earlier, it proudly reports that the tragedy was played by three different theatrical companies, but it says nothing about the author. Gradually attitudes towards the importance of the playwright, or at least of Shakespeare, changed. Only in 1598, with a quarto of *Love's Labour's Lost*, was Shakespeare's name put on the printed text of a play. Yet by 1608 the title page of the first quarto of *King Lear* was headed, in the largest typeface on the page, 'M. William Shakspeare:' followed by, '*HIS* True Chronicle Historie of the life and death of King Lear and his three Daughters'. Similarly the 1623 First Folio title page foregrounds the author's name: 'Mr William Shakespeares Comedies, Histories, & Tragedies'. With no surviving manuscripts of the plays apart from the contested pages of the unpublished *Sir Thomas More*, it is not surprising that 'The canon of Shakespeare's plays rests primarily on the authority of title-pages' (Chambers 1930: 1.205).

Besides title pages, other external evidence for Shakespeare's authorship – by 'external evidence' we mean evidence that lies outside the texts of the plays themselves – includes occasional comments by contemporaries such as Ben Jonson, who names specific plays by his friend; entries in the Stationers' Register; and Revels Accounts that list court performances, identifying some plays as by 'Shaxberd' (Chambers 1930: 2.331). (It is important to remember that in this period there was no fixed spelling of words and names: famously, Shakespeare didn't always spell his own name consistently on legal documents). The outstanding source of information about which plays were recognized as Shakespeare's in the first part of his career is Francis Meres's 1598 *Palladis Tamia*, in which Meres writes that 'As *Plautus* and *Seneca* are accounted the best for Comedy and Tragedy among the Latins: so *Shakespeare* among the English is the most excellent in both kinds for the stage'. Meres's subsequent list of comedies and tragedies serves as evidence for the existence by 1598 of the plays he includes and thus helpfully provides a *terminus ad quem* (that is, the latest possible date) for some of the canon, but since Meres begins his list of specifics with the words 'witness his', the titles that follow are examples (witnesses) of Shakespeare's excellent work rather than necessarily a comprehensive list. And Meres does not tell the modern scholar everything she wants to know. For instance, among the tragedies he includes *Richard II*, *Richard III*, *King John*, *Titus Andronicus*, *Romeo and Juliet* and *Henry IV*, but he does not specify how many parts of the last had appeared. Similarly, among the comedies he names

Two Gentlemen of Verona, The Comedy of Errors, Midsummer Night's Dream, and *Love's Labour's Lost,* but also *Love's Labour's Won,* which has frequently been thought to be an alternate title for some familiar comedy but instead seems to be a lost play, as the title has also been found in a 1603 bookseller's list of stock (Wiggins and Richardson 2014: 4.18–19).

A key problem with trusting title pages is that, once Shakespeare was established, his name or his initials appeared on a number of quartos whose publishers may have been attempting to enhance the prestige of a text written by a different playwright. The seven plays added in 1664 to the Third Folio of 1663 are a particularly notable example of the 'inclusiveness' camp. Earlier quartos of *A Yorkshire Tragedy, The London Prodigal, Sir John Oldcastle,* and *Pericles* had all borne Shakespeare's name, and the title pages of *Locrine, Thomas Lord Cromwell,* and *The Puritan* had borne the initials W.S. One might guess that Heminges and Condell, as long-time colleagues of Shakespeare and senior sharers (part owners) in the King's Men, knew enough about the authorship of these plays to reject them from the First Folio. However, their choices may also have been dictated by such practical matters as theatrical ownership of manuscripts (Stern, 2020, personal communication). As they rejected *Pericles,* a play which almost all modern scholars divide between George Wilkins and Shakespeare, they may have been attentive to work they did not consider primarily by Shakespeare. In the *New Oxford,* Taylor and Loughnane propose that the 'absence of *Pericles, The History of Cardenio,* and *The Two Noble Kinsmen* suggests that the Folio compilers generally excluded late collaborative romances' (Taylor and Loughnane 2017: 423–4). Yet the compilers' decisions do not preclude the possibility that other hands are present in the plays they did include; as the scholar E.K. Chambers writes, 'It is quite possible that they saw no harm in including without comment a play which Shakespeare had only revised, one or two for which he had a collaborator, and one to which he had contributed little, but which had long been linked to other "parts" in an historical series' (that is, *1 Henry VI*) (1930: 1.207). It is the desire to identify these collaborators, of whatever sort, that has led scholars to search for other kinds of evidence than title pages.

Internal evidence

Pericles, the 1609 quarto title page of which did carry Shakespeare's name, is now usually included in editions of Shakespeare, while the other six plays added to the Third Folio are considered 'apocryphal' (a term used for material excluded from the Bible on the grounds that it lacks adequate authority). In both Biblical and Shakespeare scholarship such rejected works are called 'uncanonical', a clear indication of the place of Shakespeare in English-speaking literature. Often such decisions have been based on an editor's or a critic's sense that a line or a passage 'sounds like Shakespeare'; in *Pericles* many sensitive readers and critics have thought that they recognize the entrance of the characteristic Shakespearean tone at the opening of the third act. But such stylistic intuitions are vague and unprovable. As a result, there have been many attempts, up to the present day, to find more 'objective' or 'scientific' methods of identifying the writing of Shakespeare.

Attempts to suggest that plays recognized as Shakespeare's may include work by other hands go back at least as far as Pope, who rejected entire sections of *Cymbeline*, notably most of what is 5.4 in modern editions. As the hero Posthumus falls asleep in prison, Pope breaks off his text and writes, '*Here follows a Vison, a Masque, and a Prophecy, which interrupt the Fable without the least necessity, and unmeasurably lengthens this act. I think it plainly foisted in afterwards for mere show, and apparently not of Shakespeare*' (1725: 6.219). The vision of Jupiter that Pope relegated to the bottom of his pages was still regarded as 'a spectacular theatrical interpolation' by Chambers two centuries later (1930: 1.486) Oddly, the possibility that the collaborator was not simply a different writer but an agent in the theatre who might add material for 'show' seems to presage a modern sense of the social text, but clearly Pope considered the vision a corruption. More rigorous than Pope was Malone, whose comment about *Henry VIII* hints at two issues that continue to absorb students of collaboration, anomalous content and variant poetic styles. Malone thought that references to King James in a speech by Cranmer must have been added after Shakespeare's retirement 'by that hand which ... rendered the versification of it of a different colour from all the other plays of Shakespeare' (1790: 7.139).

By the mid-nineteenth century this suspicion was taken up by the poet Tennyson, and then expanded in an article by James Spedding with the curiously self-cancelling title, 'Who Wrote Shakespeare's *Henry VIII?*'. Although Spedding's method was 'initially wholly intuitive' (McMullan 2000: 187), he moved on to metrical tests, counting in particular the unstressed eleventh syllables (also called feminine or weak endings) on iambic pentameter lines. Here are lines 3.1.102–5, where Queen Katherine berates the cardinals, with the final stresses marked:

> The more shame for ye. Holy men I thóught ye,
> Upon my soul, two reverend cardinal vírtues–
> But cardinal sins and hollow hearts I féar ye.
> Mend 'em for shame, my lords. Is this your cómfort?

Each line ends with an extra unstressed syllable, a recognized characteristic of John Fletcher's verse (though, confusingly, also occasionally used by Shakespeare). Because the weak endings appear only in limited sections of the play, Spedding concluded that the play had been co-written by Shakespeare and Fletcher. As the nineteenth century wore on, with the founding of the New Shakspere Society (*sic*), more and more attention was paid to specific elements of versification. Indeed, as Egan writes, 'methods for authorship attribution by the analysis of internal features of the plays remained essentially unchanged for the next 100 years. There were just two methods: counting the frequencies of certain verse features . . . and finding parallel passages showing that a work of known authorship contains the same words and/or phrases and/or sequences of ideas as the work for which the authorship is sought' (2017: 33).

Attribution by parallel passages is famously treacherous, as a parallel may arise from the context, or from one author imitating another, or from imitation of a piece of writing by an author not considered in the comparison (the so-called 'negative check'). This was an especial danger before there were electronic concordances of Shakespeare's contemporaries facilitating comparisons. The fact that the plays of John Ford are full of echoes of Shakespeare does not mean that Shakespeare wrote his plays, and passages in early Shakespeare that sound like Marlowe may result from the actor unconsciously remembering lines. Yet as time went on, there was a tendency to find more and more hands in the works of Shakespeare, with more and more plays suspected of collaborative authorship. Such analysis was brought to a considerable pause, if not an abrupt halt, in 1924 when E.K. Chambers, at work on his magisterial *William Shakespeare: A Study of Facts and Problems*, gave a talk attacking 'The Disintegration of Shakespeare'. By 'disintegration', Chambers meant the assignment of passages of the canonical plays to someone other than Shakespeare. As Egan points out, Chambers was not opposed to all metrical analysis; based on the metrics of certain passages he accepted claims that *Edward III* and *Sir Thomas More* were in part by Shakespeare. Nevertheless, claims for expanding the Shakespeare canon were less contentious than 'disintegrating' plays long assumed to be Shakespeare's alone by rejecting sections of them as non-authorial.

It was known that Shakespeare had collaborated with Fletcher, a playwright successful both alone and in collaboration with other dramatists, who eventually became Shakespeare's successor as the attached dramatist of the King's Men. *The Two Noble Kinsmen* was published under both their names in

1634, and there are later references to a lost play called *Cardenio* by both men (Taylor and Egan 2017: 583–5; Wiggins and Richardson 2015: 6.244–7). Because it was repeatedly Fletcher's hand that analysts believed they had found in *Henry VIII*, determination of the particular characteristics of the younger playwright's style was especially pertinent. Despite Chambers's warnings, or perhaps because he was dealing with dramatists considered less important than Shakespeare, E.H.C. Oliphant's 1927 study of the plays of Beaumont and Fletcher continued the attempt to determine the respective shares of the eponymous playwrights (and those of others) in the plays included in the 1647 and 1679 Folios that bore their names. Real advances, important for their methodology, came with a series of articles on the canon of the duo published by Cyrus Hoy between 1956 and 1962. In addition to charting the familiar metrical characteristics of Fletcher's writing (i.e. his use of the weak ending to iambic lines), Hoy looked at distinctive diction (*ye* instead of *you*), verb forms such as third person verbs ending *th*, and many specific contractions (*'em*, *i'th'*, *o'th' h'as* for *he has*, *'s* for *his* as in *in's*, *on's*). Hoy's findings, because they were so meticulous and because they were applied to a large corpus, were very persuasive. He was able to divide the Beaumont and Fletcher plays into those written by the original pair, those written by Fletcher alone, those written by Fletcher with Massinger, and even those that brought in three or more authors. He was, however, unable to find stylistic markers for Beaumont, a major limitation. Most significantly for Shakespeare studies, Hoy's method 'confirmed earlier divisions of *All is True / Henry VIII* and *The Two Noble Kinsmen* between Shakespeare and Fletcher' (Egan 2017: 36) (*All Is True* was an alternative contemporary title for the play called in the Folio *Henry VIII*).

Hoy's methodical work 'establishing a series of linguistic preference tests and applying them to a substantial body of drama' (Egan 2017: 37) seems to have broken through the objections propounded by Chambers, at least when applied to Shakespeare's contemporaries. Projects using similar methods were undertaken by those anxious to identify the work of Thomas Middleton, whose canon had never been carefully delineated. During their analysis of all the plays sometimes attributed to or associated with Middleton, David Lake and MacDonald P. Jackson, working separately and on different continents, each found Middleton's hand in sections of *Timon of Athens*, a play that is present in the Shakespeare First Folio. Influenced by work that had distinguished between the three authors of the American *Federalist Papers*, Jackson developed a method whereby he counted what are now known as 'function words' – *a/an*, *but*, *that*, *to*, or *with* – that a writer uses without noticing and that are less likely to be changed by compositors than, e.g., *you* and *ye*. Laboriously counting these words by hand, Jackson was able to show significant differences in each author's frequency of use, forming an identifiable fingerprint. But, as Egan writes, 'Without computer automation, the counting of linguistic features was always likely to be incomplete and error prone' (2017: 38).

Various methodologies began to be attempted using computers, but it was only with the creation of *LION*, an electronic database that contained searchable texts of much of early modern English literature and of nearly all extant plays, that full comparison of Shakespeare's work and that of other writers could be convincingly attempted and the results measured. It is possible to search *LION* not only for individual words but for 'collocations' – word groups like 'purple NEAR mantle NEAR torn' – increasing the likelihood of finding (or, just as significantly, not finding) similar uses by more than one author. Other major methods include pause tests (charting where in a line of ten syllables the pause is most likely to fall) and attention to differing grammatical forms such as has/hath or does/doth. In these tests an important refinement is the consideration of chronology. As attentive readers have noticed, Shakespeare's style changed over his career. Pauses shift to later in a line, the modern *has* increasingly replaces *hath*, there is more enjambment, that is, the carrying over of sense from line to line, as when Macbeth meditates that 'If it were done, when 'tis done, then 'twere well / It were done quickly. If th'assassination / Could trammel up the consequence, and catch / With his surcease, success: that but this blow. . .' (1.7.1–4). These changes can be quantified. However, there is a risk, the possibility of circular reasoning. If an unrecognized collaboration is used in creating the chronology it may distort the table, a particular danger if another suspected collaboration is tested against it. It is remarkable that almost all of the attributions assigned by Hoy, Lake and Jackson, working with index cards and pencilled tables, have been further confirmed when retested with electronic data. Nevertheless, these databases can only allow comparisons to literature that still exists, while large numbers of early modern plays are lost – see the *Lost Plays Database* for examples.

The early twenty-first century has seen an explosion of methods for attributing sections of early modern drama. Not surprisingly, most of these methods claim to be 'scientific', repudiating the earlier work Chambers rejected as intuitive or haphazard. Quite a few call upon an understanding of such statistical concepts as standard deviations, variability and probability. Arguments have raged over whether di-grams (two-word collocations) or tri-grams (three-word collocations) are more trustworthy. In a different approach Brian Vickers has adapted a plagiarism methodology, Turnitin, originally developed to help instructors determine whether student essays are original or copied. New ways of processing the rates of features such as function words are used by the editors of the *New Oxford*. At this writing there is, at least among those willing to imagine that William Shakespeare, like every other dramatist in his period, occasionally collaborated, considerable agreement about which 'Shakespeare' plays include sections by another hand. The first act of *Titus Andronicus* is now usually agreed to be by Peele, parts of *Henry VIII* and *The Two Noble Kinsmen* (as the quarto of the latter announces) to be by Shakespeare's successor John Fletcher, *Timon of Athens* to be in part by Middleton, and *Pericles* in part by George Wilkins.

This much agreement has not ended arguments about collaboration in the Folio plays. Recent claims in the *New*

Oxford Shakespeare, for example for Marlowe's hand in several early plays, are still being debated.[1] A somewhat separate question concerns when indications of later revision, as opposed to original collaboration, can be found in a surviving text. An outstanding case is *Macbeth*, which on the one hand no one doubts is Shakespeare's, and which nevertheless contains several anomalies in its only text. It is by far the shortest of the tragedies. It calls briefly for two songs – once '*Sing within*. "Come away, come away, *etc.*"' (3.5.35), once '*Music and a song*. "Black spirits, *etc.*"' (4.1.43) – and full lyrics for those songs are found in the manuscript of Thomas Middleton's unsuccessful and unprinted play *The Witch*. There are inconsistencies in *Macbeth*'s treatment of the witches, in particular the unprepared appearance in only one scene of the flying Hecate, a prominent figure in *The Witch*. On the assumption that the single surviving text is Middleton's revision of a lost original, *Macbeth* appears in both the *Oxford Shakespeare* and the *Collected Middleton*.

A more recent debate, revealing how a variety of methods may be called upon to identify collaboration, concerns *All's Well That Ends Well*. Inconsistencies in that play, like fluctuations in its style, confusion about the names and roles of characters such as the groups of 'lords' and 'gentlemen', and variant speech prefixes for a single character (e.g., Countess, Old Lady, Mother), have often been noted. Some critics have argued that Shakespeare wrote the play in stages, occasionally forgetting what he had intended earlier. Others have sought thematic or theatrical reasons for the apparent peculiarities of *All's Well*, for example pointing out that the tightly rhyming passages are suitably present in the more fairy-tale aspects of

---

[1]Although in a review of the *New Oxford Shakespeare* in the *TLS* Brian Vickers says its 'every attribution is false' (2020: 15), he actually means only the *New Oxford*'s newer attributions to Marlowe, Middleton and other more minor figures. In *Shakespeare Co-Author* (2002) Vickers accepts all the attributions given in the preceding paragraph.

the plot. In 2012 Laurie Maguire and Emma Smith proposed that the play was, like *Timon*, a collaboration between Shakespeare and Middleton. They found both linguistic and stylistic evidence for Middleton, including the presence of contractions characteristic of his writing but not of Shakespeare's, and noting the high proportion of rhyming lines, frequent feminine endings, and 'fondness for tri- and tetra-syllabic endings' in certain scenes. Some of the changes in speech prefixes, they suggested, coincide with places in which the authorship may have gone back and forth (Maguire and Smith 2012).

In a strong articulation of the purity position, Brian Vickers and Marcus Dahl found 'absolutely no evidence of another hand in this play'. They pointed out that the percentage of rhyming lines in *All's Well* is similar to that in some other Shakespeare comedies and argued that other Jacobean dramatists besides Middleton fit a few of the patterns noted. They corrected the claim that Shakespeare uniformly preferred *Omnes* to *All* as a speech prefix. However, they were less persuasive when they attempted to undermine Maguire and Smith's assertion that the repeated presence of certain contractions (*for't*, *on't*, *I'de*, *ha's*, *doe's*, etc.) is a sign of Middleton (Vickers and Dahl 2012).

The argument was carried out in successive issues of the *TLS*. Maguire and Smith remained persuaded that *All's Well* was written under the influence of Thomas Middleton, but conceded that whether further analysis would support merely influence or a more active partnership remained to be seen (Maguire, 2016, personal communication). Such further analysis was undertaken by the editors of the *New Oxford*, with results that present an almost Hegelian synthesis of the two opposing positions. In the *Authorship Companion* Gary Taylor, speaking for the Oxford editors, concludes that Maguire and Smith's recognition of more than one 'hand' in *All's Well* is astute, while Vickers and Dahl's objections to some of their supporting evidence and to the implication that the play is a simultaneous collaboration are also well founded. Instead,

Taylor convincingly suggests, the surviving text is based on a 'manuscript that had been annotated for a revival' (Taylor 2017a: 342). Several elements point to preparation for a revival after 1609 at the indoor theatre. The manuscript of such a revival might include new additions appearing intermittently, rather than as a sequence of scenes; the resulting text would not be a synchronic collaboration but a layered composition. Recognition that the play includes discrete additions helps explain conflicting evidence for and against the presence of a second author. Some of the unusual characteristics of the text, such as sudden rashes of un-Shakespearean contractions, need not be explained away, once their confinement to small sections is recognized as pointing to intermittent additions.

These examples demonstrate how the case for collaboration often grows with evidence of more than one type. In *Macbeth*, support for collaboration was both external – the presence of the complete song texts in a Middleton manuscript – and stylistic. In the case of *All's Well*, theatrical considerations support the possibility of revision. Two of the sections proposed as additions affect the role of the braggart soldier Paroles. The first is an extended first-act conversation between Paroles and Helen, often referred to as the 'virginity dialogue' (1.1.110–63). There is a long history of critical and theatrical objections to the passage as uncharacteristic of the heroine, and it has often been cut in performance. The same passage also includes a 'notorious textual disruption' marking the transition from the comic prose dialogue to a lengthy verse soliloquy by Helen. Taylor shows that the awkward transition can be explained as a consequence of a later insertion that can be neatly excised without disrupting the sense. The second addition is apparently an extension (4.3.242–83) to the farcical comedy of Paroles' unmasking, which theatrical history reveals became the play's most popular section. Thus the two additions implicitly support each other as interventions in one particular role intended to increase the play's popularity with audiences. These additions would require limited cue changes and alterations to very few actors' parts (or cue-scripts), exemplifying Marino's point that 'a script divided into parts is uniquely amenable to mid-sized revisions' (2020: 59). In yet a third case, *Pericles*, suspicion has always been aroused by the single text's many incoherences. The possibility that the cause was collaboration seemed supported by the discovery of George Wilkins's pamphlet, *The Painful Adventures of Pericles Prince of Tyre*, which presents itself as 'the true History of the Play of *Pericles*, as it was lately presented by the worthy and ancient Poet John Gower,' published a year before the quarto. The attribution was then further supported by comparison of Wilkins's style elsewhere (see Chapter 11).

Investigation of the 'known' Shakespeare plays for their authorship always implicitly asks, What part(s) of the texts that we have can we be sure are Shakespeare's own composition? The passage from *Hamlet* that forms an epigraph to this chapter may serve as a warning about how difficult such investigation can be. *The Murder of Gonzago* is presumably a pre-existing play – the troupe's leader immediately agrees that they can play it – by an unnamed dramatist. Hamlet asks the First Player to learn 'a speech of some dozen lines, or sixteen lines, which I would set down and insert in't', and later he gives him further instructions: 'Speak the speech, I pray you, as I pronounced it to you – trippingly on the tongue' (3.2.1–2). *The Murder of Gonzago*, or at least the section that parallels the situation at the Danish Court and therefore presumably includes Hamlet's addition, is then performed. Yet critics, using their various methods, have been unable to isolate the added speech. For one thing, the entire play-within-the-play is dramatically different in style from the rest of *Hamlet*: it is 'marked off . . . by the rhyming couplets and by an artificial elaboration of style characteristic of an older period' (Jenkins, 1982: 506). So is the insertion adjusted to that style? The futility of the search for Hamlet's insertion is further attested by analysis of the First Player's earlier speech on Pyrrhus that proved 'caviare to the general'. Theories that the Player's speech 'burlesques or emulates the style of earlier tragedy, and especially Marlowe and Nashe's *Dido*' (Jenkins 1982: 479) have not been widely accepted, but even Dryden considered it an example of the 'blown puffy style', not written by Shakespeare but quoted from 'some other poet' (1962: 2.257). Clearly, it is not easy to identify 'another hand' in the work of a playwright who could convincingly parody the grandiloquent or 'puffy' style of his contemporaries. Hamlet, like Shakespeare, seems entirely up to the task.

Enlarging the canon

The attempt to find Shakespeare's contributions to plays that historically have not been regarded as primarily his own – that is, to enlarge the canon by identifying his hand in collaborations – employs many of the same methods as those used to investigate interventions in plays recognized as Shakespeare's. Such research has been greatly facilitated by the development of electronic versions of the texts of most of the other known playwrights of his period, and by the searchable texts created by the Text Encoding Initiative. Yet research on the manuscript of *Sir Thomas More* vividly demonstrates the potential difficulties of isolating Shakespeare's contribution to collaborated plays. In the censored, revised, corrected and unfinished manuscript of *Sir Thomas More*, Jowett, the *Arden 3* editor, identifies no fewer than seven contributing hands: Anthony Munday, 'acting as copyist rather than composing a first draft'; Henry Chettle (Hand A); Thomas Heywood (Hand B); William Shakespeare (Hand D); Thomas Dekker (Hand E); Hand C (unidentified playhouse scribe and annotator); and Edmund Tilney, the Master of the Revels (2011: 351–2). The title page of the Arden edition attributes the original text to Anthony Munday and Henry Chettle. Jowett proposes that this original text dates from c. 1600 (other scholars place it in the 1590s), and that the revision, the point at which Shakespeare was brought in, dates from 1603–4 (424, 432–3).

Clearly *Sir Thomas More* had a singularly complex and unhappy history. One reasonable theory imagines that

Shakespeare, attached to the King's Men as their in-house dramatist, was asked to try to salvage a problematic original draft after Tilney, as Master of the Revels, raised his vigorous and still legible objections in the margin. Tilney's demands were specific: '*Leave out the insurrection wholly and the cause thereof, and begin with Sir Thomas More at the Mayor's sessions, with a report afterwards of his good service done being Sheriff of London upon a mutiny against the Lombards – only by a short report, and not otherwise, at your own perils*' (Jowett 2011: 5). Facing such perils, Shakespeare may have asked Heywood and Dekker to help him, or alternatively the scribe, Hand C, who seems to have managed the revisions, may have hired a group of well-known dramatists for assistance. The revisers all worked separately, on separate sheets of paper, presumably in their own styles but perhaps to an unknowable degree trying to suit the style of the already-existing play. As Jowett says, the revisions 'suggest a collaborative model of textual production centred on the theatre company' (2011: 362). Yet textual analysis does not determine which theatre company, and surprisingly Jowett suggests that this might have been Worcester / Queen Anne's Men, to which Heywood had ties (2011: 102–3). Given Shakespeare's own ties to the King's Men, this suggests yet another reason to obscure individual styles, making it even harder to determine who participated in the collaborative revision. With all of its puzzles, *Sir Thomas More* leaves us wondering how scholars could ever be certain that Shakespeare had 'touched up' other plays, or, by extension, that an actor in the King's Men had touched up the playwright's lines.

Despite these inherent difficulties, scholars continue to attempt to enlarge the parameters of the Shakespeare canon. Most recently, the *New Oxford Shakespeare* includes *Edward III*, *Arden of Faversham*, and the 'Additions' to *The Spanish Tragedy*. *Edward III* is also included in *Arden 3* and *Norton Shakespeare 3* (digitally only). Yet thirty years earlier, the *Oxford Shakespeare* listed *Arden of Faversham* and *Edward III* among 'Works Excluded from this Edition' at the end of the section entitled 'The Canon and Chronology of Shakespeare's Plays'. The 'Additions' to the *Spanish Tragedy* were not even mentioned. The intervening years have seen some claims come and go – the 'Funeral Elegy', attributed to Shakespeare by Donald Foster in 1995, has now been definitively attributed to Ford, and 'Shall I Die', attributed to Shakespeare by Gary Taylor in 1986, has been dismissed as not Shakespearean by many scholars but still appears in the *New Oxford* among poems attributed to Shakespeare in seventeenth-century miscellanies. Nevertheless, either because evidence from computerized analyses of data has proven persuasive or because, for some scholars not trained in the statistical methods, the claims have appeared too intimidating to contest, there has been a more general acceptance of the idea that Shakespeare collaborated occasionally throughout his career. Tiffany Stern's description of the patchwork nature of early modern play construction has also strengthened the belief that Shakespeare might have participated here and there in correction or revision.

The *New Oxford Authorship Companion* rethinks the 'Canon and Chronology' of the earlier *Oxford Shakespeare* and includes an updated section on external and internal evidence for collaboration in the plays. Tables show such measurable elements of style over time as rhymes, speech lengths, verse features, pause placements, and rates of hendiadys (a figure of speech in which a single complex idea is expressed by two words connected by a conjunction, as in 'sound and fury'), etc. None of the inclusions we will look at was first proposed by the Oxford editors: *Arden of Faversham* was first attributed to Shakespeare in 1770; *Edward III* was attributed to Shakespeare in a bookseller's catalogue of 1656 (Taylor and Loughnane 2017: 503) and proposed again by Edward Capell in 1760 (Proudfoot and Bennett 2017: 1). It was the project of Richard Proudfoot for decades before the *Arden 3* edition appeared in 2017. The possibility that Shakespeare wrote the 'Additions' to *The Spanish Tragedy* was proposed by Warren Stevenson in 1968 but only studied seriously in the twenty-first century. As Taylor and Loughnane say in describing research on *Arden of Faversham*, only quite recently have 'adequate techniques of authorship attribution' been applied to the problems posed by these plays (Taylor and Loughnane 2017: 488–9). All of the new conclusions depend upon a variety of these new techniques.

In their summary of the work of a number of scholars (MacDonald Jackson, Arthur Kinney, Marina Tarlinskaja, Brett Greatley-Hirsch and Jack Elliott), Taylor and Loughnane describe many of the current computational methods for determining authorship. Some, like comparing collocations in *Arden of Faversham* to those in five other plays, or prosodic and function word analysis, are now reasonably well known to textual scholars, while others, such as the 'Delta, Zeta, Nearest Shrunken Centroid, and Random Forests techniques' are sophisticated and unfamiliar. For *Arden of Faversham*, *New Oxford* believes recent scholarship has 'established solid ground for concluding that Shakespeare cannot have written scene 1 or scene 14 . . . and that he was the sole or main writer of scenes 4–8 or 4–9' (Taylor and Loughnane 2017: 490, 489). An important methodological concern is chronological comparison. *Arden* is dated earlier than any other Shakespeare play, with a 'best guess' as 1588, so comparisons must be made to Shakespeare's earliest plays. This in itself creates two problems. First, many of the plays that might serve as comparisons are, like the *Henry VI* plays, themselves collaborative. Second, there are references to many lost plays, and it is always possible that there is no surviving work of a collaborator to serve as a control. *New Oxford* is convinced that *Arden of Faversham* is a collaborative play from Shakespeare's 'early apprenticeship' but admits that 'Shakespeare's senior collaborator has not been identified . . . . the existing scholarship has effectively ruled out all playwrights with even a single extant early play of uncontested single authorship' (Taylor and Loughnane 2017: 490). In the absence of sufficient further information, the *New Oxford* assigns the play to Anonymous and William Shakespeare.

It is less surprising that *Edward III* has begun to appear in collected editions. In 1987 Taylor wrote that 'of all the non-canonical plays [it] has the strongest claim to inclusion in the *Complete Works*' (*TxC* 1987: 136), and indeed it was added to the revised edition. In the 2017 'Canon and Chronology' Taylor and Loughnane summarize the scholarly consensus that Shakespeare wrote 'at least some of the play', as supported by studies of vocabulary, imagery, rare words, and stylometrics (2017: 503). Nevertheless there is no agreement about the extent of Shakespeare's involvement nor, once again, about the identity of the other hand in the play. Like most earlier scholarship, the *New Oxford* is confident only that the scenes with the Countess of Salisbury are by Shakespeare. The inclusion of the play, then, in twenty-first century editions is a strong indication of a reversal of attitude. Admitting that a play is not exclusively Shakespeare's and including it nevertheless, thus extending the canon, is both a commercial and an intellectual rejection of the purity stance. The change of attitude is further confirmed by the presence in the *New Oxford* of the 'Additions' to *The Spanish Tragedy*. These were not even considered in the *Oxford Shakespeare*, and in an essay in the *Authorship Companion* Taylor concludes that the additions were themselves a collaboration by Shakespeare and Heywood (2017c: 260). Nevertheless, all five additions appear in the *New Oxford* due to its commitment to inclusivity.

Theoretical implications

In one sense work on collaboration in the last half century has been quite successful. Most scholars have accepted that Shakespeare, like almost every other early modern dramatist, sometimes worked with his contemporaries, and that his own drama, while admired, was nevertheless subject to the same kinds of alterations as other plays: cutting, revision, adaptation for new performers or different venues. Investigation of *Sir Thomas More* seems to indicate that he also occasionally altered or rewrote the plays of others. But work on collaboration has also strengthened a profound theoretical division in textual scholarship. Fundamentally, the success of research on attribution has depended on the persuasiveness of empirical evidence. Tables of the difference in metrics between Shakespeare and Fletcher or the different frequencies of specific contractions between Shakespeare and Middleton seem to provide objective, factual evidence, with which few scholars argue. The division instead concerns the way such facts are connected to the concept of the author.

For a theorist of 'textual intercourse' like Jeffrey Masten, collaboration was 'a prevalent mode of textual production in the sixteenth and seventeenth centuries, only eventually displaced by the mode of singular authorship'. Empirical evidence only confirms this claim. Such a view of collaboration as 'a' or 'the' early modern norm immediately reduces the status of the godlike author, even Shakespeare, to one among many. In consequence Masten proposes that scholars 'forego anachronistic attempts to divine the singular author of each scene, phrase, and word', thus rejecting the very project of those who use empirical evidence in just such attempts. Masten notes how even Hoy's apparently successful division of the Beaumont and Fletcher plays had ultimately to leave out Beaumont because his style could not be translated into data. Instead Masten urges recognition that the production of texts is always a social process, incorporating not only the writer(s) but 'discourses, figures, locations, and cultural practices' (1997: 4, 7, 27). In this view, all texts are inherently collaborations, and it is ultimately futile to search for 'authorial univocality'. It has been unfortunate for postmodern theorists of collaboration that their arguments against the efficacy of the disintegrative methods emerged in parallel with rapid developments in digital attributional methodologies which, even while they confirm the fragmented nature of early modern playwriting, tend to be inimical to work drawing on French theory.

The opposite position is represented by Brian Vickers, whose compendium of historical research on the authorship of a number of plays from the Shakespeare canon is entitled *Shakespeare Co-Author*. Vickers's coining of the term 'co-author' as an alternative to 'collaborator' is designed to reintroduce the controlling 'author' in the context of collaboration studies, which had been one of the blind spots in poststructuralist author-centred analysis. Vickers's goal is to resituate the collaborator – with all the implications that Masten gives that term – as merely a subdivision of the category author, rather than as a radical challenge to the traditional implications of that concept. Vickers accepts the results of centuries-long efforts to identify other authors who worked with Shakespeare; he just wishes to see each as an historical individual rather than, to repeat one of Foucault's striking images, an abstract 'principle of thrift' setting boundaries on part of the text. In this reaction a desire to discover 'who is speaking' through the text of an early modern drama trumps recognition of the complex social roles and circumstances that may 'speak' through that text. It also ignores the specific problem that a play is constituted entirely of the voices of its characters. Such reactions against poststructuralism seem to be gaining force and have been supported by the wider cultural effort to recognize and celebrate the tangible reality of authors who were female or of colour.

The theoretical debate about authorship has concrete implications for interpretation and, as we will see in Chapter 8, for editing. Attitudes towards the ontological status of 'the author' will affect the applicability of various kinds of criticism, most obviously biographical and psychological. For example, some analyses of Shakespeare and Fletcher suggest that the first was 'the King's playwright', the second sided with the views of his anti-court patrons; the first, whose father was a Roman Catholic, perhaps longed for the old religion, the second was the son of an Anglican Bishop and his patrons were zealously Protestant. Do these differences matter when together they write a play – *The Two Noble Kinsmen* – that ends with a long scene of prayers to Venus, Mars and Diana? Even traditional methodologies, like analysis of sources, may be in danger of circular argument based on different attitudes towards authorship. It is sometimes suggested that in *Henry VIII* the 'Shakespeare' scenes depend on the older historian, Raphael Holinshed, the 'Fletcher' scenes on a newer one, John Speed, but Gordon McMullan warns against assuming that only the younger man used the fashionable new book. It is possible that the collaborators did not work by scenes or that they revised each other's work as they proceeded. In that case, what is the implication of searching for 'an author' for these scenes?

Most affected by different theoretical positions has been the issue of what parallel passages reveal. Assuming that an individual writer tends to repeat himself across his oeuvre is a familiar method of identifying authorship, but it is discredited as a form of scholarship on collaboration because it ignores every capable writer's ability to imitate the styles of others. It also ignores the chronological development of drama in the tight theatrical world of Elizabethan and Jacobean London. For example, Lois Potter notes parallels to Shakespeare in the 'Fletcher' scenes of *The Two Noble Kinsmen*, the latter usually taken to be primarily the subplot. But these parallels prove nothing about authorship, since the Jailer's daughter's madness is descended from that of Ophelia, who had appeared in one of the most popular and oft-imitated plays of the period. Fletcher, like Wilkins and Middleton, all of whom wrote after the turn of the seventeenth century, would have seen many of Shakespeare's plays and even read some of them; certainly, in two of his early collaborations with Francis Beaumont, *Philaster* and *The Maid's Tragedy*, Fletcher created versions – tongue in cheek – of the action and characterization of *Hamlet*. Conversely, Shakespeare himself, especially in the first half of his career, acted in plays of his contemporaries, with lines that may have remained etched in his brain and thus may have formed the bases of his 'own' composition. He very obviously began his writing life by drawing on the successful style of Christopher Marlowe. Who is the author of such lines? Of the speech on the 'rugged Pyrrhus'?

In the end, whether or not modern scholars are able to – or desire to – attribute every line or scene of an early modern play to a specific author, the fact remains that collaboration was a norm of the early modern theatre. We may never identify the speech Hamlet wrote, but he claims its authorship. As he tells Horatio, if Claudius's 'occulted guilt / Do not itself unkennel in one speech / It is a damned ghost that we have seen' (3.2.76–8). The one speech works; the guilt is revealed indirectly in Claudius's rising and directly in his later confession. Shakespeare is showing us both that collaboration was done, how hard it is to trace, and how successful it could be.

7

The (In)Stability of the Text

What if the printer went to lunch?

In 1969, at roughly the same time as poststructuralists were challenging certainties about the author, the text and the work, D.F. McKenzie published 'Printers of the Mind: Some Notes on Bibliographical Theories and Printing-House Practices'. Where the poststructural theorists were primarily philosophical, McKenzie's work was primarily practical. Philosophers like Foucault were concerned to disrupt conceptions of authorship and intention as lying behind or beneath a surviving text; McKenzie was concerned to disrupt assumptions about the physical process that resulted in that text. Poststructuralists deployed an author to limit a text's possible meanings; McKenzie examined printing-house procedures to challenge 'printers of the mind', those hypothesized without examination of the actual practices that determined how a text came into being. Although their work was separate, both emerged from a *Zeitgeist* that resisted apparently long-settled ideas and viewed truth as relative. The ensuing half-century has seen the overturning of many similar certainties, with textual scholars coming to accept what McKenzie called 'the normality of non-uniformity' (1969: 12). The effect has been to bring both the stability of the Shakespeare text and the process that produced it into question.

The New Bibliographers thought that their analytic methods had firmly settled such matters as the order of printing for the pages of the Folio, the number of proof sheets pulled before imposition, and the habits of individual compositors. They therefore believed they could furnish credible information about, for example, the kinds of error most likely to emerge from a particular compositor – inferior work must come from the apprentice! – and, consequently, the kinds of emendation required in a damaged text. However, working with the detailed seventeenth-century records of the Cambridge University Press, McKenzie found patterns 'of such unpredictable complexity . . . that no amount of inference from what we think of as bibliographical evidence could ever have led to their reconstruction' (1969: 7). In particular, McKenzie, and more recently scholars such as Peter Blayney, have demonstrated that because it was normal for printing shops, and the compositors within them, to work on several different books concurrently, it is impossible to make assumptions about such matters as the typesetting rates of individual compositors, the size of editions, the relation between individual compositors and particular presses or the balance between 'composition [setting type] and presswork [physical printing] on a particular book' (McKenzie 1969: 24). Some of McKenzie's analysis challenged generally accepted technical assumptions, such as an equation between presses and skeleton formes, that is, the reused running heads and decorative materials like lines that may frame each page.

The consequences of McKenzie's radical scepticism about previous technical analysis became apparent when he turned to the Shakespeare Folio. Certainties evaporated. McKenzie attacked Hinman's deduction that the book was printed on one press with two compositors working on it exclusively, essentially as a 'self-contained operation' (1969: 35–6), as well as the conclusions Hinman drew about the number of copies printed. He re-examined the reasons for casting off – predetermining how much text would fit on each page – distinguishing between those reasons for a folio in sixes like the First Folio, where three folded sheets were inserted one within the next, and those for a quarto. For the Folio, to print so much text *seriatim* a printer would need to arrive at the seventh page before he could redistribute his type; for a quarto the problem was more likely to be type depleted due to concurrent printing of other volumes. McKenzie showed that Joseph Moxon's printing manual, *Mechanick Exercises or the doctrine of handy-works*, which included 'The Whole Art of Printing', although only published in parts between 1678 and 1683, nevertheless serves as a trustworthy guide to procedures essentially unchanged from earlier in the century.[1] For instance, Moxon described multiple stages of proofing, up to and including for a third proof. Thus McKenzie explained that the corrected sheets, carrying proofreaders' marks, that Hinman found bound into some exemplars of the Folio would have been revises used to check that the earlier corrections had been entered. These were pulled when the forme was 'virtually ready for printing and the likelihood is great that printing will begin while the revise is looked at'. Such sheets had a good chance of being 'placed on the heap and eventually bound' (1969: 47). Consequently, MacKenzie contended, Hinman's finding of relatively few corrections in the Folio was not a result of printing-house indifference to correctness but a natural result of human limitation, with errors remaining even after several earlier stages of proofing.

---

[1] Moxon's guide is itself dependent on earlier ones, particularly Hieronymus Hornschuch's 1608 *Orthotypographia* (Hargrave: 2019). Moxon's printing career began well before the *Mechanick Exercises*. His father, a Puritan printer, took the boy to Holland in 1637; when they returned to England in 1646 they established a printing partnership. Printing techniques changed little over time: later guides such as John Smith's *The Printer's Grammar* (1755) still depend upon Moxon.

In conclusion McKenzie stressed the 'conditions of enormous complexity' that prevailed even in a 'small two-press house' (1969: 54). Implicitly his technical details supported a more general argument, that inferences from the printed texts could not yield dependable information about the manuscripts underlying those texts. Subsequent investigations further upset, when they did not fully reject, the conclusions of the New Bibliographers. In particular, traditional binary thinking, which classed texts as good or bad, as reflecting the author's original or final intentions, as revised or corrupted, as theatrical or authorial, has been displaced. Analytic bibliography has of course, continued to flourish. In a new Introduction to the Norton Facsimile, Peter Blayney included a table of the compositor attributions for each page of the Folio. But many familiar generalizations no longer hold.

For example, as briefly described in Chapter 1, Paul Werstine's research has undermined the apparently logical assumption that close examination will reveal whether a printed text was based on a theatrical or an authorial manuscript. Greg had presumed that theatrical promptbooks would 'tie up loose ends, eliminate false starts, and otherwise resolve confusions'. He anticipated they would 'be reasonably consistent and unambiguous in naming roles . . . and would contain a complete and accurate complement of speech prefixes and stage directions' (Werstine 2013: 2–3). However, examining surviving theatrical manuscripts of the period, Werstine found that this was not borne out by the empirical evidence. Instead, 'all kinds of theatrical texts, manuscript or printed – scribal or authorial' (2013: 118) exhibit variations and ambiguity in naming and contain stage directions that leave important actions, even entrances, indefinite. Thus it is impossible to do as the New Bibliographers hoped, to distinguish which of two versions of a play is based on a theatrical manuscript by comparing them to each other with a view to determining which of the two is more like a promptbook (2013: 220–33). Even more disturbing to the categorical certainty of the New Bibliographers, Werstine concludes that 'when an early printed Shakespeare play is apparently set into type from a MS ... there are an array of possibilities for printer's copy: authorial MS, MS by a theatrical scribe, or MS by a non-theatrical scribe' (2013: 231). Once again the attempt to bring the reader into the undoubted presence of the author fails.

Why are some texts bad?

The New Bibliographers were interested in determining what kinds of manuscripts lie behind the printed Shakespeare texts partly as a route to discovering the origins of the bad quartos. Besides *Romeo and Juliet* (1597), *Richard III* (1597), *Henry the Fifth* (1600), *The Merry Wives of Windsor* (1602), *Hamlet* (1603) and *Pericles* (1609), the category was sometimes expanded to include the earlier versions of 2 and 3 *Henry VI* called *The First Part of the Contention betwixt the Two Famous Houses of York and Lancaster* and *The True Tragedy of Richard Duke of York*. Some of these texts notably confuse plot details and damage the play's language, whether verse or even, in the case of *Merry Wives of Windsor*, prose. If the differences cannot be explained by errors in the printshop, then what is their cause? Arguments about this question model the way that scholars form and debate a textual theory, that is, a structure of conjectures that explains the evidence under examination. Such theories attempt to appear scientific, presenting a variety of evidence to support their claims, but, like the assumptions about procedures in the printing house, they often turn out to be more exact than the evidence can support.

Early in the twentieth century Pollard suggested that the inferior texts were pirated. But who were the pirates? There were two major proposals: actors recreating the scripts of plays in which they had performed, or unknown persons taking down texts during performance. Each of these hypotheses was elaborately developed, then attacked, and finally abandoned, at least in its original form, though both eventually reappear in different guises.[2]

The textual theory that blamed the actors became known as 'memorial reconstruction'. It grew from Greg's observation that in the quarto of *Merry Wives* the text improves – that is, comes closer to the Folio text – when the Host of the Garter Inn is on stage. An actor, Greg argued, would know best his own role and perhaps might learn the lines of other characters on stage with him. He could then 'reconstruct' the play, but unevenly. As the theory developed it was extended to many other plays, so that, for example, Greg wondered whether the state of the first quarto of *Hamlet* could be explained by assuming it was reported by the actor who played Marcellus. Since Marcellus is a small part, as the theory grew so did the actor's responsibilities: the Marcellus actor was also alleged to have taken a variety of other small parts including that of First Player. Obviously an actor of small parts might also be brought on as a silent palace guard in yet more scenes; the extension of possible roles was limited only by the limitations of doubling.

Explanations for why texts might be memorially reconstructed varied. Some assumed the motives were venal, minor actors (sometimes identified as the 'hired men', as opposed to sharers in the company like Shakespeare) putting together a text to sell to a stationer. Other motives proposed were less criminal, for instance that a text was needed either because one had been accidentally destroyed or because a company on the road lacked one. In one early theory the bad quartos of the plays later known as 2 and 3 *Henry VI* were short texts used for touring in May 1593 when the London theatres were closed by plague, thus intermingling memorial reconstruction with the idea that provincial audiences accepted performances that were shorter and generally inferior to those at the theatres in London. However, Werstine effectively

---

[2]A detailed tracing of the debate and the varied contributions of scholars over nearly a century is found in Egan (2010: 100–28).

undermined the assumption that travelling troupes, finding themselves without normal materials, performed from an unauthorized book that they had memorially reconstructed. Instead Werstine found in the Hall Book of Leicester for 3 March 1583/4 an entry which requires that 'No Play is to be played, but such as is allowed by the said Edmund [Tilney, Master of the Revels], & his hand at the latter end of the said book they do play'. This strongly suggests that what companies on the road presented to the provincial authorities was the 'allowed book' from which they played in London (1998: 56). Research for the *Records of Early English Drama* (*REED*) has found no evidence that the provinces wanted or were presented with reduced texts (Werstine 1998: 62).

While the theory of memorial reconstruction accrued both more details and further candidates, an alternative suggestion proposed that the texts of the bad quartos had been taken down by stenography during performance and then re-elaborated as the basis of printed texts. Notably, such a procedure would involve memory, since 'the potentially ambiguous symbols have to be expanded in the light of what the stenographer recalled the actors saying'. Stenography, or at least 'note taking' by members of the audience, was widely practised at sermons and was known to exist in Spanish theatres. This theory was supported by Heywood's complaint in the Prologue to *1 If You Know Not Me You Know Nobody*, originally published in 1605, that 'some by Stenography drew / The plot: put it in print: (scarce one word true)' (Egan 2010: 101, 15).

Over much of the twentieth century both proposals tended to be intermingled with other possible causes, such as a presumed theatrical demand for plays that could fit into the 'two hours' traffic' of the stage mentioned in the Prologue found in both Q1 and Q2 of *Romeo and Juliet*. Yet because those two quartos differ considerably in length from one another, the argument falls apart in the process of being made (Stern 2020: personal communication). There were also varying explanations for multiple 'good' texts, like those for *King Lear*.

Support for or attacks on these theories were often piecemeal and play-specific. For example, Peter Alexander argued that key lines, a confused genealogy for the Duke of York in the quarto of *The Contention of York and Lancaster* (later *2 Henry VI*), make no sense and must result from an actor's misremembering (see below). Yet Alexander also noticed that the phrasing of a stage direction in the same quarto is essentially the same as that in the Folio stage direction. Actors do not memorize the language of printed stage directions – in the early modern theatre the parts they were given included their lines, a few words serving as a cue and, on the evidence of the sole surviving professional part, only what Stern calls 'character-specific stage directions' (2020, personal communication) – so Alexander conceded that Q's printers must 'also have had a transcript of the play'. The concept of the single piratical actor was occasionally modified, as when Greg proposed that the quarto of *Richard III* was created by 'an entire troupe recalling their lines to overcome the lack of an authorized book'. Chambers thought that the quarto of *King Lear* had 'characteristics of a reported text' but suggested it was produced 'by shorthand and not memorization' because 'it does not misplace bits of dialogue within a scene, or bring in bits from other scenes or other plays'. Greg supported Chambers on *Lear* –'if it is indeed a reported text it must have been taken down by shorthand' – but a few years later (1949) George Duthie apparently showed that Q1 *King Lear* 'could not have been made by one of the three methods of stenography available at the time', a conclusion that was accepted for the next half century (Egan 2010: 104–13).

A series of attacks on memorial reconstruction came from those who concentrated on theatrical procedures. Scott McMillin showed, for instance, that the bad quartos of *2* and *3 Henry VI* methodically reduce the number of actors required for doubling and thus may have been a product of theatrical necessity; he also noted how in some texts (Q *Othello*, 1622, Q1 *Philaster*, 1620), the female roles are reduced in the fourth act, suggesting an intention to save tired boy actors (McMillin

2005). By implication, whoever created these quartos was preparing for performance rather than mistakenly recording it.

A radical change in understanding Shakespeare's multiple texts resulted from Michael Warren's argument that the two texts of *King Lear* were not 'good' and 'bad' but varied through 'systematic artistic changes that weaken Albany and turn Edgar from "a young man overwhelmed by his experience" to . . . "a new leader of the ravaged society"' (Egan 2010: 115). Warren revived Madeleine Doran's claim that Q *King Lear* was 'much too good to be a result of memorial reconstruction' (Warren and Taylor 1983: 109); instead he suggested that the differences between the quarto and the Folio texts of that play resulted from revision. Warren's now widely accepted theory embodied a major change in attitude towards Shakespeare's artistic procedures and his two-text plays. Apparently unstable texts might represent original and revised versions. Even more radically, Warren asserted that in the case of *King Lear* the revision was Shakespeare's own. The author reappeared, doubled.

Memorial reconstruction as a general explanation for the bad quartos, and by extension for the existence of plays in two texts, was apparently given a death blow by Laurie Maguire's 1996 monograph, *Shakespeare's Suspect Texts*. Maguire worked through dramatic texts from the early modern period, looking methodically for eighteen presumed indicators of memorial reconstruction varying from repetition and 'plot unconformities' to mislined verse and factual errors, all of which had at some point been alleged as signs of the practice. Her conclusion, very like the conclusion of McKenzie about the non-uniformity of procedures in the printing house, was that there was far too much variation to justify generalizations about the source[s] of inferior texts. Indeed, 'textual disturbance caused by faulty memory . . . is identical to the textual disturbance caused by scribes, compositors, forgetful authors, revising authors, adapters, or other playhouse personnel adding to a MS' (1996: 155). In her table of forty-one plays whose texts had ever been called into question she could find no unquestionable memorial reconstruction. For four texts, including the quarto version of *The Merry Wives of Windsor* (1602) and *The Taming of A Shrew* (a 1594 play of uncertain relation to Shakespeare's *The Taming of the Shrew*), she concluded that a 'strong case' could be made for memorial reconstruction. More uncertainly, for *Hamlet* Q1 (1603) and *Pericles* (1609) she decided that a case could be made. Ultimately Maguire ruled that everything else she tested, including the other quartos usually seen as bad and the abdication scene of *Richard II*, was not the product of memorial reconstruction.

Questions about the origin of the two-text plays nevertheless persist, and proposals earlier dismissed have seen a modern revival. George Duthie's 1949 contention that the quarto of *King Lear* could not have been created through shorthand had long been accepted when, in a series of *PBSA* articles and a book on *Shakespeare in Shorthand* (2009), Adele Davidson argued that the phonetic rules outlined in John Willis's 1602 *The Art of Stenographie* correlate with anomalies found in *Pericles* (1609). Furthermore, Davidson proposed that 'unusual features and anomalous spellings' in Q *King Lear* might emerge as shorthand was expanded into text. She repeatedly emphasized the role of memory in 'short' or 'swift' writing: 'Stenographie ultimately functions for Willis as a form of memorial reconstruction from notes . . .. Willis' conflation of shorthand and mnemonics calls into question the critical binarism that too often has treated shorthand reporting and memorial reconstruction as opposing and incompatible paradigms of provenance' (2009: 26).

Davidson strengthened her case with electronic resources, using the *EEBO-TCP* database to demonstrate the rarity of some Q *Lear* variants and suggesting that 'uncommon modes of spelling, such as shorthand or abbreviated writing, may have been used' in their creation (2011: 330). Further, certain of the variant spellings in Q *King Lear* correlate with Willis's rules in *Stenographie*, such as dropping *h* and *w* in transcription or omitting silent letters such as *p* in 'accompt' and t in 'wretched'. Truncated words might derive from Shakespeare's handwriting or anomalous spelling, but 'shortened spellings' and special abbreviations for certain syllables are regular components of Willis's stenographic method. In this proposal the instability of the text comes from its transmission.

Davidson's approach to the quarto of *King Lear* has been repeatedly attacked by Richard Knowles, editor of the variorum *King Lear*, who argues that foul papers did not usually serve as printers' copies. Davidson rebuts with detailed evidence from the databases showing that many of the *King Lear* variants Knowles has identified as common have in fact 'only one or two other occurrences in *EEBO-TCP* among thousands of contemporaneous texts' (Davidson 2011: 332). Interesting examples are found in surviving uncorrected pages later corrected. For example, the uncorrected quarto has 'good deuen', which in the corrected quarto becomes 'good euen' but is 'good dawning' in F. Willis advises running 'words together in transcription' (2011: 333), and the sequence here and in other cruxes in Q may 'result not from the successful reconstruction of text written in abbreviated writing, but from errors or misapplication of rules' (2011: 345). Ultimately Davidson agrees with Maguire that play construction 'represents a variety of processes involving different kinds of agents' but cautions that 'the shorthand debate . . .. should not be prematurely or permanently closed' (2011: 344, 326).

One objection to the theory of shorthand takers has been that such persons would have been conspicuous and unacceptable in the theatre audience, but Tiffany Stern has shown that 'the theatre was, visibly, a place in which written text was created' (2008: 143). In a time before modern recording devices, spectators 'sat in the playhouse with pens and notebooks in their hands'. As evidence, Stern cites not only Heywood's complaint that 'some by Stenography drew / the plot' but the report of George Buc, Master of the Revels from 1610 to 1622, that by means of 'brachygraphy' (a form of shorthand) 'they which know it can readily take a Sermon, Oration, Play, or any long speech, as they are spoken, dictated, acted & uttered in the instant' (Stern 2013: 9). Buc, who was responsible for everything that went on in the public theatres as well as for arranging court performances, was well placed to know whereof he spoke. As Stern points out, the claim 'that whole plays could be copied during performance by spectators . . . only makes sense in a theater in which writing is too "normal" an activity to draw attention to itself' (2008: 143).

Arguing for *Hamlet* Q1 as a 'noted text', Stern extends Maguire's proposal that a 'bad' text might result from different kinds of agents employing a variety of processes. As a theatre historian Stern rejects the idea that Q1 could be a memorial reconstruction by an 'actor-pirate', showing that the alleged pirate, Marcellus, 'misremembers his own cues' (2013: 2). She points out that there is no evidence of actors from any country involved in the reconstruction of plays from memory, while Spanish examples locate 'textual theft amongst the spectators'. So she investigates 'not whether one person, using one form of shorthand, on one occasion, copied Q1 *Hamlet*, but whether some people, using any form of handwriting they liked, on any number of occasions, could have penned *Hamlet* Q1' (2013: 3–4). For the audiences of sermons, 'speedy writing became a goal'. One result was the multiplication of modes of shorthand, often mixed with longhand. Then, 'Given the habit of rewriting sermon notes at home . . . The process of note-taking in whatever form easily became (re)writing' (2013: 5–7).

In describing the evidence for 'note traces' in *Hamlet* Q1, Stern avoids the trap of scholars who 'become loyal to a single brand of shorthand'. Instead she looks for 'the techniques taught around shorthand or "swift writing"'. These include 'noting by synonyms . . . .. *Hamlet* Q1 is known for its synonyms'; noting only the first few letters of a name, as when names like Voltemand (Q2) / Voltemar (Q1) vary at their conclusions; resting while rhyme was spoken, which may explain why 'one half of a rhyming couplet is presented with relative accuracy, while the other half differs entirely'; aural errors like 'impudent' for 'impotent' or 'invenom'd speech' for 'in venom steept'. More complex errors occur when 'a correct word is in the correct place . . . but its meaning is different, as though it has been recorded 'verbatim', but the space surrounding it has been completed using inadequate memory later', or when a passage, such as Gertrude's list of the flowers in Ophelia's garlands, is summarized, or when a passage is 'stitched together' using lines from other plays (Stern 2013: 12–16). This work expands on that of Davidson, who includes a list of changes between Q and F *Lear* where new words employ similar letters, 'especially in consonant outline', but provide different meaning, such as Conying/Crying; intrech/intrince; confirming/conferring; vncleane/vnchaste (Davidson 2009: 229).

An intriguing element of Stern's theory is her explanation for the uneven 'badness' of *Hamlet* Q1, which she suggests may result from it being a text 'combined from the notes of two or more people'. Such combination by 'noters', she shows, occurred in preparing both parliamentary speeches and sermons. The various noters may have used different methods and have had different skills, some more given to verbatim copying, another tending to summarize (Stern 2013: 18). Unsurprisingly, badness, however created, remains an indefinite quality, partly established by comparing texts but never too far from aesthetic judgement.

Why – and how and when – do some texts change?

Another debate about the nature of the multiple texts concerns their relation to each other and their sequence. For Kathleen Irace certain passages in Q1 *Hamlet* 'make sense only to someone familiar with Q2 or F, a clear indication that Q1 was derived from a longer version' (Stern 2013: 16). The reverse claim, that several of the bad quartos were early drafts that Shakespeare later rewrote, also has its adherents and has been strengthened by wide acceptance of the idea that Shakespeare himself revised *King Lear*. We will take up the particulars of the *Hamlet* texts in Chapter 11, but the issue is more general.

Scholarly arguments about the creation of several of Shakespeare's earliest plays, particularly *The First Part of the Contention* (quarto 1594) and *The True Tragedy of Richard Duke of York* (an octavo rather than a quarto, 1595), are a particularly vivid demonstration of how explanations for unstable texts may be rejected and then, like the return of the repressed, reappear.

For both of these plays, the relation of the two texts is intertwined with questions of authorship. If the shorter texts represent *earlier* versions than those in the Folio (where they become 2 and 3 *Henry VI*), were they originally by Shakespeare alone? If they are memorial reconstructions of the longer Folio texts, and hence *later* than the Folio versions, can collaborative authorship still be traced in them? Division about the nature of the texts goes back to the eighteenth century: 'Pope and Theobald believed that Shakespeare had written and then revised the earlier two-part play to produce 2 and 3 *Henry VI*' (Ronald Knowles 1999: 107). Samuel Johnson speculated that the quartos were memorial reports, but Malone took the revisionist position, proposing that the plays had been written by Peele, Greene and Marlowe, and were later rewritten by Shakespeare into the forms found in the Folio. This conclusion stood 'for more than a century' (Cox and Rasmussen 2001: 45–6) but apparently fell to the argument for memorial reconstruction, voiced prominently by Peter Alexander and Madeleine Doran in the late 1920s. Later, as that theory was challenged, scholars continued to argue about the authorship.

The vacillating debate can be traced in the two Oxford editions of 3 *Henry VI*. In the 1987 *Textual Companion* to the *Oxford Shakespeare* William Montgomery rejected Alfred Hart's 1942 claim that the 'play was originally a collaboration of Marlowe with Shakespeare, subsequently revised by Shakespeare'. For Montgomery, the view that the Octavo was an early version rather than a 'report' or memorial reconstruction was not acceptable to 'modern scholars' (*TxC* 1987: 112). However, thirty years later the *New Oxford* rejects both halves of Montgomery's conclusion, essentially returning to Hart. Summarizing work that employed contemporary computer-based methods, Jowett concludes that 'the play was originally written around late 1590 ... it was revised by Shakespeare, probably c. 1595, in conjunction with the formation of the Chamberlain's Men. Shakespeare initially wrote the play in collaboration: Shakespeare is most confidently identified in Scenes 3–6, 8–12, 14, 23, and 15–19, with Christopher Marlowe probably the main author of the rest' (Jowett 2017d: Crit. Ref. 2.2559).

Uncertainties remain. The analyses of Alexander and Doran, arguing that *Contention* and *True Tragedy* were reconstructions from memory by actors, were most persuasive when they pointed out that a passage in each play has the kind of confusion that an actor depending on memory might show, but which an author working from the chronicles would avoid and which are, consequently, correct in the Folio. In *Contention* the Duke of York attempts to claim the throne by heredity, yet in the quarto his argument is pointless:

York had to prove that, although descended from the fifth son of Edward III, he was, because of his father's marriage with a descendent of the third son, more in the direct line of succession than the heirs of the fourth son [i.e. the Lancasters]. The Quarto writer by making him declare his ancestor the Duke of York to be second son to Edward III renders further argument superfluous.

Alexander, cited in Knowles 1999: 124

Urkowitz, who instead believes that both quartos were early drafts, objects that 'Alexander has shown only that the errors in the historical genealogy exist in the Quarto. He has not shown that a memorizing pirate was responsible for them'. Instead, Urkowitz suggests, Shakespeare's own 'lapse of memory could have generated' the error, or he may not have had continuous access to his sources, especially if he was on tour in the 1590s (1988: 239).

Another possible memorial disturbance occurs in *True Tragedy* when the Octavo does not agree with its source, Hall's *Chronicle*, in matching various heiresses to specific nobles, whereas the Folio 'accurately' follows the sources (*TxC* 1987: 197). This difference formed the linchpin of Alexander's argument for memorial reconstruction, which the 1986 Oxford editors did not think had been plausibly refuted. But in the *Arden 3* edition John Cox and Eric Rasmussen reject basing a conclusion on a single variant. Instead they cautiously write that links between the Octavo and its source 'might also be seen as evidence that O is an original authorial version, but . . . other explanations are certainly possible. And the fact that the textual "evidence" for memorial reconstruction can often suddenly become the evidence of authorial copy must give us pause' (Cox and Rasmussen 2001: 164). Again, their scepticism is reflected by changes between the two Oxford editions. Montgomery accepted that *True Tragedy* 'reports an abridged and possibly otherwise revised version of the F text' (*TxC* 1987: 197), but Jowett, speaking for the *New Oxford* editors, rejects Montgomery's 'assumption that the 1595 text represented a later version, incorporating early and intentional theatrical revision . . . we are now convinced that the 1623 text contains not only the fullest but also the latest recension of the play' (Jowett 2017d: Crit. Ref. 2.2559). Even more recently, Jowett argues that *True Tragedy* is a 'composite text', a 'degenerative development away from the primary co-authorial text' with 'distinctive features' that result from 'disruptive transmission followed by reconstruction that involved a limited amount of new writing in an unknown hand' (2020: 255).

In all probability arguments about Shakespeare's multiple texts will never be fully resolved. The debate about priority, though, continues in a new current, a disagreement between Richard Dutton and Lukas Erne. In *Shakespeare as Literary Dramatist* Erne rejected what he saw as a developing critical assumption, of Shakespeare's 'indifference to the publication of his plays' (2003: 26). Instead, as his title suggests, Erne believes that Shakespeare was fully conscious that his plays would be read as well as performed. Consequently, he wrote plays that 'were substantially too long and reduced them himself to manageable length in preparation for the stage'. The '"long" extant texts . . . do not appear to have been meant for performance before undergoing abridgement and adaptation for the stage' (170, 219). Erne's claim is supported by Jowett, who asserts that 'Length is usually a symptom of proximity to the early state of the play' (Jowett 2017b: Crit. Ref. 1.xlii).

Dutton, on the other hand, in *Shakespeare, Court Dramatist* argues that in the case of two-text plays, the shorter version was the one originally created for and performed in the public theatres. Shakespeare later revised these texts into longer versions specifically for court performance. Hence, the 'shorter quartos of *2* and *3 Henry VI*, *Romeo and Juliet*, *Henry V*, *Hamlet*, and *The Merry Wives of Windsor* were not created by a process of cutting from pre-existing longer quarto or folio versions, but were poorly reported versions of the plays as they originally existed, before they were transformed into the canonical versions' (Dutton 2016: 286). Dutton believes that plays obviously longer than the presumed two- or two-and-a-half-hour performance time at the public theatres come from the later part of Shakespeare's career, when the Chamberlain's/ King's Men were the chief performers at court. There 'the demands . . . were regularly for entertainment of three hours – and sometimes significantly more' (2016: 82). Thus the long versions were indeed meant for performance, but for performance at court.

Each of the arguments has weak points. Most importantly, each scholar has difficulty explaining the language of the 'bad' quartos within his theory, and each eventually falls back upon the idea that the bad texts result from report. For Erne, '"Bad" quarto language that does not match its counterpart in the "good" text may . . . reflect a version of what players spoke on stage' (2003: 213). In support, he notes Humphrey Moseley's address to the readers of the 1647 Beaumont and Fletcher Folio, which describes actors transcribing 'what they Acted' for 'private friends'. Erne concludes that the bad quartos were products of a 'communal undertaking' by actors. He acknowledges that the short texts 'make for exciting theater' but believes 'this is largely despite. . . their verbal texture' (2003: 218, 194). Dutton, who never asserts that *True Tragedy* and *Contention* were originally by Shakespeare, also imagines that the bad texts were transmitted in some way by actors and in part created aurally. Each 'bad' quarto 'is an early version of a play which was later adapted'. Each is a 'poorly reported version' . . . probably transmitted (at least in part) by actors . . . And that transmission was probably (again, at least in part) oral/aural, a form of 'memorial reconstruction'. On the other hand, the 'good' versions 'derive directly from authorial manuscripts or written versions based closely upon them' (2016: 169).

Each of these critics brings forward in support of his theory many factors – the relation between the length of public performance and the much longer court entertainments; the role of the Master of the Revels, who had to provide and oversee entertainment at court as well as to control the public theatres; possible changes in the attitude of the players towards publication; the differences between multiple-text plays like *Hamlet* where one text is 'bad' and the others are 'good' and those, like *King Lear* and *Othello*, where arguably both are good but different. Notably, both theorists fall back upon elements of 'reconstruction' and some kind of report by actors to explain the texts, although there is no proof extant of a reporting actor in any country in the early modern period. Furthermore, both theorists implicitly assume that all the changes between two texts of a play were made simultaneously. But because actors learned their parts separately, some changes were easy to make and could be introduced at any time; others (e.g., involving a number of actors and/or requiring actors to learn new cues) were much harder to make after the parts were learned. As Marino concludes, 'scholarly consensus about the provenances of particular dramatic texts should be taken with caution when such consensus ignores the evidence of parts and cues' (2020: 53).

Ultimately, both Erne and Dutton give full responsibility to Shakespeare himself, one for writing overlong plays and then cutting them, one for drafting short plays in the 1590s and then expanding them (or those by others) as the King's Men were offered opportunities to perform in the conditions at court. Dutton rejects any notion that the company's actors were responsible for major changes in the text: 'The actors were quite busy enough ... and the Chamberlain's Men ... had a resident "ordinary poet" who was better placed than anyone to change their texts' (2016: 167). Once again, the author returns, whether more prominently as a member of a theatrical company or as a literary dramatist. Where both Stern's emphasis on the fragmentation of the early modern play text, and proposals that certain texts (e.g., *Merry Wives*) were adjusted at different times for different occasions and venues, have a clear relationship with poststructuralism's heartfelt resistance to traditional belief in authorial control and textual stability, the Erne/Dutton debate is perhaps the clearest evidence of what might be viewed as the backlash – the ongoing insistence of many editors and book and theatre historians that Shakespeare the *author* must remain at the heart of their work.

8

Editing and Unediting

Editing, usually regarded as a practical endeavour, has found theoretical challenges in the issues outlined so far. Facing an apparent error in a text, editors hoping to emend must now consider not only the mechanical ways in which such an error may have arisen but the theoretical implications of deciding that what lies behind the error is the product of an author's, or some other agent's, intentions for that text. If the text is regarded as primarily a social product, with intentions and meanings dispersed, on what grounds can or should an editor intervene to 'correct' it? For instance, if the condition of an existing playtext results from censorship or performance constraints, should it be expanded, and if so, how? If the editor believes her text is the product of collaborative authorship, should she indicate the proposed authorial divisions in every scene, or isolate that information in an appendix, or even, as in the edition of *Macbeth* in the *Collected Middleton*, grey out the work of the secondary author? If there are multiple texts (usually quarto and Folio but sometimes 'good' and 'bad' quarto versions) how is an editor to choose the text that will form the basis for the edition or handle the variants? Should an editor conflate – that is, create a single edition formed from her preferred readings from multiple originals? What about standardization: should a text be modernized? How much? A powerful 'unediting' movement, identified especially with Randall McLeod and Leah Marcus, argues against many prior forms of intervention. Editorial method now divides, broadly speaking, into interventionist and hands-off, with strong theoretical commitments on both sides. As it appears that Shakespeare did set forth and oversee his long poems, *Venus and Adonis* and *The Rape of Lucrece*, writing and signing dedications to them, most debate about editing Shakespeare has concerned the texts of his plays, although the sonnets pose problems of their own (see Chapter 9). This chapter will concentrate on the editing of the plays.

The reason why Shakespeare's works need to be edited, and the traditional purpose of that editing, are both clear from Heminges and Condell's announcement that at least some of the texts in circulation are damaged ('maimed and deformed') and need to be 'cured' and made 'perfect'. Furthermore, in lauding the materials they present in the First Folio as 'absolute in their numbers, as he conceived them', Heminges and Condell anticipate the traditional editorial goal of bringing a text as close as possible to an author's conception or 'original intentions'. Had circumstances been different, 'the Author himself had lived to have set forth, and overseen his own writings; But since it hath been ordained otherwise, and he by death departed from that right' his friends 'have collected & published them'.

Heminges and Condell were indeed Shakespeare's friends, sharers (owners in common) of the company since the 1594 formation of the Chamberlain's Men. In his will he left them money to buy mourning rings, traditionally worn in memory of the deceased. It is, however, unlikely that it was their task to prepare (or 'perfect') the texts, and scholarly speculation concerns just who did undertake such editing as was done. The New Bibliographers thought that it might have been Edward Blount, a member of the publishing consortium with a 'distinctive interest in literary works' or even the printer Isaac Jaggard; others have suggested Ben Jonson, whose dedicatory poem, 'To the memory of my beloved, the author', is copious in praise of 'thy book and fame'. Sonia Massai suggests a wider variety of 'annotating hands', including John Smethwick, another of the consortium of stationers. Considering particularly plays printed from earlier quartos, Massai concludes that 'the annotation of the printer's copy for the press is best understood as function- rather than agent-specific' and proposes that the annotators included stationers and scribes (2007: 159, 155; see also Massai 2013). Yet despite whatever work the early correctors did, even relatively straightforward, Folio-only plays such as *All's Well That Ends Well* or *Timon of Athens* still contain numerous errors that range from simple compositor typos, omissions and misalignment to long-debated cruxes.

One of the most notable things about the editing of Shakespeare from the work of Rowe (1709) until the Cambridge edition of 1863–66 was the self-confidence of the editors. As Andrew Murphy has shown, Rowe 'emended as he saw fit'; Pope 'cherry-picked ... the readings he found to be most appealing'; Theobald, despite his published objections, accepted many of Pope's emendations, 'particularly his regularizations of Shakespeare's meter' (Murphy 2007a: 94–7).[1] To some extent these editors were doing consciously what those who put together the Second, Third and Fourth Folios did without explanation, 'perfecting' Shakespeare's text by clarifying cruxes and bringing the grammar, prosody and expression up to (their own) date. Even those editors, like Capell, who collated methodically and, according to Murphy, 'succeeded in clearing out a very large number of errors', nevertheless selected from the possible emendations 'whatever improves the Author' (2007a: 102–3) – or, we might say, whatever seemed best to Capell.

The 1863–66 Cambridge edition included notes that listed every textual variation from the first four Folios, the early quartos and occasional earlier editions. Hence it presented itself and its text as the product of impressive scholarly research. Nevertheless, in the prospectus for the edition the Cambridge editors admitted their ultimate subjectivity: 'When

---

[1]Tiffany Stern points out that Theobald had access only to a second Folio, not to the First Folio or any of the quartos (2020: personal communication).

the text appeared faulty, it has been altered from the subsequent
editions, the reading which has the greatest weight of authority
being chosen' (Murphy 2017a: 108). They do not explain the
source of this authority.

The apparent self-assurance of Shakespeare's editors increased
even more with the New Bibliographers, who were 'professional
scholars' rather than 'gifted amateurs'. And, as Paul Werstine
points out, their success tended to ratify itself: Greg and Pollard's
discovery of the true date of the so-called 'Pavier quartos', a
group of pamphlets with fraudulent dates and publication
history (to be discussed more fully in Chapter 9) inspired in the
New Bibliographers 'the confidence that they could discover
much more about the nature of the texts in early printings of
Shakespeare'. They became certain they could identify 'with
nearly scientific precision' foul papers, memorial reconstructions,
and 'within early printed texts exactly what Shakespeare wrote'
(Werstine 2007: 111–12, 126). Their complex and sometimes
contradictory arguments about such matters, frequently
presented with much technical analysis of variants, accounts of
printing procedures, and inferences from presumed secretary
hand, and with one hypothesis built upon another, seemed
daunting to most readers, who tended to accept whatever text
they were reading as Shakespeare's. Consequently, late-twentieth-
century students could be taught a conflated version of *King
Lear* – one in which the editor had felt free to pick and choose
readings from either the quarto or the Folio text – not very
different from that found in the Globe Shakespeare. The
assumption remained that there was, behind any Shakespeare
printed text, a single authorial version, and it was the editor's job
to recreate that version as accurately as possible.

Editing Shakespeare

Whatever his or her theoretical persuasion, a fundamental
decision for any editor of a Shakespeare play is the choice of
what is called the base- or copy-text, that is, the early printed

text which serves as the basis for the edition. This becomes the default from which any variation must be justified. As described in Chapter 2, in 1950 W.W. Greg proposed – in what seems at first a counterintuitive approach – a critical difference in the treatment of the 'substantives', that is, the actual words, and the 'accidentals', that is, the spelling and punctuation, of any early text. Recall that Greg argued that an editor should accept the accidentals of the earliest text, as most likely to reflect those of the author. But for the substantives the editor could choose, based on an analysis of how she/he believed the variants came to be (e.g., compositorial or scribal error, marginal insertion, etc.). This theory left the editor free to correct 'errors' in the chosen base text by adopting whichever words (substantives) seemed to be Shakespeare's (or, once again, best pleased the editor). This theory ruled editing for many decades, remarkably so since it was well known that spelling and punctuation were the responsibility of the compositors and hence that playwrights would expect their accidentals to be regularized in the printshop by someone over whose decisions they might have no say (unless, unusually, they were directly involved in the printing process). Whether or not Hand D in *Sir Thomas More* is Shakespeare's, its three pages give a good instance of what dramatic writing might have looked like before the compositors intervened. It has very little punctuation, irregular or uncertain speech prefixes, stage directions placed inexactly and continuous writing that does not respect the lineation of verse.

The most important effect of Greg's essay was that it 'invoked an idealist distinction between the work and a particular material embodiment of it', giving editors authority to alter the texts they were dealing with (Egan 2010: 45). The rationale justified emendations from alternative early texts or from the long history of proposed variants listed in the variorum editions. It supported the assumption that 'the work' was originally one text, although there was argument about whether its form might reflect the author's original intentions or, just possibly, be the product of later revision and hence embody final intentions.

As already mentioned, the major break came with work on *King Lear* in the collection *The Division of the Kingdoms: Shakespeare's Two Versions of King Lear* (ed. Warren and Taylor 1983). Essays in that volume proposed that the tragedy's two texts were not, as had always been assumed, each a different and inadequate reconstruction of a lost single original. Instead, the Folio text was a revision by Shakespeare himself of the earlier quarto version. Consequently any attempt to conflate the two versions would violate Shakespeare's intentions, no longer viewed as singular or stable. In the 1986 *Oxford Shakespeare* Stanley Wells and Gary Taylor carried through the implications of this new theory by editing the two texts separately. They indicated that they would have liked also to edit the texts of F and Q *Hamlet* separately but had to compromise by including lines from the Folio in their edition, which used Q2 as copy-text.

The publication of multiple texts has been greatly facilitated by the development of electronic editions. Similarities and differences in the approach of two recent collected editions, the *Norton Shakespeare 3* (2015) and the *New Oxford Shakespeare* (2016), say a good deal about the state of play in Shakespearean editing in an electronic age. Even given greater scepticism about the possibility of recreating a single original work, both editions have had to determine when two texts are sufficiently different that they should be treated separately and when surviving exemplars can or should be conflated. For *Hamlet* and *Lear*, not surprisingly, both collected editions include multiple texts electronically, though they differ in the number and choice of texts they include in their single-volume print editions. But different ideas of how to handle multiple texts are well illustrated in divergent recent treatments of *Titus Andronicus* and *King Richard II*, each of which has an anomalous added scene in its Folio text. Those cases incidentally demonstrate the role of general guidelines for collected editions in the editorial treatment of individual plays.

Titus Andronicus was first published in 1594 in a quarto that is generally imagined to be 'unusually close to a play as

Shakespeare wrote it' (Bate 2018: 95). Only one copy of Q1 survives. The second quarto (1600) concludes the play with four lines not present in Q1. It is usually thought that the compositor of Q2 was working from a damaged copy of Q1, with its final lines torn off, and may have written the conclusion himself. If so, his action 'highlights the role that compositors played in shaping the texts of Shakespeare's plays'. The lines certainly highlight the permeability of an authorial text. The four lines reappear in subsequent quartos as well as in the Folio, and the Folio text also adds a single scene, usually numbered 3.2, in which the killing of a fly is made elaborately symbolic. This scene, scholars suggest, 'was written after Q1 was printed, probably by Shakespeare for a revival of the play' (Silverstone 2015: 499).

What is to be done in presenting this play to readers? For the editors of the *RSC Shakespeare* (2007), which announces itself as an edition of the First Folio, the play appears in the Folio form, complete with the final lines from Q2 and the fly scene. Decisions were less obvious for the *Norton 3* and *New Oxford* editors. The decision in *Norton 3* was partly dependent on that volume's commitment to single-text editing; partly on editorial inference, which concluded that the quarto text was closer to Shakespeare; and finally on the knowledge that in its electronic edition the *Norton* could include both Q and F texts. As a result, the textual editor, Catherine Silverstone, chose Q1 as the base text for the print volume despite the *Norton*'s general commitment to print the longer text when two are available (Silverstone 2015). Students who consult only the *Norton* print volume will not encounter the fly scene or the added final lines. The edition, aimed at the general reader and following general guidelines, adds act numbers from the Folio text and the traditional scene numbers, as well as regularizing character names.

The *New Oxford*, on the other hand, while also basing its text on Q1, includes the fly scene in a box within the text, presumably because its criteria call for giving the text with the most Shakespeare. It does not include the final lines found in F, reifying its belief that they are not by Shakespeare. The editors criticize the *Norton 3* editor for inserting act and scene numbers into an edition of Q1 (Taylor et al 2017: Crit. Ref. 1.127), but the same numbers appear in the *New Oxford* edition. Purchasers of the print *Norton* are dependent on its electronic version for the alternative version; purchasers of the *New Oxford* are dependent for the added lines on its two-volume Critical Reference Edition, more likely to be found in a library.[2]

For *Richard II*, as described in Chapters 1 and 2, the most important difference between the texts is that the first three quartos, published before Queen Elizabeth's death, do not include the scene in which Richard yields his crown to Henry Bolingbroke (4.1.155–318). The scene first appears in an inferior text in Q4 (1608) and then again in a better text in the Folio. As already discussed, various factors suggest that the scene 'was part of the play as originally written and acted onstage but was omitted from the published versions because it was too politically sensitive to be printed' (Stewart 2015: 894). Meanwhile, each of the quartos was printed from the preceding one, and aside from the deposition scene, F itself was probably based on a 'complete exemplar of Q3' (Forker 2002: 507). Once again an editor must decide whether this situation justifies editing Q1 and F as separate texts, or whether it will be sufficient to insert the relevant passage into a text based on Q1, the text usually accepted as closest to Shakespeare's holograph.

In this case, readers of either the Norton or the Oxford print volume will have the added scene, but their texts will otherwise vary. Committed to single-text editing of the longer text, the *Norton 3* includes an unconflated F text of *Richard II* in the print volume and editions of both Q and F in the digital edition. In the opinion of the *Norton* textual editor, Alan

---

[2] The *New Oxford* denies that either *Titus* or *Richard II* qualifies for an electronic alternative version because the Folio texts of both plays are based on 'good' quartos.

Stewart, cuts in F that streamline the play, change speech prefixes and make John of Gaunt 'a less pragmatic, more sympathetic character', suggest that 'Shakespeare or another hand revised the text between 1597 and 1623, probably for theatrical performance . . .. to produce a subtly different play' (Stewart 2015: 894–5). The *New Oxford* editor, Anna Pruitt, is unsympathetic both to this view and to this method. Arguing that Folio *Richard II*, like *Titus*, comes from a 'subset of plays' with 'lightly annotated' texts, she uses Q1 as her base text, promoting an approach that comes very close to Greg's views on accidentals. She finds it 'unarguable' that the first quarto was 'closer than all other editions to the manuscript that was in all likelihood written by Shakespeare; its spellings, capitalization, punctuation, and layout belong to the same decade in which the play was written'. Nevertheless, she seems to accept that variants in the Folio 'may represent minor changes introduced by Shakespeare himself' (Pruitt 2017: Crit. Ref. 1.357–8, 366). This might easily lead to the *Norton* editor's decision to present a single-text edition of the Folio text. However, in the *New Oxford* print volume the base text is Q1, with the added scene again presented in a box. Readers are unlikely to realize how much effort, and how much textual theory, lies behind these editorial decisions, giving readers two subtly different experiences of what is meant by '*Richard II*'.

Editing collaborations

Collaboration poses specific problems for an editor, whether or not the collaboration is acknowledged. If the edition is to form part of a collected works, the editor is first of all driven to justify the play's inclusion. The Reverend Alexander Dyce, a nineteenth-century editor, included *The Two Noble Kinsmen* in his 1846 edition of *The Works of Beaumont and Fletcher*, but waited twenty more years to include it in his second edition of the works of Shakespeare. Then he only inserted it 'in deference to the opinion of more than one literary friend, who think that the works of the great dramatist can hardly be considered as complete without it'. The friends included, among others, the poet Samuel Taylor Coleridge. Interestingly, Dyce not only identified the passages that he thought were by Shakespeare, but 'conceive[d] that in some places they may have been altered and interpolated by Fletcher' (1866: 8.117–18).

The modern editor will want to present a more detailed rationale for any inclusion but encounters a difficulty in communicating the textual information. To promote accessibility for the vast majority of readers, almost all contemporary editions of early modern dramatists, for instance, the *Collected Middleton*, the *Cambridge Works of Ben Jonson*, and editions of Shakespeare except the *Critical Reference* volumes of the *New Oxford*, are in modern spelling. Thus much of the evidence employed in investigations of authorship and/or collaboration is removed. Function words will remain, but spellings, characteristic punctuation, and in some editions even variant elisions (*'um* / *'em*) vanish. This leaves the modernizing editor in the position of arguing a case without being able to show the evidence. Decisions about formatting and presentation, such as whether a passage should be displayed as verse or prose, or whether to use consistent speech prefixes (or even consistent spelling) for a character name, may obliterate evidence that a second hand was involved in the writing. For a poststructuralist editor who assumes that collaboration was a different process from solitary composition, likely to blur individuality in the creation of a social text, it will become even harder to identify authors by their personal habits.

An example of how editorial intervention masks evidence of collaboration is found in *The Two Noble Kinsmen*. Lois Potter, editing for the *Arden 3* edition, bases her argument that the collaborators on the play worked separately, without much opportunity to compare work in progress, partly on a change of a character's title. Having decided on the authorial division, she finds that in the quarto the *Jailer* of 2.1, which she identifies as a Shakespeare scene, becomes the *Keeper* in 2.2, a scene she identifies as by Fletcher. Yet in later Fletcher scenes the character is called '*Jailer*', and Potter presumes this is because Fletcher had 'discovered that this was what Shakespeare had already called him in 2.1' (2015: 29–30). Nevertheless, because the Arden guidelines call for characters to be identified consistently, this signal of collaboration disappears from Potter's text: a reader who does not attend to the textual explanations will find only *Jailer* in the stage directions and speech prefixes for this character, including in 2.2.

The editor of a text she believes is collaborative must face the issue of circularity, particularly if the text is obviously in need of intervention. Once the editor decides that a play is by Shakespeare and another, does she or does she not alter the text when a peculiarity may be a stylistic tic of the second author? To do so may make the text seem more 'Shakespearean', to leave the peculiarity may strengthen the case for collaboration. One can see how decisions about authorship affect emendation in Rory Loughnane's notes to *Pericles* (Loughnane 2017c: *New Oxford* Crit. Ref. edn). Loughnane accepts that the first eleven scenes of the play are by George Wilkins, the rest by Shakespeare. Consequently, explaining the unusual phrase 'grieve for' at 1.2.98, he compares Wilkins's *Miseries of Inforst Mariage* 'Which tell you that he knew he did you wrong, / Was greeud fort'. On the other hand, to justify retaining 'The' rather than emend to 'Thou' in Pericles' opening speech to 3.1 ('The God of this great Vast, rebuke these surges') he compares 'Shakespeare's similar use of "the" as vocative "Farewell, the latter spring" in *1 Henry IV*' (Loughnane 2017c: Crit. Ref. 1.1398, 1391). Similarly, in a note to *2 Henry VI* he follows the *Oxford Shakespeare* in emending 'a honest' to 'an honest' because the latter 'occurs in Shakespeare at least sixty-two times, "a honest" only here'. The emendation is inserted even though the note goes on to point out that the relevant scene is 'now attributed to Marlowe' (Loughnane 2017b: Crit. Ref. 2.2538). In all these cases, the procedure could be seen as circular – having decided on the authorship based on the text, the emendations to the text are brought in line with the decision.

There are many other ways in which an editor will determine the reader's experience of a possible collaboration. Does the title page proclaim that *Henry VIII* was by William Shakespeare, as in the *Arden 2* (1957), or by William Shakespeare and John Fletcher, as in the *Arden 3* (2000)? Introductions, commentary notes, and the presentation of the text can all strengthen or weaken the case for dual authorship. For example, as mentioned in Chapter 6, many scholars now believe that *Macbeth* was adapted by Thomas Middleton about a decade after its first (now lost) version. Middleton, it seems likely, decided to reuse two songs from his unsuccessful play, *The Witch*. The *New Oxford* editors believe that Middleton also introduced Hecate into 4.1 'to make it the most visually complex and spectacular episode in the play'. Returning, it seems, to the earlier Oxford's commitment to 'formulate a text presenting the play as it appeared when performed by the company of which Shakespeare was a principal shareholder', the *New Oxford* includes the full text of the songs as well as on-page notes proposing a staging in which 'Hecate may enter above or in flight' and the apparitions are performed by 'Hecate's spirit witches, appearing in the air above the stage' (Taylor et al 2016: 2543–5). Thus readers of *Macbeth* in the *Norton 3* or in the *New Oxford* will again have very different experiences, as the *Norton*, wedded to editing the unique existing text and less certain of Middleton's presence, does not include the songs or make suggestions for aerial staging, while the Oxford edition includes them all.

Unediting Shakespeare

David Bevington, writing about 'editing in practice', describes problems that keep editors up at night, such as whether to regularize the changing titles of aristocrats – what should be done about 'King Richard' in *Richard II* once Henry Bolingbroke becomes King? – or how to choose between quarto and Folio variants when, as in *Troilus*, they are nearly all 'reversible' (2007: 177). Bevington identifies himself as an interventionist editor and in his discussion of editing *Othello* puts forward a justification for that position and for the creation of an eclectic text. The play exists in two forms, an unusually late quarto (1622) and the 1623 Folio text. Bevington believes that the Folio copy was derived 'from a revision of Shakespeare's original manuscript, copied over by himself' (2007: 172). The many small changes from the quarto are characteristic of a tinkering author. Whether the Folio text was an 'updated acting version' and whether it served as a playbook – requiring entries into the acting parts – is, Bevington says, 'a matter of dispute'. The most notable change between the quarto and the Folio is the excision of profanity, presumably in response to the 1606 Act to Restrain Abuses of Players, which banned profanity on stage, although not in printed texts. Since *Othello* was written and performed prior to 1606, Bevington agrees with most modern editors that Shakespeare wrote the play with profanities. In a strong version of commitment to the author, he asserts that an editor using the Folio as his base text 'should restore the original . . . . The oaths are Shakespeare's and he should be allowed to say what he wants to say' (2007: 172–4).

How far should an interventionist editor go to restore what he or she believes a playwright wanted to say? In this case the decider was Bevington, hardly a radical. He had objected to the 1986 *Oxford Shakespeare* decision to rename the character familiar as Falstaff 'Oldcastle'. Apparently that had been Shakespeare's name for the fat knight until William Brooke, Lord Cobham, who was the Lord Chamberlain in charge of performances from 8 August 1596 until his death on 5 March 1597, objected and forced the change. A key difference in the two cases is that the profanity Bevington wants to insert into an edition of Folio *Othello* comes from the quarto, while no surviving early text of *1 Henry IV* calls the character Oldcastle. The difficulty, as always, lies in setting parameters. Some Shakespeare quartos have 'God' where the Folio text has 'Heaven'. But should all possible instances of 'Heaven' for God in the Folio be emended? Taylor argues that 'an editor who is locally judicious in rejecting the less certain of these conjectures will also be globally injudicious' in presenting texts with 'too little profanity' (1993: 94). Yet what happens when there are not clear limits is visible in the edition of *The Spanish Gypsy* in the *Collected Middleton*. Arguing that a character identified as a rake-hell 'should employ lots of offensive oaths' but in this case 'the extant text gives him none', at 4.3.52 Taylor, editing the play, adds 'Swounds', which 'immediately establishes his character' (Taylor and Lavagnino 2007b: 1117). However, the note to the emendation proposes that oaths might also have been censored in three other speeches by the same character in the same scene. No explanation is offered of why the oath is added only once. It was such arbitrary use of the editor's authority that, at least in part, brought forth the 'unediting' movement.

Acknowledgement that editorial intervention may lead only to error goes back at least to Samuel Johnson, whose 'primary instinct was to try to make sense of the text as he found it . . . and to resist emendation as far as he possibly could'. Johnson claimed to 'have rescued many lines from the violations of temerity, and secured many scenes from the inroads of correction' (Murphy 2007a: 98–9), that is, to have cleared away erroneous emendations and to have avoided creating new ones by excessive intervention. Both action and inaction have been taken as the meaning of 'unedit', a term coined by Randall McLeod. McLeod was particularly concerned with the effects of various forms of normalization – regularization of variant speech prefixes, modernization of spelling, erasure of seventeenth-century punctuation – and urged examination of photocopies, so readers or students might 'witness the vast difference between the evidence of text conveyed by photofacsimiles and what stands revealed as editorial rumors and irrelevant improvements' (1981/2: 37).

McLeod demonstrated the kinds of emendation, including conflation, he objected to by showing the differences between the texts of *King Lear* that the poet John Keats read, a facsimile of the Folio and an 1826 edition that conflated the two texts and, for example, altered the speaker of the Folio's final lines to follow the quarto. McLeod laments that editors have created a 'pervasive darkness' over Shakespeare's text. For instance, he argues, by normalizing speech prefixes editors have eliminated 'clear and evocative evidence of layering and joints', evidence which subsequent scholars have used in attribution studies. In cases where a speech prefix varies between a dramatic type and a personal name – like Braggart or Don Armado for a character in *Love's Labour's Lost* – editors who give the character just one identifier obliterate 'the specific working diction of a contemporary dramaturgic tradition' (McLeod 1981/2: 49, 52). Partly to demonstrate the irregularities of early modern printing, McLeod has published under varieties of his own name, most amusingly 'Random Cloud' and 'Random Clod'.

Others who practised unediting concentrated on the removal of previous emendations. Taylor picked up the term in the introduction to the *Textual Companion* to the *Oxford Shakespeare*, where the most radical form of unediting was undoing the traditional conflation of *King Lear* and editing the Folio and Quarto texts separately. Leah Marcus took over the term for the title of her *Unediting the Renaissance: Shakespeare, Marlowe, Milton*, which announced that it would concentrate on ways in which the texts of printed books from the Renaissance 'are transformed, often disfigured, by the twentieth-century editorial processes to which they have been subjected' (1996: 3). For example, Marcus argued that the 1602 (traditionally 'bad') quarto of *Merry Wives of Windsor* 'needs to be considered as distinct from the folio rather than a mere corruption of it, and vastly different in terms of its dramatic patterning and ideological functioning'. Yet previous editors, intent on seeing the quarto as 'dirt', worked to make one edition 'error-free while the other is discarded as refuse' (Marcus 1996: 70–1). Unlike many of her peers working in theatre history or editing, Marcus, whose work has been primarily literary-critical, explicitly affiliated her textual work with poststructuralist attitudes towards 'the author' and 'the work'. Her stated goal was to move textual studies away from the 'search for a single "authentic" point of origin and into a new discursive world'. There the author would lose authority and the work would be 'recognized as unstable, existing as an array of concrete, physical documents rather than as that elusive disembodied entity, the work as the author intended it' (Marcus 1996: 124).

Much of Marcus's scholarship has been devoted to unediting not only the text but the supplementary materials, notably commentary notes. She has analysed the ways editorial glosses on the 'blue-eyed hag' Sycorax of *The Tempest* have worked to 'cancel out its potential for disrupting the self/other binary that has characterized most readings of the play' (Marcus 1996: 6); she has argued that the contempt that editors express for the quarto of *Merry Wives* is based on social snobbery, because the quarto does not include the passages about the court at Windsor and the Order of the Garter found in the Folio. Examining editorial treatment of the two *Shrew* plays, she contends that editors' unwillingness to associate *A Shrew* with Shakespeare and to borrow its conclusion to the Sly plot is based on their anxiety about strong women and 'unwillingness to accept as partly Shakespearean or even as pre-Shakespearean a play in which the woman (and therefore the text) is less thoroughly tamed and reformed than in the standard version' (Marcus 1996: 114). In her recent work (see Chapter 4) she extends unediting to re-evaluation of editorial treatments affected by attitudes towards race and colonialism.

Cultural awareness has also been a cause of 'unediting' and rejection of traditional emendations. Both *New Oxford* and *Norton 3* reject the *Arden 2* and *3* emendation of *Othello* that reassigns Desdemona's comment, 'This Lodovico is a proper [i.e. handsome] man' (4.3.34), to Emilia, probably because a well-bred young wife is not supposed to admire men other than her husband. Both recent editions similarly reject emending Othello's Folio-only line complaining that 'My name, that was as fresh / As Dian's visage, is now begrimed and black / As mine own face' (3.3.289–91). Beginning with the second quarto many editors had made the line apply to Desdemona by having Othello allege it is 'Her name' that is blackened, an alteration which Wayne labels a function of the 'slander of women and racial Others in Western culture' (1998: 188). Barbara Hodgdon's *Arden 3* edition of *Taming of the Shrew* similarly rejects a change, proposed by Rowe and accepted in many subsequent editions, that eliminates ambiguity at the play's conclusion. To Rowe it seemed obvious that once Petruccio, having tamed the shrew, says 'Come Kate, we'll to bed' (5.2.190), his newly submissive wife would exit with him, but Hodgdon points out that altering the Folio's *Exit Petruchio* to *Exeunt Petruchio and Katherina* eliminates the text's indeterminacy as well as a variety of performance possibilities (Hodgdon 2010: 306–8).

Deciding on intervention

A useful summary of the motivations behind the unediting position comes from Erne, who divides them into 1) ideological objections to the implied politics of traditional emendations; 2) epistemological objections that there can be no certainty in the absence of original manuscripts; and 3) materialist objections that all features of an early modern text carry meaning, which editing should not efface (2015: 302–5). There are also objections raised by performers and directors, who prefer to have full freedom of interpretation and complain particularly about added stage directions. All of these objections leave editors of Shakespeare facing a conundrum. If one does not simply publish facsimiles, how can intervention be justified? How much intervention is the right amount? What, if any, emendations are necessary to allow readers to comprehend what they are reading?

One current response is the *Norton 3* commitment to 'edit the *text*, not the *work*', in other words, not to claim to reconstruct an 'imagined original'. Plays with two texts are edited separately, not conflated, to convey an elastic sense of what constitutes a play. For single-text plays, the editors stay 'as close as possible to that text when sense can be made of it', rejecting traditional emendations if they appear 'to be the product of editorial preference rather than necessary for sense'. Yet the *Norton* acknowledges that 'editors working on the basis of single-text editing must always balance their commitment to the text against the possibility of error' (McMullan and Gossett 2015: 85–8). The *New Oxford* announces a different aim: its purpose is 'to produce what an edition of Shakespeare might have looked like if it had been perfectly published in his own time, without any errors' (Taylor et al 2016: 53). However, associate editor John Jowett concedes that identifying and correcting error – in other words recognizing when emendation is justified – is 'the' challenge for editors (2017c: Crit. Ref. 1.lviii). A glance at some places where editors differ about whether and how to intervene in a single-text play, *All's Well That Ends Well*, reveals just how challenging those questions can be.

The simplest kind of correction, one on which all editions agree and which demonstrates why 'unediting' cannot be a simple clearing away of all emendations to the early text, is exemplified in the first scene, where F1 has the braggart soldier Paroles tell the heroine Helen (in original spelling) that 'there was neuer Virgin goe, till virginitie was first lost' (1.1.128–9). As early as F2 'goe' was corrected to 'got' (i.e. begot), assuming a simple one-letter error. Such an error could have been caused by a compositor misreading secretary hand, or taking the wrong type from his case, or simply misremembering the phrase as he pulled types.

Another correction is a modernization of spelling that effectively creates a different word. All modern editions agree that F's 'Virginitie . . . weares her cap out of fashion . . . iust like the brooch & the tooth-pick, which were not now' (1.1.154–7) should be emended so that 'were' becomes 'wear'. Early modern spelling was, to modern eyes, very erratic, and there are other examples of 'wear' spelled 'were'. Similarly, 'It nothing steeds vs / to chide him from our eeues' (3.7.41–2) has nothing to do with horses, requiring only the emendation of one letter to restore the meaning, 'it nothing steads us' [i.e. it profits us nothing].

Generally editors attempt to use their accumulated knowledge, both of an author's works and of the processes that brought those works to the page, to clarify passages that might challenge the reader. But not all decisions are as easy as changing steed to stead. An apparently simple word may be altered differently by different editors: for 'ore' in the Clown's lines in *All's Well*, 'and wee might haue a good woman borne but ore euerie blazing starre or at an earthquake, 'twould mend the Lotterie well' (1.3.85–7), *Norton 3* has 'or', the *Oxford Shakespeare* has 'ere' and the *New Oxford* has 'on'. John Payne Collier proposed 'one' and Alexander 'before'. For one crux, 'I see that men make rope's in such a scarre' (4.2.38), Taylor, not content with any of the twenty-five solutions offered by the original Cambridge editors, concluded that the line should be the almost incomprehensible 'I see that men make toyes een such a surrance' (Taylor 1989). Among the solutions Taylor rejects is the one the *Norton 3* accepts, 'I see that men may rope us in such a snare'. And alternative conjectures continue to be made. Editing for the *New Oxford*, Rory Loughnane adopts, 'I see that men make ropes in such a snare', because it 'connects the image of ensnaring to various versions of Psalm 139 or 140' (Loughnane 2017a: Crit. Ref. 2.2071).

It may be the failure of editors to decipher all textual cruxes, or to agree on solutions, that has led some scholars to argue for unediting. Emendations are often indicative of how much an editor is open to intervention. For example, faced with two successive lines in *All's Well* 2.4 with the identical speech prefix *Clo.*, most editors agree that a line has dropped out, although this might instead be a moment for the Clown's improvisation, with no '"scripted version" – just an outline, a plan, a series of keywords and prompts' (Preiss 2020: 77). If a line was lost, it is impossible to determine at what point this happened: did a scribe miss a short line? Did a compositor? Did the author, caught up in composition, fail to pen the line, or did he add it in a marginal note that was missed by a copyist? The question for an editor is what to do. First the Clown, Lavatch, asks Paroles a question, 'Did you find me in yourself, sir, or were you taught to find me?'. Then in his second speech he asserts 'The search, sir, was profitable, and much fool may you find in you'. Editors tend to assume that the author's intention was a coherent dialogue. Conservative editors have attempted to solve the problem without writing lines for Shakespeare; for example Sisson inserted a stage direction, '*Parolles shakes his head*'. But less conservative editors presume that the question elicited a spoken answer. The *Oxford Shakespeare* follows Taylor's proposal (1986: 34–6) that since Paroles has already called Lavatch a knave at 2.4.26, he responds, 'In myself, knave'. Yet elsewhere Paroles calls Lavatch a fool (2.4.31). Thus, striking a middle course, it seemed sufficient to me in the *Arden 3* to insert merely 'In myself'. Where missing text is being invented by editors rather than clowns, it seems best to keep it as brief as possible.

The editorial problems posed by *All's Well That Ends Well*, an apparently straightforward single-text play, reveal the challenges facing Shakespeare editors deciding when an emendation is necessary, what form that emendation should take, and how to justify it. Editors cannot escape choosing, over and over, between sometimes conflicting goals with different theoretical implications. On the one hand they usually attempt to reconstruct what they believe was the original text. This implicitly forces them to take a position regarding authorship and intention, while simultaneously considering whatever (e.g., theatrical modification, censorship, the printing process) could have impacted that original. On the other hand editors want to present a text that is comprehensible to modern readers. The call for editorial intervention can be much greater in a case like *Pericles*, which exists only in a 'bad', sometimes incoherent text and will make little sense to readers in its unedited form, or in *Hamlet*, where widely divergent texts pose questions about when to transfer words from one text into another, or how to utilize the idiosyncratic first quarto (see Chapter 11). Current editorial procedures divide between editors willing to make their presence visible and those committed, at least in theory, to 'unediting' as much as possible. Book history, to which we now turn, has played its role in this division.

9

Book History and the Text

Conservative editorial scholars have tended to offer definitions of the text that seek to argue away the aspects of poststructuralism they find troubling. G. Thomas Tanselle, for instance, makes a distinction between a text (which he defines as the words on a page), a document (the page itself), and a work (everything that we mean by saying 'Hamlet' or 'Shakespeare's sonnets').[1] The developing field of book history goes further, distinguishing between 'texts, composed of words, and books, composed of paper and ink, which act only as vehicles for texts'. This model might seem to be anathema to poststructuralists, who resist the assumption, implicit in the term 'vehicle', that meaning is distinct from the material text as it exists in the world. Yet book history functions well within poststructuralism, achieving 'its relative distinctiveness from both its emphasis upon print culture and the role of the book as material object within that culture' (Finkelstein and McCleery 2006: 1). Where much traditional textual theory sought seemingly platonic ideals, such as an author's intentions for the correct form of a crux, book history accepts, in David Kastan's formation, that 'literature exists, in any useful sense,

---

[1] For broader definitions of documents in a theatrical context, including title- and scene-boards and lost, absent, and forged documents, see articles by Steggle (2020) and by Knutson and McInnis (2020) in Stern (ed., 2020).

only and always in its materializations, and that these are the conditions of its meaning rather than merely the containers of it' (2001: 4).

Attempting to answer his own question, 'What is the History of Books' (2006), Robert Darnton created what became its iconic focus, the 'communications circuit'. Darnton's circuit traces the progress of a book from author to publisher to printers to shippers to booksellers to readers, with room in the centre of the circular image for 'intellectual influences and publicity', 'economic and social conjuncture' and 'political and legal sanctions', all represented (through arrows pointing outward to the enclosing circuit) as exerting pressure on the various participants (2006: 12). Key terms of the field are 'circulation' (or 'transmission') and 'materiality'. In a modification of the circuit, Thomas R. Adams and Nicolas Barker propose a variant in which, 'instead of the six groups of people . . . we have five events in the life of a book – publishing, manufacturing, distribution, reception and survival' (2006: 53). Book history extends McGann's idea of the social text by concentrating attention on factors far away from the traditional object of textual criticism, namely, words on a page. Indeed, looking back at several decades of book history work on Shakespeare, Jeffrey Todd Knight notes that the field 'struggles to reconcile the close attention its object [the Shakespeare text] demands with a set of methods and tools that push ever more toward distance, pattern, and diffusion' (2017: 6).

Scholars have found book history particularly important in revealing what happened to Shakespeare's texts once they were written. Book historians study the actions of stationers or publishers, booksellers, readers, collectors, annotators, correctors and curators. They attend to the paratext with which early modern books surround the dialogue of a play and the errata lists that correct that dialogue. They reconsider the validity of booksellers' claims, for instance that a text has been revised by the author himself, and the ways in which 'Shakespeare' was created by the decision of stationers to feature his name on title pages. Their new analyses of the so-called Pavier quartos have placed those little books not in the history of fraud but in a history of 'Sammelbände' or volumes of collected plays earlier than the First Folio. Work on what Tiffany Stern calls 'play patching' by documents of performance has demonstrated the importance of shorter materials, such as separately written songs or letters, which may have been used in the creation of printed materials. Some examples of the role that book history has played in textual criticism of Shakespeare follow.

Shakespeare as literary dramatist

Book history has contributed to a major debate about Shakespeare's self-image. Clearly the poet who brought *Venus and Adonis* and *The Rape of Lucrece* to his Stratford acquaintance, the printer Richard Field, and wrote and signed dedications of those poems, had every intention of seeing his manuscripts turned into books and, he surely hoped, sold. Even if, as Alexandra Halasz posits, the poems were instead brought to Field by someone in the circle of the Earl of Southampton, to whom the poems are dedicated, the dedication indicates 'the writer's release of control over a manuscript by the circulation of at least one copy' (2013: 19). Yet for a long time it was presumed that as a dramatist Shakespeare had no interest in publication and concerned himself with his plays only as scripts for performance. Furthermore, once Shakespeare became a sharer in the Lord Chamberlain's Men, the play manuscripts belonged not to him but to the company. Hence from McKerrow writing in 1939 that Shakespeare was 'producing, not plays for the study, but material for his company to perform on the stage' (Werstine 2013: 30–1) to Kastan writing more than half a century later that 'Shakespeare had no obvious interest in the printed book. Performance was the only form of publication he sought for his plays' (2001: 5), the dominant critical view was that, except for occasional excursions into poetry, Shakespeare was exclusively a man of the theatre. Furthermore, it was frequently assumed that Shakespeare's company objected to publication, jealously retaining the plays for their exclusive performance.

But as we saw in Chapter 7, in a radical challenge to twentieth-century beliefs Lukas Erne has argued that Shakespeare was a 'literary dramatist', and that he and his company had no objection to the publication of the plays. Instead they 'often actively supported it' (2003: 128). One major proof Erne adduces is the length of Shakespeare's plays, many of which are too long to be staged in the usually assumed two- to three-hour period of afternoon performances.[2] According to Erne, Shakespeare, in full knowledge that the plays would be published and read, wrote plays that were 'substantially too long and reduced them himself to manageable length in preparation for the stage' (170). In support of this theory Erne claimed that the 'bad' quartos represent 'the best witnesses we have to what would actually have been performed' (194) and the longer texts, such as the second quarto of *Hamlet*, are those prepared for reading. Although other theories of the bad quartos exist – as we saw in Chapter 7, some scholars believe they were early drafts of plays later expanded for court performance – Erne's contention that Shakespeare had equal interests in performance and publication has generated renewed understanding of Shakespeare as a 'poet-playwright'.

Erne's theory was partly dependent on his reading of elements of book history, that is, the rationale behind the decision, by Shakespeare and/or his company, to put a play into print; the stationers' economic interest in printing; the significance of the different formats. Like other scholars investigating the print history of Shakespeare's plays, Erne was indebted to a 1997 essay by Peter Blayney on 'The Publication of Playbooks'. Blayney's thesis seemed contradictory to those who imagined that early modern publishers had the same

---

[2]Performance time is widely debated; see especially Hirrell (2010) and Dutton (2016: 67–81).

respect for drama of their period that modern readers do and attained sales to match. Instead, Blayney contended that playbooks constituted only a small fraction of the early modern English book trade and the idea that a 'publisher lucky enough to acquire a play . . . would confidently expect a quick profit' was an unsubstantiated myth (1997: 384–5). To support his claim Blayney explicated the Darnton-like publication circuit for playbooks, in order 'to show what had to happen both before and after a playbook was actually printed' (1997: 416). The essay explained in detail such elements of the circuit as the role of supply and demand, the function of the Stationers' Company, the acquisition of varieties of manuscript, publishers' costs and anticipated profits, and wholesale and retail bookselling. Blayney also defined key terms such as stationer, copy, and authority and the distinction between licence and entrance in the Stationers' Register.

Blayney's thesis about the economic insignificance of playbooks to the book trade has been challenged by Alan Farmer and Zachery Lesser, who maintain that playbooks were in fact valuable commodities for a printer. Although, as Blayney showed, 'no more than one play in five would have returned the publisher's initial investment inside five years' and 'fewer than 21 percent . . . reached a second edition inside nine years' (Blayney 1997: 389), Farmer and Lesser argue that playbooks were nevertheless 'among the most successful books in which an early modern stationer could choose to invest' and turned a profit 'more reliably than most other types of books' (Farmer and Lesser 2005: 6). All three scholars agree that a publisher was most likely to make a profit if a play (or any book) went into second and subsequent editions, when a stationer had already met the costs of buying and licensing the work. But Farmer and Lesser find Blayney's analysis flawed because 'it does not systematically compare the market performance of playbooks to that of other kinds of books' (2005: 4). When they compare plays to other 'speculative books', that is, books not paid for in advance, they find that from 1576 to 1625 playbooks 'were reprinted at *more than twice* the rate' (Farmer and Lesser 2005: 20, italics in original). In a subsequent analysis of 'print popularity' Farmer and Lesser have shown that in the period, 'By far the most successful genre in terms of reprint rate, at nearly double the benchmark, was professional plays' (2013: 51). More recently, using the 'large-scale quantitative methods' of second-wave book history, Farmer has contended that printed playbooks, even the fragile quartos sometimes read to pieces, were not viewed as 'ephemera by early modern printers, publishers, booksellers and readers' (2016: 87–8). In fact, he points out, playbooks had an unusually long shelf-life, not losing appeal as they aged and sometimes being reprinted a decade or more after a first edition (2016: 115).

The traditional belief that the theatre companies objected to printing their plays and thus that Shakespeare could not regularly anticipate seeing his plays in print has also been challenged. A related claim, that publication was held back for fear of making a play available to appear on a competitor's stage, has been undermined by evidence showing that the major companies usually 'left one another's repertory holdings alone' and rather than 'pirating a playbook from another company's stock' bought a new script of their own (Knutson 1997: 469). Instead, the increase in dramatic printing after 1594, at the time of the establishment of the two major companies, the Lord Admiral's and the Lord Chamberlain's Men, and immediately after the reopening of the theatres, makes sense as a strategy of publicity. Such timing corroborates the idea that 'playhouse and book trade publications are . . . synergetic rather than in opposition to each other' (Erne 2013: 21). Stern points out that playbooks 'seem regularly to have been marketed and sold in the theater precincts', probably because they 'worked well as a marketing ploy', and so the 'players may deliberately have released scripts into the market for publicity or advertising' (2008: 139, 141). In the first part of Shakespeare's career with the Lord Chamberlain's Men, it appears that the company had a consistent policy of publishing Shakespeare's plays (when there was no unusual interruption such as plague) about two years after they first appeared on the stage. Such a rhythm suggests an attempt to revive interest in a play that might in turn (re)appear on the stage.

This pattern changed in the Jacobean period, and critics including book historians have tried to understand why, in the second half of Shakespeare's working life, the number of first editions of his plays suffered a 'vertiginous drop', with only four first editions reaching the press between 1603 and 1616 (Massai 2015: 57). Blayney suggested that there was a glut in the market caused by a large number of plays entered in the Stationers' Register in 1600 and 1601; Leeds Barroll thought that the drop was caused by repeated closures of the theatre due to plague. Sonia Massai contends that the cause was the revival of the children's companies in 1599. She suggests that 'demand for new plays by Shakespeare may have fallen dramatically after 1605, not because Shakespeare's plays had become less popular *per se*, but because the demand for plays originally staged by the adult companies shrank in comparison to plays originally staged by children' (Massai 2015: 59–60). Yet even so, the continuing republication of Shakespeare's earlier plays allows for the contrasting, if unprovable, belief that early in the new century the King's Men were already planning a collected edition of Shakespeare's plays and were saving those never printed previously for such a collection.

The creation of 'Shakespeare' through books

Shakespeare's long poems, especially *Venus and Adonis*, were enormously popular. *Venus and Adonis* went through at least sixteen editions by 1640, and even the more classical, less erotic *Lucrece* went through at least eight (Burrow 2002: 7, 43). They established Shakespeare as a poet. Whereas Greene's 1592 attack on the 'upstart crow beautified with our feathers' apparently ridiculed an actor daring to compete as a playwright, by the turn of the century, in the *Parnassus* plays performed at St John's College, Cambridge, Shakespeare is depicted primarily as a writer of erotic verse. The students mention *Romeo and Juliet* and *Richard III*, but Gullio, who promises to 'worship sweet Mr. Shakespeare ... to honour him will lay his Venus and Adonis under my pillow', and Judicio asks 'Who loves not *Adon's* love, or *Lucrece* rape?' Subsequently Shakespeare became the 'Leading playwright in print' (Farmer 2015), between 1598, when his name appeared on the title pages of four editions of three different plays, and 1608, when it was his name, rather than the play title or the name of the company, that appeared in large letters at the top of the title page of *King Lear.* Quickly enough, publication created the dramatic author.

In the second half of Shakespeare's career, even while most of his new plays were withheld, the repeated republication of such popular plays as *1 Henry IV* and *Hamlet* advertised his continuing presence in the book market and formed part of the expansion of the market for playbooks between 1598 and 1613. It was in this period that publishers apparently realized that they would sell more copies of a play if they advertised it as being 'by William Shakespeare' (Rhodes 2013: 107). Plays like *Locrine* and *Thomas Lord Cromwell* were falsely attributed to 'W.S.' and some, like *The London Prodigal*, explicitly to 'Shakespeare'. Significantly, a number of the new quartos were published by one stationer, Andrew Wise, perhaps 'the first stationer who can be described as specializing in Shakespeare' (Smith 2013: 85).

A surprising number of reprints announce that a text had been augmented or corrected by Shakespeare himself. For example, the third quarto of *1 Henry IV* (1599) promises that the play was 'Newly corrected by W. *Shake-speare*'. Book historians have challenged the traditional assumption that such statements were merely marketing ploys by stationers eager for sales. Instead, by comparing the Shakespeare quartos to those of other contemporary playwrights and then to the larger English book trade of the period, Farmer has demonstrated how rare such 'editorial pledges of revision' were. Indeed, 'the selling of Shakespeare as a revising dramatist was truly unusual in the early modern book trade . . . . [Shakespeare] was named as a revising author about three times as often as other authors were . . . [and] on a greater number of individual titles'. For Farmer, this constitutes 'ample evidence that Shakespeare was committed to the printing of his plays in corrected and enlarged texts' (2015: 98–102). Such revisions could vary from extensive rewriting, as apparently occurred between the versions of *King Lear*, to authorial tinkering – correcting a few errors, substituting words or adding stage directions – as may have occurred in *Othello*. If Farmer is right, these title-page pledges suggest that Shakespeare was 'one of the authors in the early modern book trade most concerned about the printing of his works in corrected and augmented texts' (Farmer 2015: 104). Nevertheless, Massai, examining modifications of the three plays repeatedly published by Andrew Wise, more cautiously concludes that author and publisher are equally likely to have introduced corrections (2007: 105). In any case, whether the claims for authorial correction were true or not, they presumably assisted in making these quartos bestsellers and in building Shakespeare's personal reputation.

That reputation, as a literary dramatist, was most obviously confirmed after Shakespeare's death by the appearance of the Folio. For Kastan, who believes that Shakespeare had no interest in publishing his plays, the Folio 'might be said to be the creator of Shakespeare . . . as the author he never was or wanted to be' (2001: 78, 71). Erne, on the contrary, believes in a Shakespeare who 'wanted to be published, bought, read and preserved' (2013: 9). Ultimately, what Shakespeare wanted is something we can never know. Instead, studies of the history of books have taught us how Shakespeare's reputation and authorial persona were 'created, bought, and sold by the early modern book trade' (Hooks 2016: 3). Outside factors transformed Shakespeare into 'Shakespeare', a version of himself that he might not have recognised. Book history thus seems both to confirm and to undo the author.

Readers, commonplacers
and collectors

Darnton's circuit concluded with readers, and Adams and
Barker's with 'reception and survival'. An important contribution
of book history to the study of Shakespeare has been its attention
to what happened to Shakespeare's texts *after* they were printed
and sold. Having accepted that Shakespeare was not exclusively
a man of the theatre, book historians ask what can be learned
about the reception of his works from the surviving early
modern copies of books and other material instantiations of the
Shakespeare text. One caveat is that word 'surviving': some
plays, like *Love's Labour's Won*, do not survive at all; there is
one copy of the first quarto of *Titus Andronicus* and two, found
in different countries, of the first quarto of *Hamlet*. Sermons
rather than plays were the usual choice for library collections.
Still, much can be learned from what we have.

A sense of Shakespeare's reputation as a writer can be
gleaned from the early print anthologies that included his
work and from the 'commonplace books' into which
individuals copied favourite passages. Two anthologies of
1600, *England's Parnassus, the Choicest Flowers of Our
Modern Poets*, and *Belvedere, or the Garden of the Muses*,
which has over 200 quotations from Shakespeare, contain
extracts from both the narrative poems and five plays *Romeo
and Juliet, Richard II, Richard III, Love's Labour's Lost*, and
1 Henry IV (Erne 2013: 228–9). The combination of genres is
significant because the anthologies 'give Shakespeare extensive
representation as a poet, but their publication also coincides
with his emergence as the named author of playtexts and with
the take-off in the popularity of plays as a section of the book
market' (Rhodes 2013: 116). In other words, by the end of the
sixteenth century Shakespeare was recognized and presented
as creator of both verse and drama.

The commonplace books, which survive in both manuscript
and print, reveal that readers might approach Shakespeare's

texts 'not as complete units but rather as repositories of phrases and ideas to be excerpted and appropriated' (Estill 2013: 149). In this context the author may fade, becoming a thread in the general fabric of literature. Passages were entered under headings such as 'Of Grief' or 'Of Pleasure' and might be excerpts from the writing of many individuals. The topic, rather than the author, mattered. Furthermore, as similarly revealed by variants in manuscripts of the sonnets, readers felt free to alter the texts they copied, becoming silent collaborators in increasingly social texts (*TxC* 1987: 444; Duncan-Jones 2010: 453–66).

Book historians have considered how these compendia, in manuscript or print, fit into the communication circuit. Most obviously each indicates one individual's interests and reactions, but they also may have publicized those interests if, as Stern suggests, commonplacing or the copying of dramatic passages sometimes took place in the theatre during performance. Furthermore, complicating the usual progression from writer to reader, Shakespeare may have anticipated that passages of his plays would be excerpted and hence included 'punchier quotations' intended to 'appeal to table-books' (Stern 2008: 143–4).

Printed volumes also tell a story about the reputation and creation of Shakespeare. Studies of book collections have shown that Thomas Bodley's 1612 objection to having plays in his library lest it be known that 'we stuff it full of baggage books' was not fated to last: by 1630 the Bodleian had yielded to drama and accepted the private collection of Robert Burton, which contained 'comedies, tragedies, poetry and comic works' (Hackel 1997: 113, 120). Burton was not the only prominent collector of playbooks: at his death in 1612 Sir John Harington had over 130 in his collection, including 'twenty-one of the twenty-four playbooks by or attributed to Shakespeare ... published before 1610' (Erne 2013: 198). The library of Sir William Drummond of Hawthornden similarly included plays by Shakespeare. In a reversal of Bodley's attitude, in 1626/7 the University of Edinburgh gratefully accepted Drummond's books and included 'Shakespeare *Loves Labours Lost*' in the catalogue it subsequently printed (Erne 2013: 196–7). After surveying a number of other important collections, including that of George Buc, the Master of the Revels, Erne concludes that the evidence of ownership and collecting makes it difficult to believe 'that Shakespeare's contemporaries considered his playbooks discardable ephemera or "riffe-raffe" unfit for inclusion in libraries' (2013: 214). Prominent among those whose admiration for the playbooks was notable were women, as the research of feminist scholars has revealed.

Women and Shakespeare books

Book history is one place where textual scholarship has been notably impacted by the rise of feminist criticism. Although 'the history of the book is still largely defined as a male homosocial environment' (Ozment 2020: 150), feminist research into the early modern book trade has uncovered significant levels of creative and economic activity by women, from gathering rags for paper (Craig 2020) to serving as scribes to working in printing houses to reading, editing, and collecting books. Thanks to the survival of the Stationers' Company records, we know a good deal about such women as Jacqueline Vautrollier and Jane Middleton, both of whom were the widows of printers (see also Farmer 2020). Middleton, who was not allowed to succeed to her husband's printing house 'until the warden and assistants had presented her name to the ecclesiastical commissioners' (Smith 2012: 121), was evidently highly educated: she petitioned to continue work in progress at the time of her husband's death and was permitted to complete a Greek New Testament and a work of Luther. Vautrollier followed a path not uncommon in her situation: shortly after her husband's death in 1587 she married his former apprentice (Shakespeare's acquaintance Richard Field from Stratford) and together a few years later they published *Venus and Adonis* and *The Rape of Lucrece*. It was the first of these poems that Richard Braithwaite, in *The English Gentleman and English Gentlewoman* (1641), complained that women 'carry about them (even in their naked Bosomes, where chastest desires should only lodge)' (Smith 2012: 206). Smith's research suggests that there were close supporting relationships among the women who worked in the print trade: Middleton printed six editions of an anti-Catholic letter that appeared in 1588 'under the imprint of Vautrollier and . . . Field' (123). Some of these women stationers were financially conservative, but others, Wayne argues, were 'entrepreneurial, increasing the number and types of books they issued' (2021, personal communication).

Studies of women's reading and collecting inevitably accompany each other, as most reading was done at home in private collections. Heidi Hackel cites a revealing complaint by a woman called Ann Merricke. Stuck in the country and unable to attend the theatre, Merricke laments that 'I must content myself here, with the study of Shakespeare and the history of women, All my country library' (Hackel 1997: 118). Some major collections made by elite women have been traced through household inventories or book lists taken at the time of their deaths: Frances Egerton, countess of Bridgewater (1583–1636), owned quite a few works of 'vernacular drama', including 'Diverse plays by Shakespeare'; Frances Wolfreston (1607–77) signed her name in ten Shakespeare quartos; 'Shakespeares plays' is one of six volumes in 'My Lady Temple's Custody' (Hackel 1997: 125, 122).

Egerton and Wolfreston, among the most important of these collectors, have been extensively studied. Egerton was the daughter of Ferdinando Stanley, Lord Strange, who had a company of players, some of whom later joined the Lord Chamberlain's Men. Thus Egerton had 'good reason . . . to be interested in plays, and especially in Shakespeare's plays' (Erne 2013: 205). She had many of her quartos bound into volumes of 'Diverse plays', but a number key on most of the title pages has made it possible to determine that she owned 'no fewer than twelve plays . . . almost all of Shakespeare's plays available at the time'. Using the key Lawrence Manley has attempted to reconstruct her volume of 'Diverse plays by Shakespeare', concluding that 'here, more than twenty years in advance of the First Folio, is a "complete" volume containing every one of Shakespeare's plays that were in print by 1602'; the exceptions were the bad quartos of *Henry V* and *Merry Wives* (Erne 2013: 204–6). Wolfreston, unlike Egerton, was not an aristocrat but 'a literary lady in her country house', yet at least 220 books belonging to her have been identified and she may have owned over 400. These included thirteen Shakespeare quartos, including two of *Venus and Adonis*, one the only surviving copy of Q1. There is no doubt that she read her books, as she often inscribed comments in them, e.g., in *Taming of the Shrew*, 'a very prity mery one' (Lindenbaum 2018: 196–8).

Women's reading and collection may have had an effect on the physical form of books. Most plays were published as quartos. Some of Wolfreston's quartos remained unbound, as was revealed in a later auction, but others were bound into composite volumes. However, these collections of quartos must not have been too large: the publisher Humphrey Moseley excused himself for not including anything previously published in his 1647 Folio of the plays of Beaumont and Fletcher, because 'it would have rendered the book so voluminous, that *Ladies* and *Gentlewomen* would have found it scarce manageable, who in works of this nature must first be remembered'. It is thus comforting to know that at least one woman, Elizabeth Puckering, was not put off by size from owning a Second Folio, as well as 'a respectable collection of poetry and drama' (Mayer 2018: 38).

Two material texts

Different approaches to book history, broadly conceived, and a demonstration of how textual scholars are led to sometimes duelling hypotheses using historical and physical evidence, can be found in the variety of recent theories about two controversial Shakespearean texts, the so-called Pavier quartos and two printings of Shakespeare's sonnets, the 1609 quarto and a 1640 volume entitled *Poems: Written by Wil. Shakespeare, Gent.* In both cases research into the procedures and constraints of the book trade and examination of the material books has yielded new proposals for understanding these volumes.

The Pavier quartos are a group of pamphlets dated variously and with imprints stating that in five cases they were 'Printed for T[homas] P[avier]' and in four for other stationers; three are dated 1600, two are dated 1608, three are dated 1619, and one is undated. Three of the quartos have continuous signatures but the rest do not. In 'one of the most spectacular achievements' of the New Bibliography, W.W. Greg demonstrated that these quartos, sometimes found bound together, 'were all printed on the same mixed stock of paper, and that they were therefore printed at the same time' (Massai 2007: 112). Greg concluded that they were all printed for Pavier, a well-known stationer, in 1619, including the plays with forged dates of 1600 and 1608. The nine quartos contain ten plays – the volume entitled *The Whole Contention* contains versions of the two plays known later as *2 Henry VI* and *3 Henry VI*. Despite their title-page attributions, two of the plays, *Sir John Oldcastle* and *A Yorkshire Tragedy*, are not by Shakespeare.

Greg's explanation of the forged dates seemed supported by a letter of May 1619 to the Stationers' Company from the Lord Chamberlain, who ordered that 'no plays that his majesty's players do play shall be printed without consent of some of them' (Erne 2013: 176). In what Massai calls a 'popular narrative', it was assumed that the King's Men had asked the Lord Chamberlain, William Herbert, to intercede against the piratical printing of the collection because the company itself was planning the First Folio – a Folio that four years later would be dedicated to Herbert and his brother and successor as Lord Chamberlain, Philip Herbert. The theory built on that narrative concludes that in defiance of the Lord Chamberlain's order, Pavier and Jaggard decided to go ahead with the project but to issue the plays not yet printed (those without the continuous signatures of the first three) separately and with false dates, in order to make them seem to be remainders (unsold copies) from the original printings.

The first part of this theory that has undergone new investigation is the assignment of full responsibility to Pavier, whom Pollard viewed as a pirate. Several scholars have noted that the only person connected to all ten quartos was the printer William Jaggard. As Kastan and others have pointed out, William Jaggard had a history of playing fast and loose with Shakespeare's name: he had printed *The Passionate Pilgrim* as 'By W. Shakespeare' although only four of the sonnets included were definitely by Shakespeare and several pieces were certainly by Heywood. Heywood objected and, as we saw earlier, claimed that Shakespeare was 'much offended' that Jaggard 'presumed to make so bold with his name'. Of course Shakespeare was not alive to be offended in 1623, but the oddity that the Jaggards published the First Folio after the illicit quartos has led to reconsideration of their practice.

Kastan assumed that the reason the Jaggards (William and his son and successor Isaac) were contracted to print the Folio was that they were one of the few publishers with the resources necessary to produce such a large book, while 'the impossibility of any quick profits' would repel most others (2001: 60). Blayney points out that the King's Men had to deal with William Jaggard in any case because he held the monopoly for printing playbills. Massai has gone further, arguing that Isaac Jaggard, who lived to complete the printing of the Folio, 'was inspired by Pavier's projected collection' and it was with a view to his own eventual participation in the Folio that he 'persuaded the King's Men to invoke the Lord Chamberlain's support to prevent other stationers – and *not* Pavier – from securing previously unpublished plays from their repertory' (2007: 118, 107). In Massai's view, this explains why the King's Men were willing to collaborate with Pavier on the Folio, even using an annotated copy of one of his quartos as the base text for a play in the volume.

However, technical analysis of the quartos and their place in the book trade has led to a re-evaluation of their purpose. In 2007 Peter Stallybrass and Roger Chartier pointed out that the continuous signatures of the first three plays suggest that Pavier originally intended to sell all the plays together and was only hindered by the Lord Chamberlain's letter. This would have been the 'first serious attempt to materialize Shakespeare as a dramatic author in the form of a bound book' (Stallybrass and Chartier 2007: 42). Nevertheless, in later work (2015) Lesser and Stallybrass, examining the quartos closely, raise doubts that throughout the printing the purpose remained the creation of a 'collected Shakespeare'. Pamphlets intended for individual sale have 'stab-stitch' holes, holes through which the folded sheets or signatures can be sewn together, but pages intended for binding do not. Only the first three Pavier quartos, those with continuous signatures, do not have stab-stitch holes, indicating that they were intended to form part of a bound book. Jeffrey Knight has discovered a bound copy of the quartos that originally included the 1617 edition of Heywood's *A Woman Killed With Kindness*, the only other play 'from the Shakespearean period without stab-stitch holes' (Knight 2013: 151–3), and Lesser has found 'ghost images' of the title page of *Woman Killed* in other Pavier quartos (Lesser and Stallybrass 2015: 129). By binding the Heywood play with the Shakespeare quartos of 1619, the Jaggards could make it seem that 'what might appear to be a "Shakespeare collection" is actually highly variable' (2015: 132). Yet Massai, who agrees that the bound book, with its differing dates, was intended to look like a 'nonce collection' – one combining older and newer pamphlets, not necessarily all by the same author – nevertheless believes the goal was to arouse desire for a collection of Shakespeare's plays (2007: 118–20).

Work on the Pavier quartos has thus radiated in different directions. Returning to the question of the identity of the 'stolen and surreptitious' copies to which Heminges and Condell objected, Erne has proposed that it was not earlier 'bad' texts but the bound copies of the Pavier quartos that

Heminges and Condell perceived 'as an illegitimate threat to the projected Folio edition' (2003: 257). Yet if Jaggard was the chief agent in both projects, it is odd that he would permit such an attack in the letter addressed to the reader of the Folio. Taking a different approach, Knight, studying other 'Sammelbände' or bound collections, points out that the bound Pavier volumes still include separate title pages, complete with imprint, for each quarto, while the 'real innovation' of the First Folio 'was to print a vernacular dramatist's work continuously, running from page to page' (2013: 179). Hence the Folio is rhetorically presented as the 'integrated corpus of Shakespeare and his works' (Hooks 2016: 117), once again emphasizing the role of the single author to whom all the contents can be attributed. It is for this reason that Kastan sees the book as creating Shakespeare.

Nevertheless, the First Folio is not a full corpus or collected works. Unlike the 1616 Folio of Ben Jonson often thought to be its model, it contains plays but no poems. For a different example of how recent theories in book history have impacted longstanding assumptions, we may look at changing attitudes towards Thomas Thorpe's publication, *SHAKE-SPEARES SONNETS* (1609). Most discussion of the volume has focused on biographical and interpretive puzzles: the dedication by Thorpe to the unidentified Mr. W.H., the date(s) of composition, the arrangement(s) within the sequence, and the implications of the poems for Shakespeare's sexuality. Such analyses have been central to traditional readings that see the little quarto as conveying a narrative that, properly decoded, will lead directly to the (real) author. Challenging this approach, Jane Kingsley-Smith points out how reading the sonnets in the order given in the quarto and forcing them into a gendered narrative unduly constrains the meaning of individual poems. For her, interpretations based on such 'critical orthodoxy' only work 'if we believe the Quarto sequence is Shakespeare's own, and if we subscribe to the theory that authorial intention can and should delimit the ways in which a lyric functions in the world', an attitude she calls 'nostalgic, if not reactionary' (2019: 4,

10). Once such orthodoxy is rejected, the presence of the poems in a single book does not circumscribe their meaning.

From the standpoint of a book historian, Marcy L. North strengthens these arguments, seeing the edition's 'material anomalies' as revealing the sequence as 'a cultural and generic product'. The publisher, Thorpe, diverges from the standard presentation of sonnet sequences, not printing one sonnet per page, not framing each sonnet and not including conventional prefatory materials such as an author's epistle or commendatory verses. Thus North proposes that 'rather than a sequence composed and organized for print, Thorpe acquired a partially organized collection of small côterie sequences and individual sonnets' and accordingly framed it 'partly as an organized sequence and partly as a miscellaneous gathering of small sequences and pairings' (2006: 211, 219). The oddities of the volume still may derive from Shakespeare, who North imagines tinkering 'with potential beginnings and frames'. Yet from the absence of the paratext she deduces that Shakespeare 'did not complete the final revisions before print', and hence it is an error to read the 1609 *Sonnets* as presenting a cryptic biography. Instead, to understand the collection's differences from other sequences, it must 'be set within the fullest material context that book history can provide, a context in which the sonnet sequence is primarily a print genre' (2006: 218–19).

Doubts about treating the sonnets as biographical and proposals to read them through their material presentation have had an even bigger effect on changing attitudes towards their second publication, the bookseller John Benson's 1640 collection of *Poems: Written by Wil. Shake-speare, Gent.* The usual reaction to this volume is well exemplified by Katherine Duncan-Jones, who calls it 'outrageously piratical and misleading'. She objects to Benson's 'rearrangement and titling of the sonnets, his habitual running together of two or more sonnets to give the appearance of a longer poem, together with his mingling of Shakespearean and non-Shakespearean poems throughout the volume'. Notoriously, by changing pronouns Benson makes a 'visible attempt ... to suggest that the addressee throughout is a woman' (2010: 40–1). But recently scholars have questioned whether Benson's chief concern was to conceal sexual content. For Kingsley-Smith conflation was instead Benson's 'strongest tactic in encouraging new readers to engage with the poems' (2019: 71). The titles he gave these poems, such as 'An invitation to marriage', helped readers to find a way into the material. Once the sequence was reordered, despite 'irreparable damage to Q's narrative structure' (Kingsley-Smith 2019: 69), it became possible for individual lyrics to be read as if they were unpublished poems from a manuscript culture (67).

Colin Burrow also downplays biography and sees Benson's goal as commercial, an attempt to refashion 'Shakespeare's sonnets for a market attuned to Cavalier lyric' (2002: 94). Benson did this in a variety of ways. For example, the presence of poems 'by other Gentlemen' followed the Caroline fashion for publishing collections including multiple authors (Kingsley-Smith 2019). Furthermore Benson was sensitive 'to how collections informed . . . interpretation' and restructured the sonnets to make them resemble metaphysical poems (Heffernan 2013: 73). Although his volume was published, like the 1632 Second Folio of Shakespeare's plays, by Thomas Cotes, physically the 1640 *Poems* resembles the volume of '*Poems, by J*[ohn] *D*[onne]', published posthumously by John Marriot in 1633 and reprinted in 1635 and 1639. Similarities begin with the shared title, *Poems*, and continue in the shared form, octavo. Both volumes open with lyrics or sonnets by the named author, followed by poems by others. In a specific example of 'textual mimicry', every page of the Shakespeare volume has a running title that, like the running titles in the Donne collection, includes a diaeresis (two dots over the second of two vowels which otherwise make a diphthong) in the word *Poëms* (Heffernan 2013: 90). Benson even echoed Donne's titles for his combination poems, naming one 'A Valediction'. The poems that result are essentially Shakespeare's, but the author that Benson's collection constructs lived well past 1616.

From the point of view of book history, then, Benson is not simply a distorter of Shakespeare's poetry; he is recognizably a publisher who understood how the shape and format of a collection inform its meaning. Similarly, the physical clues in the Pavier quartos – dates presenting them as remainders or indications they were to be bound separately or together – colour the reader's understanding of the texts within them. Book history thus builds its textual theories around material evidence, in cases like the sonnets and the Pavier quartos focused on those parts of the communication circuit farthest away from an imagined singular author. Original intentions are subsumed by the physical form and circulation history of a volume. Vehicle and meaning tend to merge. Ultimately, even in the case of Shakespeare it is not possible 'to pry apart a history of the book and a history of the poetic texts transmitted within those material objects' (Heffernan 2013: 97). In effect, the book, rather than the hypothesized author, creates the significance of its contents.

10

Performance and the Text

The phrase 'text and performance' may mean a number of contradictory things. On the one hand, traditionally we assume that a dramatic text determines, or at least anticipates circumscribing, performance, although specific conditions of staging such as theatre size or a particular audience (e.g., royal, provincial), and theatrical norms such as whether women actors are permitted, may affect details large or small. Some sixteenth-century plays helpfully include charts that indicate how the parts are to be doubled in performance. On the other hand the reverse is also true: printed early modern play scripts may contain elements, such as prologues, passages of dialogue, songs, or stage directions, that were introduced into or modified by, theatrical performance. More than a novel or a poem, a printed play is likely to be a social text.

From a theoretical point of view, a performance is where an author, or his putative intentions, is most often obscured if not ignored. Foucault's 'principle of thrift' often moves into other hands; in modern times these could be the director's. In Shakespeare's period a prompter controlled stage timing and words but did not impose a concept. Possibly Shakespeare, as a member of the company, had some say about performance choices. But now contemporary performances may contradict clear indications given by the text – for example, making the steward Malvolio in *Twelfth Night* or the magician Prospero in *The Tempest* female, or making the Venetian Iago black and the Moor Othello white in *Othello*. Or a staging can impose a meaning not necessarily present in the printed text, as in the Gibson *Hamlet* where the Prince climbed incestuously upon his mother in a bed not called for in either quarto or Folio, or in a production of *King Lear* where Edgar indicated that he recognized the disguised Kent. Almost all modern productions silently replace some unfamiliar diction, assumed to be the author's, but in fairly extreme cases, such as in the Oregon Shakespeare's 'translation' of Shakespeare's plays, much of the language may be openly changed. One may ask, then, in what way these performances can still be called Shakespeare's.

Modern students of adaptation and appropriation are quite open about the restricted role of the original author's words. For them, the text is only one of the 'transmedial set of objects we call Shakespeare' available for 'use'. Performance theory has moved away from 'text-based' or artifact study to concern with the transitory 'event'. '"Shakespeare" now includes performances, translations, transmediations, adaptations, appropriations, and even memes' (Lanier 2017: 295, 293). In a negative construction, the text is merely an archive behind the event, a 'decaying frayed corpse', a 'ghostly shadow', or a 'template from which performance is built' (Geddes 2019: 421). Those who object are guilty of 'fidelity discourse' (Lanier 2017: 295). More positively, Louise Geddes describes 'the interplay of text, performance, culture and reception that characterizes appropriation' (2019: 421). For scholars of performance an ephemeral event like Ivo van Hove's *Roman Tragedies* – which combined three Shakespeare plays, used a variety of media including television and Twitter, broke down the division between the audience and the theatrical space, and included two sets of surtitles creating 'continual fragmentation and reconstitution of Shakespeare language' – exemplifies how, through the 'various forms of language at work' and the 'ongoing afterlife on social media', appropriation is 'actualized in the movement between work and event' (Geddes 2019: 425–8). In such circumstances there is no reason to worry about the author. Shakespearean authenticity can 'inhabit multiple spaces simultaneously' and the performance text can be understood as 'its own entity' rather than as a re-creation of any original (2019: 423).

For Shakespearean textual scholars, the performances of particular interest remain those that have left traces in the quarto and Folio texts. Implicitly such traces reveal the methods of the early modern theatres, methods that would have been anticipated by dramatists as they wrote and that reveal some of the ways in which the texts were first appropriated. Hence this chapter will first consider evidence included in surviving early modern plays by Shakespeare and his contemporaries for methods of, and constraints on, performance. It will then turn to the textual issues that arise for modern editors as they decide whether the texts they are preparing are intended for performers as well as for readers. Given the view that any performance may be an appropriation where the text is 'in a state of perpetual coming into being' (Geddes 2019: 422), however, such concern may no longer appear appropriate.

Traces of early performance

At the end of the 1606 quarto of *The Wonder of Women or Sophonisba*, the playwright John Marston entreats the reader 'not to tax me, for the fashion of the entrances and music of this tragedy, for know it is printed only as it was presented by youths, & after the fashion of the private stage'. The phrasing paints an uncertain picture of the relation between the early modern dramatic texts that have come down to us and their original performance(s). If *The Wonder of Women* is printed *only* as it was presented by boys at the private theatres, in this case the Children of the Queen's Revels at the Blackfriars, does that imply that there existed, or could have existed, another version of the play *not* presented in this fashion? The play does give extremely detailed directions for the 'fashion of the entrances'. For example, the 'Prologus' opens as follows:

Cornetts sound a march. Enter at one door the PROLOGUE, *two* PAGES *with torches,* HASDRUBAL *and* JUGURTH, *two* PAGES *with lights,* MASSINISSA *leading* SOPHONISBA, ZANTHIA *bearing* SOPHONISBA's *train,* ARCATHIA *and* NYCEA, HANNO *and* BYTHEAS. *At the other door two* PAGES *with targets and javelins, two* PAGES *with lights,* SYPHAX *armed from top to toe.* VANGUE *follows.*
These thus entered stand still, whilst the PROLOGUE, *resting between both troops, speaks.*

Here the play assumes the presence of the usual two tiring-house doors, that is, functional doors in the back wall of the stage that led to the 'tiring' or attiring (dressing) room. Later scenes will use the balcony, the trap, and a large curtained bed. There are unusually elaborate directions for music beside the cornetts: the fourth act requires three separate consorts, one above, one below, and one 'within the canopy'. Marston's self-exculpatory phrasing might suggest either that in writing his tragedy he anticipated the physical structure and the musical strength of the Blackfriars' company – he owned a part-share in the theatre lease and in the company, the Children of the Queen's Revels, playing there – or that the quarto recounts the eventual performance, which was out of the author's hands.

The possibility of different 'fashions' of presentation – and information about how these may impact a text – is even clearer from the history of Marston's *Malcontent*. There were three quartos published, all in 1604, the third advertising itself as 'Augmented by Marston. With the Additions played by the Kings Majesties servants. Written by John Webster'. These additions include an induction (opening scene) in which named members of the King's Men (including Richard Burbage, Henry Condell and William Sly, but unfortunately not Shakespeare) answer a gallant who demands to know how they can perform the play given that 'another company', that is, the Children playing at the Blackfriars, has 'interest in it'. Condell explains 'Why not Malevole in folio with us, as Jeronimo in decimo-sexto with them? They taught us a name for our play: we call it *One for Another*. The gallant – who appears to know that a private theatre play would need expansion for performance at the Globe where, unlike at the Blackfriars, there were no musical intervals – asks, 'What are your additions?' and Burbage replies, 'Sooth, not greatly needful; only as your sallet to your great feast, to entertain a little more time and to abridge the not-received custom of music in our theatre' (Marston 1975: Ind. 76–84). Comparing the quartos reveals that the additions include the amusingly self-referential induction and two scenes presumably added to avoid the conventionally forbidden exit and immediate re-entrance of a character, a problem circumvented at the Blackfriars by entr'acte music. Augmented passages include those extending the role of the central character, Malevole, played by Burbage; a new court fool, Passarello; and scenes that feature Bilioso ['an old choleric marshal') and his witty wife. These additions suggest that the roles of a leading actor and/or of one or two amusing characters, particularly the clown, were those likely to be amplified. Nevertheless, without the quartos to compare, we might not realize how much each text of *The Malcontent* was structured by the demands of specific theatres. As it is, we have two different texts each of which might be considered to reveal an 'original' performance and each of which is a 'correct' text.

Webster's comments in the *Malcontent* induction align with a general scholarly view that the practical realities and different audiences of the various venues in which the Chamberlain's/King's Men performed Shakespeare's plays – the early Theatre, the Curtain, the Globe, the indoor Blackfriars, the Inns of Court, at Court and presumably also on the road – may explain the existence of different texts, including short quartos and longer, usually Folio, versions. One explanation is offered by Andrew Gurr, who calls the longer texts 'maximal' and explains them theatrically: he imagines that the company was best served by obtaining the approval of the Master of the Revels for the full(est) text, which could then undergo cutting for performance, even different cuttings for different venues. Among Shakespeare's plays, indications that texts were adjusted for different performance venues or occasions seem most obvious in *Merry Wives of Windsor*, which exists in two texts with considerably different final acts. The quarto is often called bad and various theories, as discussed in Chapter 7, have been invoked to explain it, but there is no reason to doubt its title page, which advertises that the play 'hath been diverse times acted by the right honorable my Lord Chamberlain's servants: Both before her Majesty, and elsewhere'. The 'elsewhere' is often argued to be at a feast to celebrate an election of knights to the Order of the Garter, England's highest honorific, either in 1597 or in 1604, either in Windsor Castle itself or at Westminster Palace (see Dutton 2016: 245–58). A lengthy Folio-only speech by Mistress Quickly as the Queen of the Fairies, praising the Order and commanding the elves to strew good luck in 'every sacred room' in Windsor Castle so that it may stand 'Worthy the owner and the owner it', suggests that the Folio text records a special performance before the monarch. Such material only partially accords with the tone of Shakespeare's most 'citizen' comedy, and whether the Folio was expanded from the quarto with the addition of a masque-like finale, or the quarto was a cut-down version of the Folio text for public playing, there seems little doubt that, like *The Malcontent*, *Merry Wives* was adjusted for different audiences at different venues.

Although many actions must have occurred on the stage that have left no trace on printed texts, occasionally they do give glimpses of how plays in performance could deviate from the author's original. As we have seen, before it was printed, a dramatic text was not a single, stable document but a series of separate units: songs, actors' parts, paper scrolls with letters or other documents, backstage plots, prologues and epilogues, any one of which might have been altered in performance and then found its way into the eventual printing. Songs were especially labile, with songbooks serving as 'theatrical source material' that could be adapted as needed. Consequently, on occasion a song has been mistakenly printed with its cue lines incorporated, and sometimes it appears that the printer

received 'a song document in a form further from the moment
of performance than the rest of the text' (Stern 2009: 160–4).

Songs might even be unfamiliar to the play's original author,
revealing his limited authority over a text once it went into
performance. In the second issue of the 1623 quarto of John
Webster's *The Duchess of Malfi*, next to a song which in the
first issue is simply identified as 'The Hymn', there is a marginal
note: 'The Author disclaims this ditty to be his'. Although
Webster sounds outraged, it was common for songs to be
supplied either from traditional music or from songbooks.[1]
They might even be brought in by an actor: in Heywood's
Rape of Lucrece (1608) a note states 'we have inserted those
few songs, which were added by the stranger that lately acted
Valerius his part' (Stern 2009: 132). Hence stage directions in
plays by Shakespeare and others that read simply 'Song' may
accurately reproduce the author's instruction to the company
to find and insert an appropriate song. Or such a direction
might instead indicate that the copyist did not have the song,
which existed in a different manuscript or on a separate sheet
of paper. Webster does not say (or perhaps did not know) who
wrote the ditty he objected to, but it was likely to derive from
the performance, not the printer.

The unique Folio text of *Twelfth Night* reveals what could
happen when a script was only partially adjusted to performance
constraints. Although the shipwrecked Viola claims she will
deserve to serve Duke Orsino because she 'can sing / And speak
to him in many sorts of music' (1.2.54–5), in fact, she never
does sing. Instead, when Orsino asks 'good Cesario' (Viola's
name in disguise) for 'that piece of song . . . we heard last night',
a courtier intervenes, telling Orsino 'He is not here . . . . that
should sing it, Feste the jester. . . . He is about the house'
(2.4.2–13) This, as Stern points out, is a surprise for three

---

[1]Ross Dutton, *Shakespeare's Songbook*, includes a collection of the ballads
and songs that appear in or are alluded to in Shakespeare's plays. All are
played by the electronic *Norton Shakespeare 3*.

reasons: because Feste, the lady Olivia's fool, is not a member of Orsino's household; because Orsino misremembers who sang the previous night; and because the song ultimately produced differs from Orsino's description of it. Instead, the song showcases 'the company's new singing clown', Robert Armin, who joined the company around 1599, and probably rescues a boy player whose voice had changed (Stern 2009: 147–8). If indeed Shakespeare (or someone in the company) inserted the courtier's lines because the maturing boy could no longer sing, he forgot to alter Viola's earlier boast. It is likely that in the 1622 quarto of *Othello* the omission of the willow song and surrounding lines that are found in the Folio version of the scene (4.3) similarly reflects a performance when the boy playing Desdemona could no longer sing. The same casting problem may also explain the awkward moment in *Cymbeline* when the brothers Arviragus and Guiderius discuss the ceremony for burying the apparently dead Fidele. First they plan to sing, although 'our voices / Have got the mannish crack', but when Guiderius announces flatly 'I cannot sing. I'll . . . word it with thee', they agree to 'say our song' (4.2.234–53).

Material in a number of Folio-only plays may derive from later performances, that is, revivals. The addition to *Macbeth* of Hecate and songs from *The Witch* I have already discussed.[2] Scenes featuring the braggart soldier Paroles in *All's Well That Ends Well* seem also to have been expanded (see Chapter 6). The *New Oxford* proposes that the only surviving text of *Measure for Measure* follows the same patterns: once again the Folio includes part of a song (the first verse of 'Take oh Take those lips away') found in full in a later play, Fletcher's *Rollo Duke of Normandy or The Bloody Brother*, and its text contains, they believe, expanded roles for an ambiguously

---

[2] The *New Oxford Shakespeare* prints 3.5 and 4.1 with the words of both songs. In the case of the song from 3.5, 'Come away, come away', it also prints the musical setting by the composer Robert Johnson, who regularly supplied music to the King's Men.

satiric figure – Lucius – and the Clown, Pompey. *Measure for Measure* is usually dated 1603/4 and *Rollo*, although not printed until 1639, is dated 1617 (Bentley 1956: 3.332–6). Taylor and Loughnane argue from topical references in 1.2 that the revision of *Measure*, with the song added, dates from 'the last months of 1621 or very early 1622' (Taylor and Loughnane 2017: 556). For the Oxford editors, the revision of all three plays was performed after Shakespeare's death by Thomas Middleton, but the claim for Middleton's responsibility is actually separate from the more general conclusion that the texts that have come down to us have been modified in performance. To use Marston's phrase, each is 'printed only as it was presented' for a revival. None of these alterations could the dead Shakespeare disclaim.

Editing for performance

Given theoretical uncertainty about the ontological status of a performance, is it, as appropriation theorists suggest, a text in itself, 'its own entity', or is it an instantiation, a completion and fulfilment of something that existed previously, either in the author's intention or, less hypothetically, as printed on the page? Is the printed text (only) a blueprint for future performance? These practical as well as scholarly questions arise for editors attempting to create modern editions that will be used by actors and directors as well as by readers. Even if 'post-textual' Shakespeare has become a 'site of interpretive play', most productions begin playing on the basis of an edited text.[3] The Van Hove production, for example, was 'streamlined but left structurally consistent with the print editions' (Geddes

---

[3]As Douglas Lanier writes, 'every adaptation must be shown to have some degree of fidelity to a source for it to count as an adaptation', even if the source has been 'edited, performed, transmediated, subjected to multiple prior interpretive operations' (2014: 296–7).

2019: 424–5). So how are textual scholars to create these print editions in the twenty-first century? The underlying theoretical issue, often not acknowledged, is whether it is an editor's place to socialize a text to the modern day theatre, or, conversely, to 'unsocialize' a text if scholars have demonstrated that it includes elements that derive from early performance but probably not from the original (i.e. author's) script. Typical debates are about how and how much to modernize language, how much and where to provide stage directions, how to handle two-text plays, and whether to prepare texts for the technical capabilities of the modern stage or instead as if for production on a seventeenth-century stage or one that, like Shakespeare's Globe, attempts to replicate the conditions of such a stage. Scholarly editions that record textual variants from earlier editions may also describe variant performance treatments, whether current or as recorded in eighteenth-century editions based on promptbooks.

Generally speaking, editors of Shakespeare retain most of his language, although they know that almost every contemporary performance will modernize some words or omit those that the audience will not recognize. For example, the 'good' quarto of *Romeo and Juliet*, Q2, the usual basis of scholarly editions, has Romeo address Juliet as 'My Neece', which logic says cannot be right. The *Arden 3* and *New Oxford* alter this to 'My nyas', the *Norton 3* to 'Mine eyas'. Yet a director may believe that either term – both mean 'a young hawk' – will confuse audiences and therefore choose to follow the 'bad' quarto, Q1, having Romeo simply call out 'Madame'.

A difficult editorial decision regards elements that may have crept in from early performance. What is the editor saying about authorship by including or excluding such elements? An example is found in *The Winter's Tale*, where an irrelevant dance of satyrs, 'one three' of whom, a Servant announces, 'hath danced before the King' (4.4.342–3), is clearly copied from Jonson's 1611 *Masque of Oberon*, recently performed at court. The *Arden 3* editor, John Pitcher, assumes that 'Shakespeare lifted the satyrs and their dance wholesale into

The Winter's Tale' (2010: 70), but as we have only the 1623 Folio text of the play it is impossible to know either by whom or when the decision to insert the masque dance was made; we cannot be certain that Shakespeare did the 'lifting'. Pitcher reads the Servant's line within the fiction, as referring to the play's King Polixenes, but the line is equally likely to have alerted an early audience that they were about to be treated to a dance performed for King James, an example of the King's Men offering what Paul Yachnin calls 'populuxe theatre' (2003: 49). The decision to insert could easily have been made by other members of the company eager to please. Yet – as in the case of *Macbeth* – we have no other text, and no editor has proposed omitting the dance. So who is the author here? The blunt editorial principle of 'more is better', ostensibly designed to provide the reader with as much Shakespeare as possible, may in fact increase the quantity of not-Shakespeare within the text. Practice thus crashes into theory.

In this theoretical context, it is harder still to know what to do when preparing a text such as *The Malcontent* or *The Spanish Tragedy*, where texts with and without additions are tied to different performances. Further complicating matters, in *The Spanish Tragedy* some of the 'additions' first found in Q4 (1602) replace material in Q1 (1592). Consequently editors of modern editions divide: some place the 'additions' in an appendix; others follow the good text (Q2) but insert the Q4 additions marked off typographically. In effect this produces an edition that implicitly refers to two different performances, one based on the play's earliest manifestation and one on a later.[4] The same problem arises less overtly about conflation of different texts – *Hamlet* and *King Lear* are the key examples – when on the one hand editors hesitate to eliminate any words written by Shakespeare and on the other hand the resulting

---

[4]This is true regardless of who was the author of the additions, who has been proposed as Jonson, Shakespeare, and most recently Shakespeare and Heywood (Taylor 2017b).

text may be too long for performance before a modern audience. The recent trend to publish separate editions of Shakespeare texts that, like *Merry Wives*, are obviously tied to different performances has not usually extended to the plays of Shakespeare's contemporaries such as Kyd and Marston. The reason, far from depending on an esoteric theoretical premise, is commercial – Kyd and Marston do not sell enough copies to make it practical for a publisher to give them the same treatment they give to Shakespeare. As so often, economics proves to be the fundamental underpinning of the negotiation between textual theory and practice.

A common problem for editors is modulating between a reconstruction of an early performance and creating an edition with directions actable on a hypothetical modern stage. Editors may disagree about how much it is possible to reconstruct an early production or even one presumably intended. Occasionally a direction found only in a 'bad text' is critical, as in a key example from the Q1 text of *Romeo and Juliet*: '*Tybalt under Romeo's arm thrusts Mercutio in* [i.e. stabs him] *and flies*'. It is such directions that have led to claims that the bad quartos, like those of *Romeo* and *Hamlet*, are tied to performance. Plays with lengthy battle scenes, such as *Macbeth*, *3 Henry VI* and *Antony and Cleopatra*, present special problems, particularly about how to treat 'Alarums' when they may indicate exits and/or entrances. As a result the fifth act of *Macbeth* is divided into seven scenes in the Folio and eleven in the *New Oxford*. *Antony and Cleopatra* has neither act nor scene divisions in the Folio text, but the section conventionally treated as the fourth act has fifteen scenes in the *Arden 3* and sixteen in the *New Oxford*. These divisions are based on the editor's theoretical understanding of what constitutes a scene, in the Anglophone tradition a section of the action that ends with a cleared stage. Yet for a director, such divisions may not present meaningful ways to convey the confusion of battle, and are often ignored.

Editors who implicitly take on the role of director have varying success. The stage directions they add usually arise from a desire to assist readers to envision a play's basic action as indicated in the dialogue. As their most crucial task, such directions must ensure that all the necessary characters come on and off the stage as required. Even this is not always unambiguous in early texts. Classical 'massed' entrances, that is, opening stage directions that list all the characters who will appear at any point in a scene, were used in the Roman tragedies and comedies studied in early modern grammar schools, such as the one in Stratford-upon-Avon. They were a preference of Ralph Crane, the scribe thought to have prepared five of the Folio plays, including the first three, *The Tempest*, *Two Gentlemen of Verona*, and *Merry Wives*. Massed entrances leave modern editors to distribute entrances as seems most logical, but the moment of particular entrances may be uncertain. For example, in *Two Gentlemen* 4.2 Crane lists an opening entrance for six characters, but in modern editions the scene begins with a 17-line soliloquy and there are at least three other entrances in the scene, not all the same in modern editions.

Other missing entries and re-entries can also be problematic. For example, in the quarto of *Richard III*, Richard's servant Catesby is directed to exit at 3.7.89. Neither Q nor F mark his re-entrance. It must occur before he speaks at 3.7.202, but when? Modern editors usually direct that he enters 'below' at the same moment that Richard appears 'aloft, between two bishops' (93 SD), but while this is a logical staging it is not the only one possible. A different complication for editors and directors arises in the so-called balcony scene of *Romeo and Juliet*. Towards the end of the scene as it is usually edited, the Nurse three times calls out to Juliet from 'within', the second and third time saying 'Madam'. Yet the implied staging and even the identification of the unseen speaker are not evident in any early text. In Q1 none of the directions or lines are included. In Q2 there is no direction for the Nurse to 'call within' at 2.2.136 but the word 'Madam', without a speaker, appears marginally twice, at 2.2.149 and 2.2.151. It is only the Folio that has 'cals within' and twice, '*within*: Madam', still without identifying the speaker. Many directors have ignored 'within', for instance allowing the Nurse to put her head into what is perceived as Juliet's bedroom, and hypothetically someone else could call the girl. An editor who includes the stage directions may theorize that they come from an early performance but has no way to know whether they go back to Shakespeare's original script or reflect his intentions. Effectively the editor is writing them herself.

Even standard entrances pose problems. A repeated sequence in the Folio (and thus probably in the manuscripts lying behind the Folio) has a character recognized by others before the direction for him or her to enter: 'Who comes here?' *Enter Parolles* (*All's Well* 1.1); 'Call Coriolanus.' OFFICER: 'He doth appeare'. *Enter Coriolanus*' (*Coriolanus* 2.2) or most confusingly, from *King Lear*, 'Oh you Sir, you, come you hither. Sir, who am I Sir?' *Enter Steward*. STEWARD: 'My Ladies Father' (1.4). The difficulty may arise from manuscript stage directions written marginally to save space. The logical modern editor wants to move such entrances so that characters enter before they are seen, but the early modern dramatic text may also be acknowledging that in some of these cases a character is visible before he is verbally acknowledged. Editing *Coriolanus* Peter Holland notes how a 1984 production at the National Theatre made use of the delay, when Coriolanus 'was momentarily seen brooding in the corridor beyond the Senate-Chamber's door' (2013: 2.2.128–9n.). Dealing with these moments requires negotiation between the underlying theoretical premises that drive the editor's textual practice and the needs of the reader, which become especially acute with respect to scenes that make immediate sense when directed on a stage but can be confusing when read on the page.

Exits are a different challenge: they are the directions most frequently absent from early modern texts. Because the bookkeeper could manage entrances but not exits from his position in the tiring house, the promptbook was more likely to contain entrances (Stern, 2020, personal communication). Consequently, many exits, especially mid-scene and especially for minor characters, are uncertain. Does the Clown remain on stage in *All's Well* 3.2 to hear the Countess receive news of her son's flight? Does the Porter remain on stage for the conversation between Lennox and Macbeth (*Macbeth* 2.3)? After the bedroom scene in *Hamlet*, does Queen Gertrude exit as Hamlet leaves, 'tugging in Polonius', or does she remain on the stage? Q2 follows a singular 'Exit' with the direction 'Enter King, and Queene, with Rosencraus and Guyldensterne', which requires that Gertrude exit with Hamlet. This clears the stage and by modern editors has been taken to mean that the third act ends with their joint exit. Yet, as *Hamlet* was written for the Globe, where there were no act intervals, the text would seem to call for Gertrude to exit and immediately re-enter, violating the so-called 'law of re-entry'. (Recall that when *The Malcontent* was transferred to the Globe the adapters were obliged to write extra scenes to avoid immediate re-entry.) The Folio, on the other hand, sends only Hamlet off and its subsequent direction is '*Enter King*', suggesting that the Queen remains and the scene (and third act) continue. The problem is notorious, prompting a ten-page appendix in the *Arden 3* edition, which ultimately evades the issue because its separate editions of F and Q allow it to number scenes of F and Q differently. The director of a modern performance, however, will have to choose one or the other: actors and directors typically have little time for the productive ambiguities that critics and editors alike can cherish in a text. Here again, textual theory and performance practice may clash.

Editorial directives risk stepping into performance practice, as two examples of 'aside' reveal. The first is the one about which Marcus complains, when Shylock's line 'I hate him for he is a Christian' is editorially marked 'aside', although Antonio articulates his hatred of Jews openly. The second is Hamlet's first line. In response to Claudius's 'But now, my cousin Hamlet, and my son—' the Prince comments, 'A little more than kin and less than kind' (1.2.64–50). Is the line an 'aside', as traditionally marked? Claudius continues as though he doesn't hear Hamlet. Or is it a confrontational interruption that the wily king chooses to ignore, as implied by the lack of punctuation in the Folio? Of course, performance always interprets – staging Caliban as a monstrous fish, a dark-skinned savage or a Native American will silently influence audience reaction – but textual editors, striving to present a 'correct' text, often don't see how small textual interventions may be interpretive when staged.

One final example comes from *All's Well That Ends Well*. When the presumably dead Helen unexpectedly reappears, she gives Bertram his ring and announces she will read the letter in which he stated his conditions for consummating their marriage: 'This it says: / *When from my finger you can get this ring / And are by me with child*, etc. This is done. / Will you be mine, now you are doubly won?' (5.3.309–12). The 'etc.' poses an editorial problem. Should it be filled in from the original letter? Normally letters were on separate scrolls so they could be handed over and re-read as needed (Stern 2009: 192–3). But Bertram's letter, which Helen read aloud earlier (3.2.57–60), called for her to '*show me a child begotten of thy body that I am father to*'. In the source the heroine appears with twin sons. Helen, however, has not actually met Bertram's challenge. For her to read the original scroll again would remind the audience of her failure, so it seems more likely that the lines in the playscript, which accord with the situation (her visible pregnancy proving she is 'with child') should not be modified. Furthermore, the verse, which here replaces the prose of the original letter, suggests that 'etc.' is not spoken, leaving a pentameter line: 'And are by me with child. This is done.' Alternatively, an actress may say 'etc.' with a gesture indicating that the remaining details are insignificant. In this case, it is probably best if a textual editor does not attempt to regulate performance.

As this chapter has shown, in practice it can prove almost impossible to prepare texts with an eye to future or past performance: an editor is driven to intervene too much or too little. One sympathetic theatre historian, having demonstrated how the insertions of editors close down performance possibilities, has announced that therefore he ignores what 'today's editors present in terms of act–scene divisions, stage directions, or place–locale signals in favor of the evidence found in the early printed texts' (Dessen 2015: 340). On the other hand, another scholar faults the New Textualism for rejecting all editorial intervention as invasive. He objects that proposals to put stage directions to the side of a page, to leave out stage directions altogether, to avoid regularizing speech prefixes or to fail to supply a missing exit can produce unperformable scripts (Egan: 2010: 211–14). Resolution of this debate may come from recognizing that the needs of readers of different levels, and those of a professional actor, will vary. An experienced stage director may stage the final battle of *Macbeth* with videos and uninterrupted fighting; another may invent a new way to handle 'etc.'. Van Hove combined three plays, moved the action to a TV studio, used screens to show what was not on stage, and displayed Caesar's body as a photograph, none of which was indicated in the printed texts from which he began. As we will see in the concluding chapter, digital media may go even further, allowing every reader to create his or her own performance text. But first-time student readers are usually grateful to receive a coherent presentation that enables them to imagine one performance, even when alternative stagings are possible.

11

Textual Theories and Difficult Cases:

Hamlet and *Pericles*

Two of Shakespeare's plays, *Pericles* and *Hamlet*, between them illustrate almost all the ways in which our understanding of 'Shakespeare' implicitly or explicitly depends upon some form of textual theory. These are extreme cases: *Pericles* exists only in a single damaged text; it was very popular, published in four quartos between 1609 and 1619, but nevertheless does not appear in the Folio; its title page states that the play is 'by William Shakespeare', but its authorship has been repeatedly challenged. Finally, there exists a prose pamphlet of 1608 by George Wilkins that claims to recount 'the Play of Pericles, as it was lately presented' but diverges in many details from the surviving text of the drama. *Hamlet*, on the other hand, exists in three texts, one only discovered in 1823, whose history, sequence, and interrelationship are all deeply contested. Theories about the *Hamlet* texts have been used as evidence for the chronology of Shakespeare's literary production, his attitude toward publication, his willingness to revise, his reaction to the deaths of his son and his father, and even his development from an angry adolescent to a mature company sharer. In the case of

Hamlet the most consistent debates, traceable over hundreds of years, concern the relationship between the texts; in the case of *Pericles* the debates focus most frequently on authorship. Both plays have elicited editions that diverge widely not only in their theoretical underpinnings but even in their very words, and different textual theories have been tested, supported or dismissed by evidence from these plays. This chapter will recapitulate the structure of this book, discussing how these two plays exemplify the problems described earlier and how various textual theories have been applied in each case.

Shakespeare's texts and early editions

Clearly there is something strange about, or wrong with, the text of *Pericles*. In the opinion of the eighteenth-century editor Edmond Malone, 'no play of our author's, perhaps I might say, in the English language, [is] so incorrect as this' (1780: 2.4). For example, as Pericles recalls his dying father's description of his armour, both syntax and meaning break down: he 'poynted to this brayse, / For that it saued me, keepe it in like necessitie: / The which the Gods protect thee, Fame may defend thee'. Prose and verse are muddled, and mislineation is everywhere. Fundamental issues of plot and action – which of the characters hears the music of the spheres; what the medical magician calls for to revive Pericles' presumably dead wife Thaisa; how the goddess Diana appears – are never resolved. Another peculiarity are the choruses by Gower, which divide the play into seven sections. These at first seem to represent the fifteenth-century author's late medieval style – 'To sing a Song that old was sung, From ashes, auntient *Gower* is come' – but the imitation is not consistent. Although at first the choruses are in rhymed tetrameter couplets, eventually they become pentameter. The sixth chorus, in pentameter with alternating rhymes and a considerable number of enjambed lines, seems to emerge from a different stylistic period: '*Marina* thus the Brothell scapes, and chaunces / Into an *Honest-house* our Storie sayes: / Shee sings like one immortall, and she daunces / As Goddesse-like to her admired layes'.

Complicating the problem is the Wilkins pamphlet, *The Painful Adventures of Pericles Prince of Tyre*, which proclaims itself 'the true History of the play of *Pericles*'. Copies of this pamphlet were only rediscovered in the nineteenth century, an oddity which uncannily parallels the textual history of *Hamlet*. There are considerable discrepancies between the play and Wilkins's account, which itself depends on an earlier narrative, Laurence Twine's *The Pattern of Painful Adventures* (entered in the Stationers' Register in 1576 but only known from copies from 1594 and a republication in 1607). A fundamental question of the textual history of *Pericles* is whether to treat the Wilkins narrative, which has scattered rhythmic lines or 'verse fossils' within the prose, as a second account of the play's text, and if so whether to invoke it throughout, or only when it appears to reflect a better or more accurate report, or only in sections where it is alleged that Wilkins was Shakespeare's collaborator.

Notably, *Pericles* is not included in the First Folio. But why is uncertain. It cannot be because the stationers putting together the 1623 Folio could not obtain rights to a text. The play had originally been entered in the Stationers' Register by Edward Blount, one of the consortium of stationers who sponsored the Folio, and the fourth quarto had been printed only a few years earlier (1619) for Thomas Pavier by William Jaggard. The Jaggards leased other Pavier quartos for use as they printed the Folio. Another explanation sometimes proposed is that the Folio consortium rejected *Pericles* because the only available text – the one we have – was imperfect. Yet stationers normally did not concern themselves with the quality of texts unless they could brag that they were bringing out a good text to replace an imperfect one. Thus the most likely explanation is that Heminges and Condell knew something about the play, presumably that Shakespeare did not write it, or did not write a significant portion of it, that made them exclude the play. In retrospect we can infer that a similar logic lies behind the exclusion of *The Two Noble Kinsmen*, which first appeared in 1634 in a quarto that stated on the title page that the play was 'Written by the memorable worthies of their time, Mr John Fletcher, and Mr William Shakespeare Gent'.

Whatever kept *Pericles* from the First and Second Folios did not inhibit the compilers of the second issue of the Third Folio, who in 1664 added *Pericles* along with six other plays to the contents of the earlier Folios (1623, 1632, 1663). All of the new plays had previously appeared in quartos identifying the author as 'W.S.' or 'William Shakespeare', and all were owned by Pavier. Paulina Kewes proposes that the enlargement was motivated by a desire to make the Folio look 'thorough and comprehensive' (1998: 187). In the event, however, only *Pericles*, with all its defects, has entered the canon.

Unlike *Pericles*, where the textual problem basically revolves around a single dramatic text, the textual problems of *Hamlet* revolve around the existence of three texts, the quarto of 1604–5 (Q2), the Folio, and what is now known as Q1, a text printed in 1603 and only rediscovered in 1823. Eventually two copies of Q1 were found, one missing the first leaf and one missing the final leaf, thus conveniently supplying a complete copy. The rarity of the quarto is not unique: recall that there are only single surviving copies of Q1 *Titus Andronicus* and Q1 *Venus and Adonis*. The finding of Q1 *Hamlet* retrospectively explained the title page of Q2, which announces that it contains the play 'Newly imprinted and enlarged to almost as much again as it was, according to the true and perfect copy'. The sequence is comparable to that for *Romeo and Juliet*, where the second quarto (1599) announces it is 'Newly corrected, augmented, and amended', presumably improving the bad quarto of 1597.[1]

---

[1]The earliest existing quarto of *Love's Labour's Lost* (1598) also claims to be 'newly corrected and augmented by W. Shakespeare', persuading many scholars that there was an earlier edition. None has ever been found.

Q2 and F *Hamlet* each supply passages not included in the other. These passages may be cuts from, or additions to, an original version – both have been argued – but in general each is a good text. Q1, on the other hand, is notoriously an unsatisfactory text, with such infamous lines as 'To be or not to be – ay, there's the point' and, using Laurie Maguire's term, extensive 'wrecked verse'. However, Q1 also has plot variants that seem coherent and have proved playable, most notably a scene without parallel in the other texts in which Horatio recounts Hamlet's interrupted voyage and elicits from the Queen an unambiguous assertion that she was not involved in her first husband's murder. Q1 also contains a number of stage directions that have been adopted into almost all subsequent editions and performances: '*Enter the ghost in his nightgown*'; '*Enter Ophelia playing on a lute, and her hair down, singing*'; in the grave scene, '*Hamlet leaps in after Laertes*'; perhaps most important, '*They catch one another's rapiers, and both are wounded. Laertes falls down, the Queen falls down and dies*'. No other text supplies a direction for the Queen's death.

For the past two centuries textual theorists have struggled to explain the condition of the three *Hamlet* texts as well as the relationship between them. Is Q1 a report, a reconstruction from memory by actors or by note-takers using some form of swift writing? Or has it been damaged in the printshop? Does it report a version of *Hamlet* as it was cut and adjusted for performance, possibly on tour? Or is it, on the contrary, an accurate reproduction of the *Hamlet* mentioned in the late 1580s? If so, was that *Hamlet* written by a youthful Shakespeare and later revised into the forms found in Q2 and F? In that case, is Q1 'bad' at all? The dates of the three printed versions are sequential – 1603, 1604, 1623 – but there are striking parallels between sections of Q1 and F. Is it therefore possible that 1603 is a report of the text that underlies the Folio, and therefore the sequence is actually Q2, F, Q1?

Enter the New Bibliography

In 1909, in *Shakespeare Folios and Quartos*, A.W. Pollard argued that Heminges and Condell's dismissal of 'surreptitious copies, maimed and deformed', referred not to all the quartos printed prior to 1623 but to a subset of pirated and inferior volumes. Both *Pericles* and Q1 *Hamlet* fell into this category. The next step came when Greg proposed that *Merry Wives* was a surreptitious memorial reconstruction by one of the actors and this theory was then extended, with various modifications, to the other quartos in the group.[2] As we have seen, the New Bibliographers were intent on lifting 'the veil of print', and once they had classified *Pericles* and *Hamlet* Q1 as memorial reconstructions, they set about doing so for these texts.

For *Pericles*, uniquely among this group, there was no other quarto to compare with the bad one. (The only significant reprint is Q4, one of the Pavier quartos, and there is no reason to believe that whoever corrected it had anything but his wits to assist him.) That meant that all proposals for change had to stand on their own persuasive merits. For example, some scholars thought that the text gave evidence of aural errors that resulted either from dictation or, in another view, from mishearing by theatrical reporters. Often such errors are difficult to untangle: when Antiochus's daughter tells Pericles before he attempts to solve the riddle, 'Of all sayd yet, mayst thou prooue prosperous / Of all sayd yet, I wish thee happiness' (1.1.60–1) is she referring to all who have 'said' or explained the riddle, or to all who have ''ssayed' or essayed to solve it?

Reported texts or 'memorial reconstructions', in the theory originally propounded by the New Bibliographers, were the responsibility of 'rogue' actors, that is, those who for whatever reason did not respect the company's exclusive ownership of its scripts. For *Pericles*, the theory was elaborately applied in

---

[2]See Egan (2010: 100–28) for details of the theory's development.

the *Oxford Shakespeare*, where the reporting was blamed on the boy who played Marina and a hired man who took a sequence of small parts, including the Pander. Such memorial reconstruction was also the explanation of the New Bibliographers for *Hamlet* Q1. In this case blame fell upon the actor of Marcellus, present in a number of scenes that were 'well reported', that is, scenes that closely resembled their parallels in Q2 or F. The play-within-the-play, when Marcellus is not present, is also well reported, so Greg suggested that this actor doubled as one of the players. By the 1950s the New Bibliographers' 'theory of memorial reconstruction was firmly established as an orthodoxy that accounted for the bad quartos', including *Pericles* and *Hamlet* Q1 (Egan 2010: 113). Meanwhile, for *Hamlet* the most important effect of the New Bibliographers' scholarship was the support their theories gave to a traditional view of authorial agency, agency that extended over all three texts. They had no doubt that there had once been a single, original *Hamlet* lying behind at least Q2 and F; the major questions facing scholars and editors, then, were first, how to excavate the authorial text hidden beneath the different reports in the two quartos and the Folio, and second, how best to make a conflated, eclectic text on that basis.

The challenge of poststructuralism, or authorship, authority, and intention

Solving the textual problems of the single bad text of *Pericles* and of the relation between Q1 and the other *Hamlet* texts had always seemed to require attempting to determine Shakespeare's intentions or what he 'meant' the words to be. For *Pericles* the hunt would be for the correct words that lay behind those misrepresented in the quarto; for *Hamlet* Q1 a further, or perhaps a prior, question would be how the words in that text relate to the words in Q2 and F, that is, whether Q1 is a separate text or a deformed version of one of the others. In one account the author's intentions changed over time; in another they were distorted, by scribes, or actors, or printers. The New Bibliographers assumed such intentions existed and were the goal of any editorial work.

Poststructuralism, as we have seen, challenged the idea of the author's singular control or authority over his text, although of all authors Shakespeare proved the hardest to give up. Much of the scholarship on *Pericles* tried to prove that Shakespeare or his intentions alone could not be responsible for the surviving version, proposing instead a different or collaborating author, an author's rough draft or foul papers not well understood, dictation, notetaking, or errors in the printshop. Even when memorial reconstruction was generally rejected as an explanation for bad texts, it remained in view for *Pericles* and, often, *Hamlet* Q1, with Maguire allowing that for *Pericles* 'a case can be made' and privately acknowledging that it was 'the most likely source' of the current text. Meanwhile Adele Davidson revived the theory that the *Pericles* text was taken down in shorthand. In most cases readers, editors, and performers attempting to solve the cruxes in the text, to undo the errors of memory or shorthand, found it difficult to do so without bringing intention, somebody's intention, into play.

Furthermore, *Pericles* revealed how difficult it is to separate an author's intentions from a social text, especially a text socialized in the theatre. For example, in 2.5 King Simonides tells Pericles 'I am beholden to you / For your sweet music this last night. I do / Protest, my ears were never better fed / With such delightful pleasing harmony' (24–7). No performance of music is mentioned in the quarto, but Wilkins's *Painful Adventures* describes how Pericles 'to pass away the tediousness of the night' called for an instrument from which 'presently he began to compel such heavenly voices . . . such cheerful notes . . . that they had power to have drawn back an ear, halfway within the grave, to have listened unto it'. On this basis the 1986 *Oxford Shakespeare* inserted a short scene (8a) in which

Pericles 'plays and sings' (10 SD2). It is unclear whether the editors therefore reconstructed the text following the author's original intentions, or restored the text as it was socialized in the theatre, or in fact 'unsocialized' what the company performed but did not necessarily produce the text Shakespeare authorized. And, of course, if this section of the play is not by Shakespeare (as is now usually believed), the entire question of authorial intentions becomes even more problematic.

Turning to *Hamlet* Q1, poststructuralism challenged assumptions about both the author and the text. If Q1 is an early version of the play, possibly the one mentioned in references to a Hamlet play as early as 1589, is it originally by a youthful Shakespeare, as Bourus (2014) argues, or a text by someone else that he later revised? If it is originally by Shakespeare, the creator and his intentions are implicitly as mobile as the text. If it isn't, agency and intention are multiplied. On the other hand, if Q1 reports a theatrical reconstruction, in which, notably, the nunnery scene and 'To be or not to be' have been moved from the beginning of the third act to the second, it displays a 'socialized text', possibly rearranged for a specific performance. Some of the parallels suggest that it is a cut-down version of the Folio text, and if so it may reflect not the author's original intentions but some or all of his or his company's final intentions.

According to Zachary Lesser, the uncertainties raised by poststructuralism lead directly to Ann Thompson and Neil Taylor's *Arden 3* edition of *Hamlet* (2006), which presents each text independently. Where Harold Jenkins's earlier, conflated *Arden 2* edition (1982) was the culmination of the New Bibliographic approach, implicitly restoring Shakespeare's intended text, the *Arden 3* is a product of the New Textualism. Consequently the name 'Shakespeare' is 'enmeshed in and formed by early modern print and theatrical culture' (Lesser 2015: 207), and what is offered is 'a detailed examination of the texts in all their variation, and an insistent refusal to speculate about textual origins'. This leaves the three texts separate and, most disturbingly, offers 'no way to explain precisely how (or even *that*) they are "the same" play' (2015: 211). In a challenge to such agnosticism, for Lesser at least it 'simply does matter whether the text of Q1 was created before or after the text of Q2, whether it was a rough draft, some intermediate stage in Shakespeare's revision of an earlier play, a stenographic or memorial report of Shakespeare's version attested by Q2, or something else that we have not considered' (2015: 218). This nostalgic desire for certainty suggests that poststructuralism has not carried all before it.

Textual and other theories

Textual work on *Hamlet* and *Pericles* has inevitably been affected by developments in other forms of critical theory. For *Pericles* the strongest influence has been feminist analysis. As I argued in the *Arden 3* edition, 'Diana is the presiding deity of *Pericles*', and a focus on Diana 'alters the male-centred Christian reading' that dominated many earlier interpretations. The feminist approach affects the text in ways large and small. For example, rather than retaining the quarto's version of Pericles' vow as it appears in the original ambiguous spelling, 'till she be married, / Madame, by bright Diana whom we honour, / All vnsisterd shall this heyre of mine remayne' (3.3.28–30), relineation makes clear that Diana is worshipped by the various members of Pericles' family – 'By Bright Diana whom we honour all' – which also restores the pentameter rhythm. Based partly on the construction in Wilkins's text, I accept the usual emendation of the next line to 'Unscissored shall this hair of mine remain' but on the basis of the play's 'buried concern with sisterhood' reject another traditional emendation. In the description of how Philoten 'Would ever with Marina be / Be't when they weaved the sleided silk', Malone, followed by most editors, changed 'they' to 'she' at 4.0.21. Removing the image of the girls weaving together obscures the way the passage parallels descriptions of feminine friendship in *A Midsummer Night's Dream* and *The Two Noble Kinsmen*; hence 'they' remains.

Several stubborn cruxes yield to a feminist interpretation. For instance, the postpartum Thaisa's recollection that she was 'shipped at sea . . . even on my learning time' cannot be right, but common emendations such as 'bearing time' have been unpersuasive and or even, like 'eaning time' (F3) offensively animalistic. It took a twentieth-century feminist scholar to point out that 'groaning time' was a common Elizabethan phrase for childbirth, one that is found in North's translation of Plutarch and seems to lie behind the Provost's concern for 'the groaning Juliet . . . . very near her hour' (*Measure for Measure* 2.2.17–18). The facts of infant mortality and wet-nursing untangle a crux in which Q1 reports Dionyza saying, 'Nurses are not the fates to foster it, not ever to preserve'; the comment becomes coherent with only small changes: 'Nurses are not the fates. / To foster is not ever to preserve' (4.3.14–15). Finally, Marina's pledge 'If fires be hot, knives sharp, or waters deep, / Untide [*sic*] I still my virgin knot will keep' (4.2.138–9) contradicts the entire plot, but editors had simply retained it. Yet the crux is probably the result of a graphic error, the omission of one letter, so that Marina intends to keep her virgin knot or maidenhead not 'untied' or opened but 'untried' or unattempted, a goal she will fight for in her confrontation with the eager Lysimachus.

For *Hamlet* much textual work has addressed discrepancies between the three versions. This analysis may be technical, for example tracing a crux to a mistake of the actor/notetaker/printer, and usually the explanations form part of an overriding theory, either that Q1 is a rough draft of what Shakespeare later expanded, or a reduction of a later version either licit (e.g., by the company) or illicit (e.g., by an actor). However, some of this work implicitly depends upon historicist analysis or, on the contrary, on editors projecting attitudes of their own historical period. For instance, tracing different treatments of Q1's 'contrary matters' where Q2 and F had 'country matters', Lesser shows how the nineteenth-century editor S.W. Singer, who usually based his edition on the theory that Shakespeare revised Q1 into the Q2/F version, proposed instead that the vulgar pun was introduced by an actor because 'country matters' was unworthy of Shakespeare (2015: 101–5).

Because many theories about *Hamlet* Q1 implicitly depend on its date of composition, much attention has been given to possible contemporary references in the text. Bourus, arguing for composition by 'young Shakespeare', connects Q1 to the drowning of a Katherine Hamlett in 1580 and the visit in 1586 to Denmark by English actors later associated with Shakespeare. Finding theatrical allusions 'compatible with performance in the late 1580s', she notes that the roles listed in Q1 for the actors visiting Elsinore – King, Knight, Clown, Lady – are, as Thompson and Taylor write, 'stereotypes of the stage in the 1580s and early 1590s', whereas Q2's addition of 'the Humourous Man' she relates to the rash of humours plays by George Chapman and Jonson at the end of the 1590s. For Bourus Q1's extended passage on clownage 'alludes, unmistakably, to Richard Tarleton, the great Elizabethan Clown', who died in 1588. Hamlet's criticism of the acting style that tears 'a passion to tatters . . . to split the ears of the ignorant' (Q1 9.7–8) she believes satirizes the style of the early Queen's Men, predominantly a touring company, whereas Q2's 'split the ears of the groundlings' (3.2.10) 'presupposes the architecture of the London amphitheatres' (Bourus 2014: 167–76).

Both theatrical and political history are used by Gary Taylor to date the text in Q2. He accepts Roslyn Knutson's hypothesis that 'the late innovation' that has caused the actors to travel refers to the period of plague after Elizabeth's death, rather than (as in other interpretations) to the period after the Essex uprising of February 1601 or the Privy Council decree of June 1600 that restricted the playhouses to two performances weekly. Hence Taylor maintains that the 'material common to Q2 and F dates the play no earlier than mid-1603'. Taylor supports his argument by reading Fortinbras's campaign against Poland as an allusion to the siege of Ostend, 1601–4, 'the most famous land battle in Europe in Shakespeare's lifetime' (Taylor and Loughnane 2017: 542–3). Ann Thompson and Neil Taylor instead continue to believe that the lines about the boy actors, present in both F and Q1, refer to the revival of the children in 1599, and thus, as Jenkins wrote, references to the 'war of the theatres' must date the play 'about or soon after the middle of 1601' (Thompson and Taylor 2006: 52). Disagreements about the historical background and date of each quarto primarily affect not the wording of the text but interpretation and glossing, while differing theories about the relation between the texts affect how much and how often editors are willing to emend from each of them. If all three texts 'are imperfect descendants of the single lost holograph' – the traditional, New Bibliographical belief –, editors are more willing to alter one from another, but if, like Thompson and Neil Taylor, they believe that Q2 and F are based on separate manuscripts, with Q1 just 'an anonymous reconstruction of a performance based on the text behind F' (2006: 509), they will be more hesitant to do so.

Attribution and collaboration

Hamlet and *Pericles* are ostensibly at opposite ends of the spectrum in arguments about whether Shakespeare collaborated or whether another 'hand' is present in the surviving text(s). No one imagines that Shakespeare had a collaborator for *Hamlet*; the authorship of *Pericles* is so dubious that, as we saw, it was not included in the early Folios and was treated as apocryphal or doubtful in many subsequent editions. Yet there is now general, if not unanimous, agreement about the dual authorship of *Pericles*, whereas arguments about the creation of Q1 implicitly cast doubt on the attribution of *Hamlet* to Shakespeare alone.

Fundamentally, for *Hamlet* the question of authorship only arises if Q1 is believed to represent an early draft later revised by Shakespeare. In that case, was the draft by Shakespeare or by another author of the late 1580s or early 1590s? There are early references to a Hamlet play but none is sufficiently convincing to end the debate. Malone believed that Thomas

Nashe's 1589 claim that 'English Seneca read by candlelight
. . . will afford you whole Hamlets, I should say handfuls of
tragical speeches' in a paragraph that later refers to 'the Kid in
Aesop' (Nashe 1966: 3.315) proved that the – or an – earlier
Hamlet was by Thomas Kyd. Late-nineteenth-century critics,
such as F.G. Fleay and J.M. Robertson, accepted Kyd as the
original author and assumed that Shakespeare had modified
the earlier dramatist's 'crude play' (Lesser 2015: 173–7).

Another early reference to a *Hamlet* comes from a 1596
quote by Thomas Lodge, who described a devil who 'looks as
pale as the Vizard of the ghost which cried so miserally at the
Theater like an oyster wife, *Hamlet, revenge*'. Bourus is
persuasive that Lodge's subsequent praise of Lyly, Spenser,
Daniel, Drayton and Nashe implies that none of them can be the
author of the dreadful devil, but less convincing when she alleges
that Lodge could not have been satirizing a dead author and
hence also eliminates Greene, Watson, Marlowe and Kyd (2014:
144–8). A note by Gabriel Harvey referring to Shakespeare's
'Venus and Adonis . . . his Lucrece, and his tragedy of Hamlet'
is no help because it is undated. Yet if the early version is by
Shakespeare, why did Meres not include it in his list of
Shakespeare's plays? Bourus proposes that the play was too
early (2014: 159), but Meres's list praising Shakespeare as 'most
excellent' for tragedy mentions *Titus* (1592) and *Richard III*
(1593); it seems likely to have included *Hamlet* along with other
plays of the early 90s had it been on the boards.

The view that Q1 is early Shakespeare has been defiantly
rejected by those who, like Lukas Erne, object that the quarto's
'linguistic texture . . . is difficult to reconcile with Shakespeare's
language elsewhere' (2003: 202). But recently analysis of the
quarto's language has been extended to what MacDonald P.
Jackson calls the 'best bits', places where the texts of Q1 and
Q2/F 'run closely parallel [and] Q1 is stylistically so good and
so exemplary of Shakespeare's *mature* style' (2018: 18).
According to Jackson, these lines provide evidence that 'Q1 is
unlikely to have been based on an early draft or "first sketch"
of any kind' (2018: 19). Aided by computer counts, Jackson

examines passages of Q1 which statistically reflect Shakespeare's usage of figures of speech, run-on lines, pauses, and rare vocabulary around the date of the canonical *Hamlet*, that is, 1602/3. He concludes that 'if Q1 is based on a *Hamlet* composed by Shakespeare about 1589, it cannot preserve the early play in unmodified form, but must incorporate the extensive beginnings of a process of Shakespearean revision and expansion' (2018: 26). Looking closely at Q1 passages such as the Queen's account of Ophelia's death, Jackson argues that the speech's 'blandness, crudity, and confusion', interspersed with 'words and phrases that both seem typically Shakespearean' and are found in other positions in Q2 'resist explanation except as the result of textual corruption' (2018: 28–30). Although Jackson refuses to endorse a 'fully fledged theory about the genesis of Q1', he concludes that the theory of 1980s editors, 'that Q1 presents an abridged and corrupted text ultimately derived from Q2', allows for 'Q1's theatrical merits, its often humdrum language, its definite errors, and the Shakespearean quality of its verse when it closely agrees with Q2's' (36). In essence, Jackson's work accepts Q1 *Hamlet* as a damaged report, implicitly a social text bearing the imprint of a reviser, and/or a theatrical performance, and/or an audience note-taker, and/or a stenographic writer.

Attitudes towards the authorship of *Pericles* are in every way different. That the play was not the product of Shakespeare's single hand was already assumed in the eighteenth century by editors and critics beginning with Rowe; Malone, too, came around to this view. The suggestion that Shakespeare's collaborator was the minor playwright George Wilkins, author of the pamphlet which claims to recount the play, also goes back to the eighteenth century and has been strengthened by modern methods of analysis. Collaboration fits well with the stylistic differences between the first two and the last three acts. Indicators of Wilkins include a high frequency of rhymes, omission of the relative pronoun in the nominative case (e.g., 'To evil [which] should be done by none' 1.0.28), and an un-Shakespearean use of assonance. The case has been built gradually as various methods, like function word tests and stylometry or statistical computation of such elements as first words of speeches, were introduced. Jackson's *Defining Shakespeare: Pericles as Test Case* (2003) summed up previous research and introduced what was then a newly possible method, electronic searching of databases (at that point *LION*) that include most literature of the period and thus allow comprehensive comparisons.

Most scholars of *Pericles*, I among them, accept the conclusion that Wilkins is responsible for the first two acts and that Shakespeare is heard as the third act opens in the midst of the storm: 'The god of this great vast, rebuke these surges / Which wash both heaven and hell, and thou that hast / Upon the winds command, bind them in brass' (3.1.1–3). Yet questions remain. The New Cambridge editors Doreen DelVecchio and Antony Hammond maintain that the stylistic differences do not constitute 'conclusive evidence of collaboration' (1998: 11). But even accepting that Shakespeare collaborated with the younger man, a pattern that seems to have recurred at various points in his life,[3] both the method of collaboration and the attribution of certain sections of the play, particularly the choruses, can be disputed. Was this a collaboration from the start? Or did Shakespeare take over a play that Wilkins had begun, either because the younger dramatist had writer's block or because the company called upon its attached dramatist for help? Loughnane calls the latter scenario 'much desired by those readers who find it improbable that Shakespeare would deign to actively collaborate with Wilkins' but 'less likely' than active collaboration (Loughnane 2017c: Crit. Ref. 1.1351). Or did Shakespeare become interested in a text submitted to the company and (with or without Wilkins's agreement) rewrite it from the beginning of the third act? What do the variations in

---

[3]See Gossett (2004: 58–9), and the discussion of *Sejanus* in the *New Oxford Shakespeare*.

Painful Adventures imply about the text in the quarto? Even the stylistic evidence is inconclusive: Jackson believes that only the Gower Choruses of acts 1 and 2 are substantially by Wilkins and that his hand can be found in the brothel scenes, but other critics detect Wilkins in later choruses and believe that Shakespeare wrote the brothel scenes alone. Given the state of the text, even the most elaborate methodology may never be able to provide a final determination.

Printing unstable texts

There are anomalies in the printing history of both *Hamlet* and *Pericles*, although it is uncertain how unusual these are or whether they can account for the state of the texts. *Pericles*, for instance, was entered in May 1608 in the Stationers' Register by Edward Blount, but Blount did not publish the play and later, as one of the consortium behind the First Folio, he did not invoke any rights to it. It is unclear whether Blount's failure to print is connected to the fact that a different stationer, Nathaniel Butter, printed Wilkins's *Painful Adventures* in 1608.

In any case the play was published in 1609, without any notice of the transfer from Blount, by Henry Gosson. Gosson had never published a play before. He had it produced by two different printers, William White and Thomas Creede. Different running heads, type founts, and numbers of lines per page reveal what seems an odd division: sheets forming signatures ACDE were printed by White, sheets forming signatures BFGHI by Creede. Successive damage to types and headlines reveals that Creede printed signature B last, which may mean that an original printing by White had to be redone. Perhaps White was no longer available. Variants in capitalization, spelling, punctuation and the abbreviation of speech prefixes indicate that the first group of sheets was set by one compositor, the second by two. The significance of these compositor and printing-house studies – a model of what may be gained by analysis of a printed text – was summarized by Taylor and Jackson for the *Oxford Shakespeare*: 'The division of work on Q between (certainly) two printers and (probably) three compositors provides the strongest possible evidence that the deficiencies of the text – present in the work of both printers – originate in the manuscript copy, not in the process of printing' (*TxC* 1987: 556). Consequently, printing history cannot help determine the nature of that manuscript or explain the text that it conveys.

There may also be something strange about the first printing of *Hamlet*, that is, Q1, that parallels the oddities of *Pericles*. The play was entered in the Stationers' Register on 26 July 1602 by James Roberts, but Q1 was instead printed for Nicholas Ling and John Trundell by Valentine Simmes. Various explanations have been offered, for instance that Roberts's entry was a 'blocking' one, possibly desired by the company to keep anyone else from publishing, or that Ling had some sort of business arrangement with Roberts, who entered other playtexts in the Register that he did not print (Bourus 2014: 30–2). Apparently supporting the latter explanation, a year later Ling employed Roberts to print the second quarto, which advertised on the title page that it was 'enlarged to almost again as it was, according to the true and perfect copy'.

Almost all the arguments about the three *Hamlet* texts thus concern not their printing but their interrelationship and the nature of the underlying texts. Nevertheless, studies of the printing may have implications for these questions. For example, it has been convincingly demonstrated that the compositors of Q2 occasionally 'made use of an exemplar of Q1', and although the *Oxford Shakespeare* concluded that 'the cumulative weight of evidence . . . makes it demonstrable that Q2 did not serve as printer's copy for F', they nevertheless do not rule out 'occasional consultation of a quarto by the Folio compositors' (*TxC* 1987: 396–7). (Thompson and Neil Taylor believe that the consulted quarto was 'Either Q3 or Q4' (2006: 481). Ultimately, compositor studies on these texts may explain certain of the errors but not their fundamental nature and connections.

Editing and unediting

Pericles and *Hamlet* offer good examples of the divergence between interventionist and hands-off editing. In both cases there is more than one text to consider; in both cases at least one of the texts is undeniably defective. We have already seen an example of editorial interference in the addition of scene 8a to *Pericles* in the 1986 *Oxford Shakespeare*. In the *Textual Companion* to that edition Taylor and MacDonald P. Jackson argue the case for editorial activism. Against Fredson Bowers's warning that the editor of a bad quarto is essentially able only to 'emend errors which there is some reason to assign to the compositor', they claim that a *Pericles* editor, based on knowledge of the sources, the author(s) styles, the nature of memorial corruption elsewhere and the two reports – *Oxford* treats *Painful Adventures* as a 'substantive' reported text – 'is in a far better position to reconstruct something closer than Q to an authentic text of the play'. Hence they offer what they freely call a 'reconstruction'. In general they make 'much more editorial use of *Painful Adventures* in what we believe to be Wilkins's share of the play', including the scene of Pericles' playing, but they also expand material that occurs in the 'Shakespeare' share, notably the unsatisfyingly brief interview between the governor Lysimachus and Marina. In justification they argue that for that section Q represents the censored text of the play, while *Painful Adventures* gives 'in essence, the more dangerous and more dramatic original' Consequently they attempt 'a scholarly reconstruction of the censored material' using the Wilkins text (*TxC* 1987: 557–9).

The opposing position was strongly maintained by DelVecchio and Hammond a decade later. As noted, the New Cambridge editors expressed 'the gravest doubts that Wilkins had anything to do with *Pericles*' (1998: 9). While they admit that many readings in the text 'cannot be right', they propose that the play was 'transcribed from foul papers, the second half being in much fouler condition', and explain 'mistakes' in Q as 'the usual errors of misreading a difficult script or compositorial error' (199–207). They reject *Painful Adventures* as an unreliable report and scornfully object that Taylor and Jackson rewrote Q 'for trivial reasons'. Instead, they propose to 'edit the text of the quarto of *Pericles*: just that and nothing more, defending its readings where we can do so; emending them . . . when we cannot' (209–10). This sounds like a commitment to single-text editing, but unfortunately they frequently claim that Q's lines are explicable when they are not. Regularly they reject emendations that go back to the eighteenth century, maintaining for example the illogical lines in which the previous martyrs advise Pericles 'to desist for / Going on death's net', which Malone recognized should have been 'desist from going', and keeping Cleon's lament that 'Those palates who not yet two savours younger / Must have inventions to delight the taste', which Steevens had already emended to palates 'not yet two summers younger', a time similarly calculated in *Romeo and Juliet* 1.2.10. In their eagerness to prove that the entire play is by Shakespeare, DelVecchio and Hammond reject 'a tradition of conservative emendation dating back to Rowe and Malone' (Loughnane 2017c: Crit. Ref. 1.1346).

Few scholars have accepted the claims that *Pericles* is entirely by Shakespeare and that Q's errors are 'usual', yet the reconstruction in the *Oxford Shakespeare* has also seemed too radical. Therefore the recent decisions of the *New Oxford* editor, Rory Loughnane, are interesting as responses. Loughnane does not 'attempt to recreate *Pericles* as it might have been first written or performed'. He does not 'supplement the text by introducing additional passages or new scenes', but he nevertheless recognizes the need 'to emend *Pericles* extensively'. He borrows readings from *Painful Adventures* 'only where error is obvious in the copy and where disruptive transmission could explain this error'. Most importantly, he is not inclined to 'trust the text' and hence refuses 'rationalizing defences of the copy text readings in cases where emendation based on the assumption of easy error readily solves the textual problem' (Loughnane 2017c: Crit. Ref. 1.1348). One might say, then, that after the radical editions of the late twentieth century, the *New Oxford* and my own *Arden 3* versions are based on textual theories that accept the uncertain provenance of the surviving material and do not claim to have restored either the authors' intentions or the early socialized text.

For editors of *Hamlet* the problem has always been whether, or how much, to conflate the two good texts, and after 1823 what, if any, use to make of Q1. Here again editing has depended on textual theory. Jenkins, who saw Q1 as a memorial reconstruction, Q2 as based on Shakespeare's autograph, and F as deriving from a playhouse transcript but also to some extent from Q2, created the 1982 *Arden 2* edition according to New Bibliographic methodology: 'While following Q2's fuller version, I naturally include also anything preserved in F which I take to have been lost from Q2; but all words and phrases in F which I judge to be playhouse additions to the dialogue ... I omit'. Jenkins found Q1 most useful in 'suggesting the source of corruption where the two better texts are at variance' (1982: 18, 75–6). The result is a conflated edition, based, as Jenkins freely admits, on the editor's judgement. In contrast, the *Arden 3* (2006) *Hamlet* presents three separate texts, pushing forward the 'New Textualist tendency to resist editing' by refusing to create a stemma (a genealogical chart, rather like a family tree) and treating the three texts as 'remarkably distinct entities'. Although Lesser praises the edition's 'rigorous attention to the materiality of Shakespeare's printed editions' and its 'detailed examination of the texts', he is unhappy, as mentioned earlier, about its 'refusal to speculate about textual origins'. Consequently, in one view, the *Arden 3* edition demonstrates 'the simultaneous culmination and exhaustion of the New Textualism' (2015: 211–13).

Arden 3 was followed by the *Norton 3* and the *New Oxford*, both of which admit to uncertainty about the source, sequence and interrelationship of the *Hamlet* texts. Consequently, both editions take advantage of their electronic platforms to offer separate editions of all three texts. At the same time, each presents only one *Hamlet* in a single-volume edition presumably meant for the classroom or the individual purchaser, and both sidestep decisions on stemma by choosing a copy-text primarily on the basis of length. For *New Oxford*, Q2 'meets the present edition's criteria of inclusivity (i.e. length) and authoriality (i.e. reliability in relation to Shakespeare's hand)' (Jowett 2017a: Crit. Ref. 1.1115). For 'plays that exist in significantly different texts', *Norton 3* prints 'the text that is most complete and apparently most finished' (McMullan and Gossett 2015: 85); once again the choice is Q2. However, treatment of these texts differs. Norton's classroom text is a hybrid, offering a Q2 text 'augmented by passages from F of a line or more'. Thus, in contrast to the *New Oxford* or *Arden 3* Q2 text, the *Norton 3* print edition includes, in a different typeface, the passage where Hamlet questions Rosencrantz and Guildenstern about why they have come 'to prison' in Denmark and another about the 'eyrie of children' whose success explains the players' travel. The textual editor for *Hamlet*, Anthony Dawson, points out that this hybrid is not a traditional conflation, in which an editor like Jenkins chooses 'word by word, from the surviving texts, according to a view of which one was better' but rather fits the desire to 'provide as many as possible of the lines readers expect to find in *Hamlet*' (2015: 1762). However, despite the differences in these texts, a similar but unspoken theory, perhaps of 'intention to mean', must underlie identical emendations in all three contemporary editions. For example, for the Q2 line, 'the lady shall say her mind freely or the black verse shall halt for't', all follow F and Q1 and emend 'black verse' to 'blank verse'.

Book history and the text

A striking similarity in the history of *Pericles* and *Hamlet* is the nineteenth-century discovery of a second or associated text – *Hamlet* Q1, *The Painful Adventures* – at which point textual theories regarding each play were somewhat upended by the contents of the new books. George Wilkins's *Painful Adventures* is in considerable sections dependent on the earlier prose narrative by Laurence Twine, and in many places it varies from the play. Yet it uses the Shakespearean names and can seem helpful in emending incoherent passages. But even if we accept Wilkins as Shakespeare's collaborator, questions remain about the method and consequences of collaboration. If Wilkins's hand is only found in the first two acts, how much did he know about the rest? In a time of handwritten play manuscripts produced singly and submitted to the theatrical company, Wilkins is unlikely to have had a copy of the entire script and possibly not even of his own pages. When he gives a prose summary of Lysimachus's conversation with Marina (4.5.70–121), is he remembering, misremembering, or inventing? Thus the additional quarto adds to the mystery of the *Pericles* text but does not 'solve' it.

Pericles was not only popular on stage but as a reading text. Printed six times in the seventeenth century, *Pericles* was the 'most popular play excluded from the Folio', and Adam Hooks suggests that 'its continuing popularity in quarto' rather than its inferior text or collaborative authorship may be the cause of its omission (2016: 132–3). Erne has attempted to explain the transactions between stationers for the repeated printing of the successive *Pericles* quartos, including the probable yielding of Blunt's rights to Gosson for the first quarto. Yet the limitations of book history work are revealed through the occasionally uncertain meaning of imprints in early modern books: does the imprint of Q3 *Pericles* – 'Printed at London by S.S.' – mean that Simon Stafford 'published the play' or instead that he 'printed it for Gosson, Pavier, or another publisher' (Erne 2013: 141). The popularity of *Pericles* is further confirmed by studies of the personal libraries of collectors. *Pericles* appears regularly, sometimes even when *Hamlet* does not, as in the case of the seventeenth-century collector Edward Conway, and it is also found in collections made by 'commoners with antiquarian interests' (Mayer 2018: 33).

A book history approach to *Hamlet* Q1 allows Lesser and Stallybrass to offer an unfamiliar view of that quarto, often assumed to be an imperfect acting version. They focus on the title-page claim that the play had been acted in the Universities of Cambridge and Oxford, and note that this is the first play of Shakespeare's printed with marginal commas. In performance texts such marks normally signify cuts, but Lesser and Stallybrass instead identify those in *Hamlet* Q1 as commonplace markers, 'a distinguishing feature of plays for the learned and scholarly reader'. Consequently they describe Q1 as a '*literary text for reading*' and maintain that it 'cannot be considered simply a performance text'. Instead 'it is the first play of Shakespeare's to assert such a literary claim' (2008: 376, 380, 410–11). Lesser and Stallybrass describe a rapid spread of commonplacing in professional playbooks from 1600 to 1613. Typically, the markers, except in the plays of Ben Jonson, were not authorial but created by readers, 'including the London stationers who published these playbooks'. Thus the commonplace indications in both Q1 and Q2 *Hamlet* were unlikely to be Shakespeare's but look 'more like the spotty practices of two different readers' (Lesser and Stallybrass 2008: 404). Such analysis does not explain the condition of the text found in Q1 but usefully suggests its place in the literary world of 1603, just as the publication of *Painful Adventures* does not explain the condition of the *Pericles* quarto but creates a different context in which to understand it.

Performance and the text

Both *Hamlet* and *Pericles* are informative about the range of early modern performance. Even ignoring the claim of *Painful Adventures* to report the play 'as it was lately presented at the Globe on the Bankside', contemporary records reveal how different productions of that play could be. Zorzi Giustinian, the Venetian Ambassador from 1606 to 1609, took the French ambassador and the Secretary of Florence to see the play at the Globe, evidence that *Pericles* was considered fit entertainment for the upper classes and supporting Jonson's complaint that audiences 'prefer some mouldy tale / Like Pericles' to his more learned fare. The play again served as diplomatic entertainment in 1619 at the elaborate leave-taking of another French ambassador. First there was a feast in the Queen's great chamber, then French singing, and finally 'In the King's great chamber they went to see the play of Pericles, Prince of Tyre, which lasted till two o'clock. After two acts, the players ceased till the French all refreshed them . . . after the players began anew' (Chambers 1930: 2.335, 346). Certainly this private court performance made no attempt to keep the play within 'the two hours traffic of the stage', but there is no information about how, if at all, the text was modified for performance in the 'great chamber'.

Quite different was the mounting of *Pericles* by a group of recusant actors, the Cholmley Players, who in the Christmas season of 1609–10 travelled with a repertory that included *King Lear*, *The Travails of the Three English Brothers* (a Wilkins collaboration), and a 'St Christopher play'. We cannot know exactly how the plays were staged, though these daring actors apparently did not hesitate to include in *Travails* a scene in which the Pope is addressed as 'That stair of men's salvations'. The performances led to a court case in which there were charges and counter-charges about the religious content of the plays performed. One player confessed that the St Christopher play was played according to the text when they played 'open in the town' but with additions when they played in the homes of persons 'popishly affected'. None of the testimony is reliable, but it seems quite likely that *Pericles* was modified, either verbally or silently, to promote a Catholic interpretation. The boy player testified that in the St Christopher play he took an angel's part. If in *Pericles* he also stood as a protective angel behind Marina during her encounter with Lysimachus in the brothel, that would create a providential view of the contest and point Marina's similarity to female saints and martyrs. One importance of this testimony lies in the assertion by the boy player that the 'book' of the St Christopher play had been brought from London. This would suggest that actors on tour used, or might use, the theatre's approved text or even a printed copy, which weakens any argument that bad or very short texts were specially created for performances on tour. On the other hand, the tale suggests how much a performance might nevertheless vary from the approved book (Gossett 2004: 87–8).

In analysing the relation between text and performance, the significance of the *Hamlet* texts derives as usual from their differences, however explained. In all texts, Hamlet, like Webster, is irritable about actors' textual insertions, instructing the players to 'let not your Clown speak more than is set down' (Q1 9.23–4 / Q2 3.2.36–7), apparently a plea against improvisation, the 'dark matter of early modern theatre' (Preiss 2020: 69). But Q1 *Hamlet* considerably expands the passage. At first it parallels Q2 and F:

> There be of them, I can tell you, that will laugh themselves to set on some quality of barren spectators to laugh with them – albeit there is some necessary point in the play then to be observed. O, 'tis vile and shows a pitiful ambition in the fool that useth it.
>
> *Hamlet* Q1 9.24–9

But what follows is found only in Q1:

> And then you have some again that keeps one suit of jests – as a man is known by one suit of apparel – and gentlemen quotes his jests down in their tables before they come to the play, as thus: 'Cannot you stay till I eat my porridge?' and 'You owe me a quarter's wages!' and 'My coat wants a cullison!' and 'Your beer is sour!' and, blabbering with his lips and thus keeping in his cinquepace of jests when, God knows, the warm Clown cannot make a jest unless by chance . . . masters, tell him of it.
>
> *Hamlet* Q1 9.29–38

Who wrote these lines? Richard Preiss notes that 'Hamlet's clown is not quite improvising' since the gentlemen 'already know, from prior attendance, what to expect' (2020: 86). For Bourus, the lines allude to Richard Tarleton and the Queen's Men and thus help date the 1603 quarto (2014: 175). From a different theoretical point of view, the description of the spectator who 'quotes' or jots down the lines in his 'tables' incidentally reveals how such material might travel from performance to a printed text.

Q1 *Hamlet* is particularly important for its traces of early modern performance. Not only does it include stage directions describing the appearance of the ghost and of the mad Ophelia, but it clarifies essential action at the tragedy's finale. Only in Q1 are there directions for the final duel and deaths: '*They catch one anothers Rapiers, and both are wounded, Laertes falles downe, the Queene falles downe and dies*'. How many readers would notice the Queen's death if there were no direction pointing it out? Yet we do not know what performance, if any, these directions report. The final direction recalls the one explaining how Tybalt kills Mercutio, found uniquely in Q1 of *Romeo and Juliet*. While directions in both texts reflect theatrical practice of the period, it is uncertain whether they were written by Shakespeare and present in the texts from the start, or written in by someone in the company (the bookholder?) before the manuscript was given to the printer, or for *Romeo* even written by Henry Chettle, a contemporary playwright who served as the printer's assistant (see Weis 2012: 110–15).

The stage directions in *Hamlet* Q1 adapt themselves to multiple theoretical explanations. Unlike some of the text, they are convincing and do not seem 'bad'. But do they simply recount standard practice? Or are they from a performance in specific conditions or at a particular moment? Both the texts assume a ghost under the stage ('in the cellarage' in Hamlet's words at 1.5.151) and none requires a balcony. Bourus thinks that the direction that Hamlet leaps into the grave 'after Laertes', found in Q1 and F but not in Q2, is a clue to the date(s) of the play. In the late 1580s Burbage would have been in his early twenties, when such stage gymnastics would have been easier for him, and she proposes that later Shakespeare adjusted the play 'with his leading actor's girth in mind' (2014: 104–5). Yet both Q2 and F have the Queen note that Hamlet – played by Burbage – is 'fat and scant of breath' (5.2.269), and it is usually thought that F is somehow related to Q1. Thus even with information about performance, no simple theoretical explanation satisfies.

Hamlet and *Pericles* have been studied, performed, and edited over the centuries, sometimes on well-articulated theories. But their texts nevertheless remain in flux. In neither case can you guarantee what you will read or hear if you pick up a modern text or attend a modern performance. This uncertainty has only increased with the advent of electronic Shakespeare, as we will see in the concluding chapter.

CODA

The Immaterial
Text

12

Textual Studies After the Digital Turn

Shakespeare is always 'a proving-ground for new information technologies and practices' (Galey 2014: 100), so of course the Shakespeare text has migrated from material 'books, composed of paper and ink' to electronic screens and files composed of bits and bytes (Finkelstein and McCleery 2006: 1). The move has caused considerable disruption and has radically altered the communication circuit. A flurry of articles and books has examined the consequences of the developing relationship between 'Shakespeare' and digital media, with authors divided between optimists who stress new possibilities and pessimists who fear the loss of intellectual accuracy and supporting financial structures. For some, the technical ease of digital modification is an advantage; for others it impinges on key goals of textual studies. The argument has been both theoretical and practical, and it is changing as rapidly as new resources appear and others become obsolete. By definition, the conclusion is the portion of this book that will age most rapidly. It will, in all likelihood, already have aged a little in the time between the completion of the typescript – or, given our topic, the electronic file – and publication.

For the optimists, the advent of the digital has been particularly important in its provision of new tools useful in research both textual and related. Where once scholars were grateful to have merely the images provided by Early English Books Online (EEBO), now EEBO-TCP is searchable, as are such tools as the English Short Title Catalogue (ESTC), the Database of Early English Playbooks (DEEP), British Library Manuscripts Online (BLMO), the Folger Digital Texts, and the Records of Early English Drama (REED) sites called Early Modern London Theatres (EMLoT) and Patrons and Performances. These accompany such older resources as the World Shakespeare Bibliography (WSB), now online. Recent digital scholarship includes the project known as Early Print, which aims to improve TCP further by transforming the English print record from 1473 to the early 1700s into a linguistically annotated and more deeply searchable text corpus, and Critical Editions for Digital Analysis and Research (CEDAR), which will provide in addition to discursive text all of a printed copy's 'epigraphic features', such as mise-en-page, markings of provenance, and indications of reader use. CEDAR is using *The Taming of the Shrew* as one of its experimental models, further decentring the singular author and authorship more generally by identifying 'common parlance' and recycled bits of other plays within the text.

Availability of these resources has affected textual studies of Shakespeare in both practical and less obvious theoretical ways. The provision of databases that contain all the texts of early modern playwrights other than Shakespeare has facilitated studies of attribution and collaboration. Editors who wish to trace theatre history can create a spreadsheet of performance texts (see Malone 2018). For glosses, editors can use not just the *OED* online but the 'hard word annotator' of the Lexicon of Early Modern English (LEME) to discover which words were unfamiliar and problematic for Shakespeare's audience (see Lancashire and Tersigni 2018). To look for large rhetorical schemas, Michael Ullyot and Adam J. Bradley have invented a tool included in their university's Text Analysis Portal for research (TaPoR3); to search for patterns of genre in Shakespeare's writing Michael Witmore and Jonathan Hope have experimented with the computer program Docuscope. Yet, as Ullyot and Bradley warn, such tools will be useful, changing 'our experience of Shakespeare's words', only when they are 'integrated into the places and habits of literary criticism' (2018: 152–3). Indeed, for many traditional Shakespeare scholars, those who were not 'born digital', learning to use these tools can require a re-education as challenging as learning older techniques of textual analysis such as creating collation formulas, tracing the reuse of skeleton formes, or operating a Hinman collator.

Some scholars see the benefits of the digital turn in ideological terms. Writing in 2006, Christie Carson foresaw scholars wresting their work 'away from the jaws of commercialisation' due to 'the free distribution channel of the internet' (179). In one example, to create a 'social edition' of the Devonshire Manuscript, an anthology of poems from the court of Henry VIII, academics and members of the public together built 'a scholarly edition on the principles of open access, editorial transparency . . . and public engagement'. The result was published on Wikibooks (Siemens et al 2018: 194). For the Devonshire Editorial Group, their edition 'models a new kind of scholarly discourse network' at the intersection of 'digital humanities, the history of the book, social knowledge creation, and the growing cross-fertilisation of academic and wiki culture'. The editors announce themselves pleased with the 'destabilising effect' of presenting a 'scholarly text as a process rather than a product' (Siemens et al 2018: 198). However, the theoretical implications of such Wiki editions for textual work on Shakespeare are uncertain. The Devonshire Manuscript includes poems by many poets, some not identified. It is hard to see how the same intellectual model would work for a single author, let alone for Shakespeare. The destabilized text seems to accord no agency and almost no recognition to the author.

Much of the positive excitement about the electronic text grows from its immense flexibility, and here the theoretical implications of moving from print to the web are revealed. Digital Shakespeare resists precisely the stability offered by the material book. Publishers have made their electronic

Shakespeare texts inviting by investing in programs that allow readers to click through from an edited text to images of the Folio and quartos or to turn apparatus such as glosses and textual variants on and off. Some of these innovations are, admittedly, not open-ended – the images and the glosses are unchanging – but others link through to such sites as those just described. The full possibilities of moving from print to the web were articulated in the *Internet Shakespeare Editions*' assertion – found on their website until 2018 – that their editions strive 'toward the goal, not of a definitive, authoritative play text, but of the "postmodern edition" ... presenting plural texts that reject "totalizations of all kinds"'. Thus an Internet Shakespeare Edition offered the reader a choice of whether to show textual variants by accessing them in a pop-up box or within the line. If within the line, the variants appeared in different colours, with their sources (e.g., F4, Capell, Taylor) included, as here at a crux from *All's Well That Ends Well*:

I see that men make ropes in such a scar[xxx] rope's in such a scarre, [F1] make Hopes in such Affairs [Rowe] make hopes in such a scene [Malone] may cope's in such a stir [Tannenbaum] may rope's in such a snare [Sisson]

Such an apparatus visually embodied the challenge of poststructuralism to any concept of textual stability. In fact, in some electronic editions the communication circuit turns around on itself so that the author becomes a creation of his readers, who are given agency to choose which of the solutions they wish to insert in 'their' edition of 'Shakespeare'. An electronic edition may go even further: students using the electronic *Norton 3* can not only adjust the text but also insert selective commentary notes and glosses, gradually creating, for example, a post-colonial or feminist or queer edition of the play at hand that may differ from that of every other student in a class. Depending on one's point of view, this is either ideal freedom or an instructor's nightmare.

The imaginary student's creation of her own edition and possibly her own text exemplifies the other characteristic of the electronic text that is widely praised, its 'interactivity'. Such texts are conceived not with the 'reader' but with the 'user' in mind; they are 'interfaces between digital technology and [the] embodied reader' (Bloom 2020: 9). The digital medium, foregrounding the mutability of the text, invites intervention. Furthermore, digital texts increasingly contain embedded links to other sites such as the Map of Early Modern London (MoEML) or Early Modern London Theatres (EMLoT), encouraging active engagement in these extratextual contexts. Many of those happiest about the possibilities opened up by web editions are scholars of performance, whose editions – or websites – can include photographs, videos, and links to other websites like those maintained by Shakespeare's Globe and the RSC. Such editions implicitly argue for understanding the Shakespearean text as fully created (only) through its use in a range of theatrical productions.

Textual instability is at the heart of the debate about what Katherine Rowe has called 'the good-enough text', a term that emerges from a study of representative sampling as an investigative method. Her concern began when, due to a failure in part of the communication circuit, in this case the purchasing system, her college bookstore did not receive the uniform text ordered for the class. Consequently students arrived with a variety of editions, including four electronic ones, which Rowe calls 'digital incunables' because they are 'emergent technologies'. The result was lively discussion of textual variation, thus fulfilling 'some of the principles animating late-twentieth-century editorial interests in textual instability'. Rowe found the result stimulating and praises the way that replacing 'single textual authorities with ambiguous alternatives' brought students into the process of analysis (2014: 147–8). She thus aligns herself with the uneditors who concentrate on what is lost, rather than gained, in the editing process. There was apparently no attempt to settle on a single text as 'correct' or perhaps, even 'better'. The various texts were all 'good enough' for teaching purposes.

Rowe concludes by asking 'Whether Shakespeare studies . . . will accept the idea that 'good' should now mean 'scholarly-utilizable-flexible' rather than 'scholarly-accurate' (2014: 157). It is precisely the suggestion of abandoning the scholarship of centuries, and the accuracy for which it strived, that troubles textual scholars. For example, John Lavagnino, a pioneer in the field of digital humanities, has expressed concern about 'the rise of the haphazard, which represents the majority of digital texts now available'. Writing in 2014, he notes how many digital texts, for example those in Project Gutenberg or the 'Moby' text of Shakespeare, which is based on the Cambridge (Globe) edition, are merely digital reproductions of out-of-copyright nineteenth-century editions. Even worse, those texts have frequently been read in through optical character recognition (OCR), which is highly inaccurate. In some cases good digital projects have been discouraged 'by the wide availability in digital form of outdated books: non-experts couldn't see the difference' (Lavagnino 2014: 20–1). As Eleanor Collins of Oxford University Press asks, are we ready to move away from the 'established centres of knowledge' that traditionally confer authority? (2014: 135). Of course in the past few years major scholarly texts embodying such knowledge – notably the *New Oxford* and *Norton 3* editions – have been put on the web, but these electronic editions are only available behind a paywall, either individual or through a university. Students, accustomed to the idea that everything they read on the web is free, resist paying when they can access the free Moby text instead. As Rebecca Niles and Michael Poston, describing their work in creating the corpus of Folger digital texts, ruefully note, 'Readers will use whatever digital texts are available' (2016: 117–18). Perhaps it is in answer to this challenge that Taylor and Bourus write an essay at the beginning of the *New Oxford* called 'Why Read *This* Complete Works?' (2016).

Digital textual projects constitute intellectual arguments rather than merely providing improved technology (Estill and Silva 2018: 131). They shape the way that users conceptualize texts and the text. In response to objections like Lavagnino's, Hope and Witmore (2010) defend their use of the Moby text as suitable for their machine-assisted attempt to 'discriminate plays into groups' because the linguistic evidence they use is so frequent that 'the differences between the Globe and a modern text are likely to be very small' (Rowe 2014: 156). In other words, the digitally conveyed language is 'good enough' for the purpose, furnishing adequate representative samples, even if textual scholars looking to deal with the fine grain of Shakespeare's poetry might not find it so. More radically, from the point of view of those who use social media, blogs, and websites to offer texts for widespread consumption, 'the notion of the stable text as an essentialist, purist artifact [is] not only fallacious, but elitist' (Geddes 2019: 424). Typically divided reactions were elicited by the RSC and Google Creative Lab's production of *A Midsummer Night's Dream*, a complex multimedia event based partly in social media. For the Creative Lab director, it was a success because 'new audiences encountered a Shakespeare whose language and modes of communication matched their own'. Yet this was Shakespeare as plot and character but not poetry. For Christie Carson and Peter Kirwan, 'the Shakespearean text remained frustratingly concealed beneath the veil of "contemporary" language' prioritized by the Google team (2014a: 239–40). Although only sometimes acknowledged, the division is once again based on fundamentally different understandings of what is meant by 'Shakespeare'.

Rowe's classroom experience raises two great concerns of those pessimistic about the digital turn in textual studies. The first is the question of standards, or the abandonment of the textual goals, whether original intentions, final intentions, or merely an error-free text, for which centuries of editors have striven. Andrew Murphy, while praising the utility of the tools added to the Moby text in the *Open Source Shakespeare*, nevertheless concludes that 'without *editing* the text, the heart of Open Source Shakespeare remains fundamentally (and often fatally) outdated' (2010: 404). The second is the breakdown of the comfortably familiar communication circuit for Shakespeare's texts. To Rowe in 2014, it appeared that the 'Shakespeare textbook industry has collapsed' (145). Although this diagnosis proved too drastic – the *Norton 3* was published in 2015 and the *New Oxford* in 2016, and these anthologies have been accompanied ever since by a flow of single-volume editions from various publishers – clearly her experience derived from massive changes in publishing, production, shipping, and purchasing, felt by wholesalers, bookstores, and individual faculty and student buyers alike. In a pessimistic reading of the economic situation, the availability of free texts, as well as a lack of interest in high culture leading to low sales, means that publishers, not earning a return on their investment, will cease to fund editions. In recent years work on major editions of playwrights other than Shakespeare has been funded by grants from bodies such as the National Endowment for the Humanities in the US, the Arts and Humanities Research Council in the UK and the Social Sciences and Humanities Research Council in Canada. If such sources also dry up, individual academics and independent scholars will abandon textual work because they will have neither the time to undertake the research nor the expectation of gain from it, either in professional standing or in royalties and improved salaries. Wikibooks is unlikely to replace these supported projects. Much depends on whether publishers see themselves as venture capitalists or as professional allies committed to the intellectual work they traditionally facilitate, in which case there is hope that they will find ways to participate in the digital change.

Both publishers and scholars have reason to worry about the many kinds of instability caused by the advent of the electronic. In an older example, the Middleton *Collected*

Works, a massive scholarly enterprise, took nearly two decades to complete, finally appearing in 2007. In the period of the book's creation, computers, software programs, electronic files and methods of storage all changed repeatedly, so that it is now nearly impossible to access the original materials used in creating the edition. This could impact publishing decisions such as whether – or whether it is possible – to create spin-off volumes for elements of the collection like single plays, originally foreseen as a financial support for the whole edition. On the other hand many electronic textual projects operate on an assumption of constant change, expecting to be continually updated as new research is incorporated. Such projects accept the instability of their materials while simultaneously requiring a different kind of stability: continuously available space on a server and funds to pay for it. It may be doubts about committing to such space in perpetuity that have made publishers like Oxford and Norton hesitant to promise that the electronic versions of their newest Shakespeare texts will be permanently available. Furthermore, it is always possible that a publishing house will abruptly move to a new electronic platform on which earlier publications no longer function as they originally did. In the age of electronic texts, the final element of Adams and Barker's circuit, survival, can become an urgent question.

For Shakespeare scholars, a dramatic example of how textual work is endangered by a commitment to poststructural fluidity while assuming stable technical support is provided by the history of the *Internet Shakespeare Editions*. A massive project to which 'hundreds of people contributed their labour, expertise, and credibility', the ISE developed its own coding language and applications as it worked toward the postmodern editions it promised. Eventually, however, the website posed a security risk to its host institution. A security update was incompatible with the systems used, and 'one of the oldest and most visited Shakespeare websites in the world went dark' (Jenstad 2020). This situation has led to two results. First, fortunately, is the creation of Linked Early Modern Drama

Online or LEMDO, a platform that will host the remediated *Internet Shakespeare Editions*. LEMDO uses the XML markup language of the Text Encoding Initiative (TEI) rather than the 'boutique markup language' previously created by the ISE (Jenstad 2020). But the theoretical implications are equally important. The crisis posed by the ISE collapse has led to fundamental rethinking about the future of textual work in the digital humanities, with the results embodied in the significantly named 'Endings Project'. Because, as Janelle Jenstad writes, 'Repeated loss and disappearance does nothing for the credibility of digital editions', the Endings Project plans 'to develop practical strategies for concluding and preserving scholarly digital projects' (Jenstad 2020). For Shakespeare's texts, Jenstad suggests, this might mean avoiding 'the bad habit of dragging everything along with each new iteration' of a textual project. Instead, just as the *Arden 3* volumes are 'complete and safely archived' while *Arden 4* begins, there will come a moment when the digital texts will be similarly 'staticized'. Although this vision focuses not on the line-by-line variants possible in an electronic edition but on full volumes, its ramifications push back significantly against the idea that perpetual flux is the most desirable form for scholarly work and accepts the possibility of stable 'totalizations' at different intervals.

Ultimately, the digital turn will have differing effects on different aspects of textual studies. Some but not all are positive. Scholars of text and performance can illustrate a line or a speech with video. Historians of theatre can consult the Lost Plays Database. Attribution scholars can access databases of Shakespeare's contemporaries and choose between competing statistical methodologies to determine the authorship of a passage or an entire play. Book historians can consult DEEP to study 'the publication, circulation, and reception of books in early modern England' or use the more fine-grained *Shakespeare Census*, which identifies particular copies for close analysis. On the other hand, digital images cannot convey the physicality of an actual book, as Bruce

Smith complains (2014). Most of all it is unclear what the effect of putting all texts on screen will have on the individual student and the scholar of the 'text itself'. Rowe comments that online environments 'tilt all reading towards the high-volume efficiencies of skimming and scanning' (2014: 152). These appear to be precisely the opposite of the time-consuming inefficiencies of close reading and analysis, traditionally thought of as necessary for both the understanding and the full enjoyment of Shakespeare's plays and poems. The work of textual scholars is equally slow and careful, whether in investigating the spelling of a compositor, the cause of a crux, or the collation of copies. Machines will help verify conclusions, but as Alan Galey notes, digital projects are more promising when they 'emphasize discovering over verifying' (2010: 311).

In the end, as new generations become more and more accustomed to reading on screens, electronic texts are likely to become standard methods of communication. They may, like the 'baggage' quartos that Sir Thomas Bodley once rejected, become valued objects of study. Consequently, some book historians will become screen historians. Galey and Niles promise that 'it is possible to combine the perspective of a book historian and a text encoder to understand the continuities in Shakespeare editing' (2017: 34). Similarly, the 'Encoder-Remediators' at LEMDO found that their work 'rapidly shades into editorial labour' (Jenstad 2020). Investigating new Shakespeare texts and Shakespeare texts anew, digital scholars will consequently face many of the same theoretical issues – variant texts, copies with fraudulent dates or publishers, questionable attributions – that confronted earlier textual scholars. Yet new challenges will call for newer skills. This was confirmed in 2019 when it was revealed that Amazon was distributing books (the example was George Orwell's *Animal Farm*) that upon inspection did not contain the original text. Some books had been openly altered, others were 'worded slightly different' [*sic*]. Many, it seemed, had been produced using optical scanners, resulting in such readings as 'Homepage' for 'Homage' and 'Fair' for 'Fairy'. Here the electronic means of production, rather than, say, an errant compositor, was creating variant texts. Furthermore, Amazon had already demonstrated the potential instability of *all* electronic texts when, in an argument with one publisher, it had effectively 'unshipped' its books, electronically 'wiping' certain copies from customers' Kindles (Streitfeld 2019: B6). With its self-publishing arm, its customers' reviews and its control of servers, Amazon thus could take over all five events in the life of a book either material or electronic – publishing, manufacturing, distribution, reception and survival. Precisely how such material control by a gigantic modern stationer will affect the future publication of Shakespeare texts remains to be seen. There is no way to know.

And where does this take us in respect of textual theory? In textual work on Shakespeare, it appears that we have ceased to believe many things about which earlier scholars were certain. Throughout this book we have repeatedly seen widespread scholarly convictions overturned. We no long believe that bibliographic analysis can convincingly reveal all the details of the manuscript that lies behind the printed text we read. We no longer claim we can determine and restore an author's intentions for a text, even while we continue to edit and emend that text. We no longer believe we know exactly what happened in the printshop when Shakespeare quartos and Folios were in production. The number of compositors who allegedly produced the First Folio has repeatedly changed. The motives behind the Pavier quartos have become murkier. The 'bad' quartos may no longer be so bad. We cannot agree whether Shakespeare wrote short plays that he later expanded, or long ones that were cut for performance. We no longer teach that Shakespeare never revised his plays, and beliefs about the presence of his hand in the plays of others, and the presence of other hands in his texts, constantly change. We are uncertain whether we want our texts in postmodern flux or 'staticized'. So, as I write in 2021, we also cannot know the eventual consequences of our current methodologies or how soon they will become outdated. Digital tools for textual analysis, having brought much new information to light, turn out to have their own risks. Many methods have been superseded by newer ones, and older ones sometimes reappear. Yet discoveries continue to be made. We can only look forward, then, to new methodologies, new textual questions and new answers – in other words, to new developments in textual theory – enabled as Shakespeare's works become electronic.

REFERENCES

Place of publication is London unless otherwise stated.

Adams, Thomas R. and Nicholas Barker (2006), 'A New Model for the Study of the Book', in David Finkelstein and Alistair McCleery (eds), *The Book History Reader*, 2nd edn, 47-65, New York: Routledge.

Barthes, Roland (2006), 'The Death of the Author', in David Finkelstein and Alistair McCleery (eds), *The Book History Reader*, 2nd edn, 277-80, New York: Routledge.

Bate, Jonathan, ed. (2018), *Titus Andronicus* (rev. ed.), Arden.

Bentley, Gerald Eades (1941–56), *The Jacobean and Caroline Stage*, 7 vols, Oxford: Clarendon.

Bevington, David (2007), 'Working with the Text: Editing in Practice', in Andrew Murphy (ed.), *A Concise Companion to Shakespeare and the Text*, 165-84, Malden MA: Blackwell.

Blayney, Peter W.M. (1991), *The First Folio of Shakespeare*, 2nd edn, Washington DC: Folger.

Blayney, Peter W.M. (1996), 'Introduction to the Second Edition', *Norton Facsimile of the First Folio*, New York: Norton.

Blayney, Peter W. M. (1997), 'The Publication of Playbooks', in John D. Cox and David Scott Kastan (eds), *A New History of Early English Drama*, 383-422, New York: Columbia University Press.

Bloom, Gina (2020), 'Theater History in 3D: The Digital Early Modern in the Age of the Interface', *ELR* 50: 8-16.

Bourus, Terri (2014), *Young Shakespeare's Young Hamlet: Print, Piracy, and Performance*, Palgrave MacMillan.

Brayman, Heidi, Jesse M. Lander and Zachary Lesser, eds (2016), *The Book in History, The Book as History: New Intersections of the Material Text*, New Haven, CT: Yale.

Burrow, Colin (2002), *The Oxford Shakespeare: Complete Sonnets and Poems*, Oxford: OUP.

Carson, Christie (2006), 'The Evolution of Online Editing: Where will It End', *Shakespeare Survey* 59: 168-81.

Carson, Christie and Peter Kirwan (2014a), 'Digital Dreaming', in Christie Carson and Peter Kirwan (eds), *Shakespeare and the Digital World: Redefining Scholarship and Practice*, 238-57, Cambridge: CUP.

Carson, Christie and Peter Kirwan, eds (2014b), *Shakespeare and the Digital World: Redefining Scholarship and Practice*, Cambridge: CUP.

Chambers, E.K. (1924), *The Disintegration of Shakespeare*, British Academy Lecture.

Chambers, E.K. (1930), *William Shakespeare: A Study of Facts and Problems*, 2 vols, Oxford: Clarendon.

Cheney, Patrick (2004), *Shakespeare, National Poet-Playwright*, Cambridge: CUP.

Collins, Eleanor (2014), 'Unlocking Scholarship in Shakespeare Studies: Gatekeeping, Guardianship and Open-Access Journal Publication', in Christie Carson and Peter Kirwan (eds), *Shakespeare and the Digital World: Redefining Scholarship and Practice*, 132-43, Cambridge: CUP.

Cox, John D. and Eric Rasmussen, eds (2001), *King Henry VI Part 3*, Arden.

Craig, Helen (2020), 'English Rag-women and Early Modern Paper Production', in Valerie Wayne (ed.), *Women's Labour and the History of the Book in Early Modern England*, 29-46, Bloomsbury.

CWBJ (2012) *The Cambridge Edition of the Works of Ben Jonson*, ed. David Bevington, Martin Butler, and Ian Donaldson, 7 vols, Cambridge: CUP.

Darnton, Robert (2006), 'What Is the History of Books?' in David Finkelstein and Alistair McCleery (eds), *The Book History Reader*, 2nd edn, 9-26, New York: Routledge.

Davidson, Adele (2011), '"Common Variants" and "Unusual Features": Shorthand and the Copy for the First Quarto of *Lear*', *PBSA* 105: 325-51.

Davidson, Adele (2009), *Shakespeare in Shorthand: The Textual Mystery of King Lear*, Newark: University of Delaware Press.

Dawson, Anthony B. (2015), 'Textual Introduction' to *Hamlet*, in Stephen Greenblatt et al (eds), *The Norton Shakespeare*, 3rd edn, 1760-63, New York: Norton.

De Grazia, Margreta (1991), *Shakespeare Verbatim*, Oxford: OUP.

De Grazia, Margreta and Peter Stallybrass (1993), 'The Materiality of the Shakespearean Text', *SQ* 44(3): 255-83.

DelVecchio, Doreen and Antony Hammond, eds (1998), *Pericles*, Cambridge: CUP.

Desmet, Christy, Jim Casey and Natalie Loper, eds (2014), *Shakespeare/Not Shakespeare*, New York: Palgrave Macmillan.

Dessen, Alan C. (2015), 'Divided Shakespeare: Configuring Acts and Scenes', in Margaret Jane Kidnie and Sonia Massai (eds), *Shakespeare and Textual Studies*, 332-41, Cambridge: CUP.

Drakakis, John, ed. (2010), *The Merchant of Venice*, Arden.

Dryden, John (1962), *Of Dramatic Poesy and Other Critical Essays*, 2 vols, Everyman's Library.

Duncan-Jones, Katherine, ed. (2010), *Shakespeare's Sonnets*, rev. edn, Arden.

Duthie, George (1949), *Elizabethan Shorthand and the First Quarto of King Lear*, Oxford: Blackwell.

Dutton, Richard (2016), *Shakespeare, Court Dramatist*, Oxford: OUP.

Dutton, Richard and Jean E. Howard, eds (2003), *A Companion to Shakespeare's Works*, 4 vols, Malden MA: Blackwell.

Dyce, Alexander (1866), *Works of Shakespeare*, 2nd edn, vol. 8.

Egan, Gabriel (2010), *The Struggle for Shakespeare's Text*, Cambridge: CUP.

Egan, Gabriel (2017), 'A History of Shakespearean Authorship Attribution', in Gary Taylor and Gabriel Egan (eds), *The New Oxford Shakespeare Authorship Companion*, 27-47, Oxford: OUP.

Eggert, Paul (2019), *The Work and the Reader in Literary Studies*, Cambridge: CUP.

Erne, Lukas (2003), *Shakespeare as Literary Dramatist*, Cambridge: CUP.

Erne, Lukas (2013), *Shakespeare and the Book Trade*, Cambridge: CUP.

Erne, Lukas (2015), 'Emendation and the Editorial Reconfiguration of Shakespeare', in Margaret Jane Kidnie and Sonia Massai (eds), *Shakespeare and Textual Studies*, 300-13, Cambridge: CUP.

Estill, Laura (2013), 'Commonplacing Readers', in Margaret Jane Kidnie and Sonia Massai (eds), *Shakespeare and Textual Studies*, 149-78, Cambridge: CUP.

Estill, Laura, Diane K. Jakacki and Michael Ullyot, eds (2016), *Early Modern Studies after the Digital Turn*, Toronto: Iter and Tempe Arizona, ACMRS.

Estill, Laura and Andie Silva (2018), 'Storing and Accessing
    Knowledge: Digital Tools for the Study of Early Modern Drama',
    in Janelle Jenstad, Mark Kaethler, and Jennifer Roberts-Smith
    (eds), *Shakespeare's Language in Digital Media*, 131-43,
    Routledge.

Farmer, Alan B. (2015) 'Shakespeare as Leading Playwright in Print,
    1598-1608/9', in Margaret Jane Kidnie and Sonia Massai (eds),
    Shakespeare and Textual Studies, 87-104, Cambridge: CUP.

Farmer, Alan B. (2016), 'Playbooks and the Question of
    Ephemerality', in Heidi Brayman et al (eds), *The Book in History,
    The Book as History: New Intersections of the Material Text*,
    87-125, New Haven, CT: Yale University Press.

Farmer, Alan B. (2020), 'Widow Publishers in London, 1540-1640',
    in Valerie Wayne (ed.), *Women's Labour and the History of the
    Book in Early Modern England*, 47-73, Bloomsbury.

Farmer, Alan B. and Zachary Lesser (2005), 'The Popularity of
    Playbooks Revisited', *SQ* 56: 1-32.

Farmer, Alan B. and Zachary Lesser (2013), 'What is Print
    Popularity? A Map of the Elizabethan Book Trade', in Andy
    Kesson and Emma Smith (eds), *The Elizabethan Top Ten:
    Defining Print Popularity in Early Modern England*, 19-54,
    Burlington, VT: Ashgate.

Finkelstein, David and Alistair McCleery, eds (2006), *The Book
    History Reader*, 2nd edn, New York: Routledge.

Forker, Charles, ed. (2002), *Richard II*, Arden.

Foucault, Michel (2006), 'What is an Author', in David Finkelstein
    and Alistair McCleery (eds), *The Book History Reader*, 2nd edn,
    281-91, New York: Routledge.

Galey, Alan (2010), 'Networks of Deep Impression: Shakespeare and
    the History of Information', *SQ* 61: 289-312.

Galey, Alan (2014), *The Shakespearean Archive: Experiments in
    New Media from the Renaissance to Postmodernity*, Cambridge:
    CUP.

Galey, Alan and Rebecca Niles (2017), 'Moving Parts: Digital
    Modeling and the Infrastructures of Shakespeare Editing', *SQ* 68:
    21-55.

Gaskell, Philip (1972), *An Introduction to Bibliography*, Oxford:
    OUP.

Geddes, Louise (2019), 'Some Tweeting Cleopatra: Crossing Borders
    on and off the Shakespearean Stage', in Christy Desmet et al

(eds), *Shakespeare/Not Shakespeare*, New York: 420-31, Palgrave Macmillan.

Gossett, Suzanne, ed. (2004), *Pericles*, Arden.

Gossett, Suzanne and Helen Wilcox, eds (2019), *All's Well That Ends Well*, Arden.

Greenblatt, Stephen (1998), *Shakespearean Negotiations: The Circulation of Social Energy in Renaissance England*, Berkeley: University of California Press.

Greenblatt, Stephen, Walter Cohen, Suzanne Gossett, Jean E. Howard, Katharine Eisaman Maus and Gordon McMullan, eds (2015), *The Norton Shakespeare*, 3rd edn, New York: Norton.

Greg, W.W. (1931), *Dramatic Documents from the Elizabethan Playhouses: Stage Plots, Actors' Parts, Prompt Books*, 2 vols, Oxford: Clarendon.

Greg, W.W. (1939), *A Bibliography of the English Printed Drama to the Restoration*, For the Bibliographical Society at the University Press, Oxford.

Greg, W.W. (1950–51), 'The Rationale of Copy-Text', *Studies in Bibliography* 3: 19-36.

Gurr, Andrew (2008), 'Did Shakespeare Own His Own Playbooks', *RES* n.s. 60: 207-27.

Hackel, Heidi Brayman (1997), '"Rowme" of its Own: Printed Drama in Early Libraries', in John D. Cox and David Scott Kastan (eds), *A New History of Early English Drama*, 113-30, New York: Columbia University Press.

Halasz, Alexandra (2013), 'The Stationers' Shakespeare', in Marta Straznicky (ed.), *Shakespeare's Stationers: Studies in Cultural Bibliography*, 16-27, Philadelphia: University of Pennsylvania Press.

Hargrave, Joscelyn (2019), *The Evolution of Editorial Style in Early Modern England*, Cham, Switzerland: Palgrave Macmillan.

Heffernan, Megan (2013), 'Turning Sonnets into Poems: Textual Affect and John Benson's Metaphysical Shakespeare', *SQ* 64: 71-98.

Hirrel, Michael J. (2010), 'Duration of Performances and Lengths of Plays: How Shall We Beguile the Lazy Time?', *SQ* 61 (2): 159-82.

Hodgdon, Barbara, ed. (2010), *The Taming of the Shrew*, Arden.

Holderness, Graham, Brian Loughrey and Andrew Murphy (1995), '"What's the matter?" Shakespeare and Textual Theory', *Textual Practice* 9: 93-219.

Holland, Peter, ed. (2013), *Coriolanus*, Arden.

Honigmann, E.A.J. (1965), *The Stability of Shakespeare's Text*, Edward Arnold.

Hooks, Adam G. (2016), *Selling Shakespeare: Biography, Bibliography, and the Book Trade*, Cambridge: CUP.

Hope, Jonathan and Michael Witmore (2010), 'The Hundredth Psalm to the Tune of "Green Sleeves": Digital Approaches to Shakespeare's Language of Genre', *SQ* 61: 357-90.

Hoy, Cyrus (1956–62), 'The Shares of Fletcher and his Collaborators in the Beaumont and Fletcher Canon I-VII', *Studies in Bibliography* 8: 129-46; 9: 143-62; 11: 85-106; 12: 91-116; 13:77-108; 14: 45-67; 15: 71-90.

Jackson, MacDonald P. (2003), *Defining Shakespeare: Pericles as a Test Case*, Oxford: OUP.

Jackson, MacDonald P. (2018), 'Vocabulary, Chronology, and the First Quarto (1603) of *Hamlet*', *MRDE* 31: 17-42.

Jenkins, Harold, ed. (1982), *Hamlet*, Arden.

Jenstad, Janelle (2020), 'The Politics of Remediation', unpub. SAA seminar paper.

Jenstad, Janelle, Mark Kaethler and Jennifer Roberts-Smith, eds (2018), *Shakespeare's Language in New Media: Old Worlds, New Tools*, Abingdon: Routledge.

Jowett, John, ed. (2000), *The Tragedy of Richard III*, Oxford: OUP.

Jowett, John, ed. (2011), *Sir Thomas More*, Arden.

Jowett, John, ed. (2017a), *Hamlet*, in Gary Taylor et al (gen. eds), *The New Oxford Shakespeare*, critical ref. edn, 1.1115-1228, Oxford: OUP.

Jowett, John (2017b), 'Shakespeare, Early Modern Textual Cultures, and This Edition: An Introduction', in Gary Taylor et al (gen. eds), *The New Oxford Shakespeare*, critical ref. edn, 1.xxiii–xlviii, Oxford: OUP.

Jowett, John (2017c), 'Shakespeare and the Kingdom of Error', in Gary Taylor et al (gen. eds), *The New Oxford Shakespeare*, critical ref. edn, 1.xlix–lxiv, Oxford: OUP.

Jowett, John, ed. (2017d), *The Third Part of Henry the Sixth*, in Gary Taylor et al (gen. eds), *The New Oxford Shakespeare*, critical ref. edn, 2.2559-2642, Oxford: OUP.

Jowett, John (2020), 'The Origins of *Richard Duke of York*', in Rory Loughnane and Andrew J. Power (eds), *Early Shakespeare, 1588-1594*, 235-60, Cambridge: CUP.

Kastan, David (2001), *Shakespeare and the Book*, Cambridge: CUP.

Kesson, Andy and Emma Smith, eds (2013), *The Elizabethan Top Ten: Defining Print Popularity in Early Modern England*, Burlington, VT: Ashgate.

Kewes, Paulina (1998), *Authorship and Appropriation: Writing for the Stage in England 1660-1710*, Oxford: OUP.

Kidnie, Margaret Jane and Sonia Massai, eds (2013), *Shakespeare and Textual Studies*, Cambridge: CUP.

Kingsley-Smith, Jane (2019), *The Afterlife of Shakespeare's Sonnets*, Cambridge: CUP.

Knight, Jeffrey Todd (2013), *Bound to Read: Compilations, Collections and the Making of Renaissance Literature*, Philadelphia: University of Pennsylvania Press.

Knight, Jeffrey Todd (2017), 'Economies of Scale: Shakespeare and Book History', *Literature Compass* 2.

Knight, Leah, Micheline White and Elizabeth Sauer, eds (2018), *Women's Bookscapes in Early Modern Britain: Reading, Ownership, Circulation*, Ann Arbor: University of Michigan Press.

Knowles, Ronald, ed. (1999), *King Henry VI Part 2*, Arden.

Knutson, Roslyn Lander (1997), 'The Repertory', in John D. Cox and David Scott Kastan (eds), *A New History of Early English Drama*, 461-80, New York: Columbia University Press.

Knutson, Roslyn L. and David McInnis (2020), 'Lost Documents, Absent Documents, Forged Documents' in Tiffany Stern (ed.), *Rethinking Theatrical Documents in Shakespeare's England*, 241-59, Bloomsbury.

Lancashire, Ian and Elisa Tersigni (2018), 'Shakespeare's Hard Words, and Our Hard Senses', in Janelle Jenstad et al (eds), *Shakespeare's Language in New Media: Old Worlds, New Tools*, 27-46, Abingdon: Routledge.

Lanier, Douglas (2017), 'Afterword', in Christy Desmet et al (eds), *Shakespeare/Not Shakespeare*, 293-305, New York: Palgrave Macmillan.

Lavagnino, John (2014), 'Shakespeare in the Digital Humanities', in Christie Carson and Peter Kirwan (eds), *Shakespeare and the Digital World: Redefining Scholarship and Practice*, 14-23, Cambridge: CUP.

Lesser, Zachary (2015), *Hamlet after Q1: An Uncanny History of the Shakespearean Text*, Philadelphia: University of Pennsylvania Press.

Lesser, Zachary and Peter Stallybrass (2008), 'The First Literary *Hamlet* and the Commonplacing of Professional Plays', *SQ* 59: 371-420.

Lesser, Zachary and Peter Stallybrass (2015), 'Shakespeare Between Pamphlet and Book, 1608-1619', in Margaret Jane Kidnie and Sonia Massai (eds), *Shakespeare and Textual Studies*, 105-33, Cambridge: CUP.

Lindenbaum, Sarah (2018), 'Hiding in Plain Sight: How Electronic Records Can Lead Us to Early Modern Women Readers' in Leah Knight et al (eds), *Women's Bookscapes in Early Modern Britain: Reading, Ownership, Circulation*, 193-213, Ann Arbor: University of Michigan Press.

Loffman, Claire and Harriet Phillips, eds (2018), *A Handbook of Editing Early Modern Texts*, Routledge.

Loughnane, Rory, ed. (2017a), *All's Well that Ends Well*, in Gary Taylor et al (gen. eds), *The New Oxford Shakespeare*, critical ref. edn: 2.2067-2039, Oxford: OUP.

Loughnane, Rory, ed. (2017b), *2 Henry VI*, in Gary Taylor et al (gen. eds), *The New Oxford Shakespeare*, critical ref. edn: 2.2471-2558, Oxford: OUP.

Loughnane, Rory, ed. (2017c), *Pericles, Prince of Tyre*, in Gary Taylor et al (gen. eds), *The New Oxford Shakespeare*, critical ref. edn: 1.1340-1432, Oxford: OUP.

Loughnane, Rory and Andrew J. Power, eds. (2020), *Early Shakespeare, 1588-1594*, Cambridge: CUP.

Maguire, Laurie E. (1996), *Shakespeare's Suspect Texts*, Cambridge: CUP.

Maguire, Laurie E. (2000), 'Feminist Editing and the Body of the Text', in Dympna Callaghan (ed.), *A Feminist Companion to Shakespeare*, 59-79, Malden MA: Blackwell.

Maguire, Laurie E. and Thomas L. Berger, eds (1998), *Textual Formations and Reformations*, Newark: University of Delaware Press.

Maguire, Laurie E. and Emma Smith (2012), 'Many Hands: A New Shakespeare Collaboration', *TLS*, 19 April 2012.

Malone, Edmond (1780), *Supplement to the Edition of Shakespeare's Plays Published in 1778*, 2 vols.

Malone, Edmond (1790), *The Plays and Poems of William Shakespeare*, 10 vols.

Malone, Toby (2018), 'A Digital Parallel-Text Approach to Performance Historiography', in Janelle Jenstad et al (eds),

Shakespeare's Language in New Media: Old Worlds, New Tools, 105-23, Abingdon: Routledge.

Marcus, Leah S. (1996), *Unediting the Renaissance: Shakespeare, Marlowe, Milton*, Routledge.

Marcus, Leah S. (2007), 'Editing Shakespeare in a Post-Modern age', in Andrew Murphy (ed.), *A Concise Companion to Shakespeare and the Text*, 128-44, Malden, MA: Blackwell.

Marcus, Leah S. (2017), *How Shakespeare Became Colonial: Editorial Tradition and the British Empire*, Abingdon: Routledge.

Marino, James J. (2011), *Owning William Shakespeare: The King's Men and their Intellectual Property*, Philadelphia: University of Pennsylvania Press.

Marino, James J. (2020), 'Parts and the Playscript: Seven Questions', in Tiffany Stern (ed.), *Rethinking Theatrical Documents in Shakespeare's England*, 52-67, Bloomsbury.

Marston, John (1975), *The Malcontent*, ed. George K. Hunter, Methuen.

Massai, Sonia (2007), *Shakespeare and the Rise of the Editor*, Cambridge: CUP.

Massai, Sonia (2013), 'Edward Blount, the Herberts, and the First Folio' in Marta Straznicky (ed.), *Shakespeare's Stationers: Studies in Cultural Bibliography*, 132-46, Philadelphia: University of Pennsylvania Press.

Massai, Sonia (2015), 'The Mixed Fortunes of Shakespeare in Print', in Margaret Jane Kidnie and Sonia Massai (eds), *Shakespeare and Textual Studies*, 57-68, Cambridge: CUP.

Masten, Jeffrey (1997), *Textual Intercourse: Collaboration, Authorship, and Sexualities in Renaissance Drama*, Cambridge: CUP.

Masten, Jeffrey (2016), 'Glossing and T*pping: Editing Sexuality, Race and Gender in *Othello*' in Valerie Traub (ed.), *The Oxford Handbook of Shakespeare and Embodiment*, 570-85, Oxford: OUP.

Mayer, Jean-Christophe (2018), *Shakespeare's Early Readers*, Cambridge: CUP.

McGann, Jerome J. (1983), *A Critique of Modern Textual Criticism*, Chicago: University of Chicago Press.

McLeod, Randall (1981/2), 'Un"Editing" Shakespeare', *SubStance* 10/11: 26-55.

McKenzie, D.F. (1969), 'Printers of the Mind: Some Notes on Bibliographical Theories and Printing-House Practices', *Studies in Bibliography* 22: 1-75.

McMillin, Scott (2005), *The First Quarto of Othello*, Cambridge: CUP.

McMullan, Gordon, ed. (2000), *King Henry VIII*, Arden.

McMullan, Gordon and Suzanne Gossett (2015), 'General Textual Introduction', in Stephen Greenblatt et al (eds), *The Norton Shakespeare*, 3rd edn, 75-92, New York: Norton.

Mowat, Barbara (1998), 'The Problem of Shakespeare's Texts', in Laurie E. Maguire and Thomas L. Berger (eds), *Textual Formations and Reformations*, 131-48, Newark: University of Delaware Press.

Moxon, Joseph (1677), *Mechanick Exercises or The Doctrine of Handy-works*.

Murphy, Andrew, ed. (2007a), *A Concise Companion to Shakespeare and the Text*, Malden, MA: Blackwell.

Murphy, Andrew (2007b), 'The Birth of the Editor', in Andrew Murphy (ed.), *A Concise Companion to Shakespeare and the Text*, 93-108, Malden, MA: Blackwell.

Murphy, Andrew (2010), 'Shakespeare Goes Digital: Three Open Internet Editions', *SQ* 61: 401-14.

Nashe, Thomas (1966), *Works*, ed. Ronald B. McKerrow, corrected F.P. Wilson, 5 vols, Oxford: OUP.

Newcomb, Lori Humphrey (2020), 'Frances Wolfreston's Annotations as Labours of Love', in Valerie Wayne (ed.), *Women's Labour and the History of the Book in Early Modern England*, 243-66, Bloomsbury.

Niles, Rebecca and Michael Poston (2016), 'Re-Modeling the Edition: Creating the Corpus of Folger Digital Texts' in Laura Estill et al (eds), *Early Modern Studies after the Digital Turn*, 117-44, Toronto: Iter and Tempe Arizona, ACMRS.

North, Marcy (2006), 'The Sonnets and Book History', in Michael Schoenfeldt (ed.), *A Companion to Shakespeare's Sonnets*, 204-21, Malden, MA: Blackwell.

Oliphant, E.H.C. (1927), *The Plays of Beaumont and Fletcher: An Attempt to Determine Their Respective Shares and the Shares of Others*, New Haven, CT: Yale University Press.

Orgel, Stephen (1981), 'What is a Text', *Research Opportunities in Renaissance Drama* 24: 3-6.

Ozment, Kate (2020), 'Rationale for Feminist Bibliography', *Textual Cultures* 13: 149-78.

Pitcher, John, ed. (2010), *The Winter's Tale*, Arden.

Pollard, Alfred W. (1909), *Shakespeare Folios and Quartos: A Study in the Bibliography of Shakespeare's Plays, 1594-1685*, Methuen.

Pope, Alexander (1725), *Works of Shakespeare*, 6 vols, Tonson.

Potter, Lois, ed. (2015), *The Two Noble Kinsmen*, rev. edn, Arden.

Preiss, Richard (2020), 'Undocumented: Improvisation, Rehearsal, and the Clown', in Tiffany Stern (ed.), *Rethinking Theatrical Documents in Shakespeare's England*, 68-88, Bloomsbury.

Proudfoot, Richard and Nicola Bennett, eds (2017), *King Edward III*, Arden.

Pruitt, Anna, ed. (2017), *Richard II*, in Gary Taylor et al (gen. eds), *The New Oxford Shakespeare*, critical ref. edn, 1.357–447, Oxford: OUP.

Purkis, James (2015), 'Shakespeare's "Strayng" Manuscripts', in Margaret Jane Kidnie and Sonia Massai (eds), *Shakespeare and Textual Studies*, 39-53, Cambridge: CUP.

Rhodes, Neil (2013), 'Shakespeare's Popularity and the Origins of the Canon', in Andy Kesson and Emma Smith (eds), *The Elizabethan Top Ten: Defining Print Popularity in Early Modern England*, 101-19, Burlington, VT: Ashgate.

Rowe, Katherine (2014), 'Living with Digital Incunables, or a "Good-enough" Shakespeare Text', in Christie Carson and Peter Kirwan (eds), *Shakespeare and the Digital World: Redefining Scholarship and Practice*, 144-59, Cambridge: CUP.

Seary, Lewis (1990), *Lewis Theobald and the Editing of Shakespeare*, Oxford: Clarendon.

Shillingsburg, Peter (1996), *Scholarly Editing in the Computer Age*, 3rd edn, Ann Arbor: University of Michigan Press.

Siemens, Raymond, Constance Crompton, Daniel Powell, Alyssa Arbuckle with the Devonshire Manuscript Editorial Group (2018), 'Social Editing and the Devonshire Manuscript' in Claire Loffman and Harriet Phillips (eds), *A Handbook of Editing Early Modern Texts*, 193-8, Routledge.

Siemon, James, ed. (2009), *Richard III*, Arden.

Silverstone, Catherine, ed. (2015), *Titus Andronicus*, in Stephen Greenblatt et al (eds), *The Norton Shakespeare*, 3rd edn, 491-554, New York: Norton.

Smith, Bruce R. (2014), 'Getting Back to the Library, Getting Back to the Body', in Christie Carson and Peter Kirwan (eds), *Shakespeare and the Digital World: Redefining Scholarship and Practice*, 24-32, Cambridge: CUP.

Smith, Helen (2012), *Grossly Material Things: Women and Book Production in Early Modern England*, Oxford: OUP.

Smith, Helen (2013), '"To London All"? Mapping Shakespeare in Print, 1593-1598', in Margaret Jane Kidnie and Sonia Massai (eds), *Shakespeare and Textual Studies*, 69-86, Cambridge: CUP.

Smyth, Adam (2018), *Material Texts in Early Modern England*, Cambridge: CUP.

Stallybrass, Peter and Roger Chartier (2007), 'Reading and Authorship: The Circulation of Shakespeare 1590-1619', in Andrew Murphy (ed.), *A Concise Companion to Shakespeare and the Text*, 35-56, Malden, MA: Blackwell.

Steggle, Matthew (2020), 'Title- and Scene-boards: The Largest, Shortest Documents', in Tiffany Stern, (ed.), *Rethinking Theatrical Documents in Shakespeare's England*, 91-110, Bloomsbury.

Stern, Tiffany (2007), '"I Do Wish You Had Mentioned Garrick": The Absence of Garrick in Johnson's Shakespeare', in Eric Rasmussen and Aaron Santesso (eds), *Comparative Excellence: Essays on Shakespeare and Johnson*, 70-96, New York: AMS.

Stern, Tiffany (2008), 'Watching as Reading: The Audience and Written Text in the Early Modern Playhouse', in Laurie E. Maguire (ed.), *How to Do Things with Shakespeare*, 136-59, Oxford: OUP.

Stern, Tiffany (2009), *Documents of Performance*, Cambridge: CUP.

Stern, Tiffany (2013), 'Sermons, Plays and Note-Takers, *Hamlet* Q1 as a "Noted" Text', *Shakespeare Survey* 66: 1-23.

Stern, Tiffany, ed. (2020), *Rethinking Theatrical Documents in Shakespeare's England*, Bloomsbury.

Stewart, Alan, ed. (2015), *King Richard II*, in Stephen Greenblatt et al (eds), *The Norton Shakespeare* 3rd edn, 885-956, New York: Norton.

Straznicky, Marta, ed. (2013), *Shakespeare's Stationers: Studies in Cultural Bibliography*, Philadelphia: University of Pennsylvania Press.

Streitfeld, David (2019), 'Big Brother is Botching: Orwell Gets a Rewrite', *New York Times*, 19 August: B1–6.

Tanselle, G. Thomas (2005), *Textual Criticism Since Greg: A Chronicle, 1950-85*, Charlottesville, NC: Bibliographical Society.

Taylor, Gary (1986), 'Inventing Shakespeare', *Deutsche Shakespeare-Gesellschaft West: Jahrbuch*: 26-44.

Taylor, Gary (1989), 'Textual Double Knots: "Make Rope's in Such
     a Scarre"', in Ronald L. Dotterer (ed.), *Shakespeare: Text,
     Subtext, and Context*, 163-85, Selingsgrove, PA: Susquehanna
     University Press.

Taylor, Gary (1993), ''Swounds Revisited', in Gary Taylor and John
     Jowett, *Shakespeare Reshaped 1606-1623*, 51-106, Oxford:
     Clarendon.

Taylor, Gary (2017a), '*All's Well That Ends Well*: Text, Date and
     Adaptation', in Gary Taylor and Gabriel Egan (eds), *The New
     Oxford Shakespeare Authorship Companion*, 337-65, Oxford:
     OUP.

Taylor, Gary (2017b), 'Artiginality: Authorship after
     Postmodernism', in Gary Taylor and Gabriel Egan (eds), *The
     New Oxford Shakespeare Authorship Companion*, 3-26, Oxford:
     OUP.

Taylor, Gary (2017c), 'Did Shakespeare Write *The Spanish Tragedy*
     Additions?', in Gary Taylor and Gabriel Egan (eds), *The New
     Oxford Shakespeare Authorship Companion*, 246-60, Oxford:
     OUP.

Taylor, Gary and Terri Bourus (2016), 'Why Read *This* Complete
     Works', in Gary Taylor et al (gen. eds), *The New Oxford
     Shakespeare*, 45-58, Oxford: OUP.

Taylor, Gary and Gabriel Egan, eds (2017), *The New Oxford
     Shakespeare Authorship Companion*, Oxford: OUP.

Taylor, Gary, John Jowett, Terri Bourus and Gabriel Egan, gen. eds
     (2016), *The New Oxford Shakespeare*, Oxford: OUP.

Taylor, Gary and John Jowett, Terri Bourus and Gabriel Egan, gen.
     eds (2017), *The New Oxford Shakespeare*, critical ref. edn,
     2 vols., Oxford: OUP.

Taylor, Gary and John Lavagnino, eds (2007a), *Thomas Middleton:
     The Collected Works*, Oxford: OUP.

Taylor, Gary and John Lavagnino, eds (2007b), *Thomas Middleton
     and Early Modern Textual Culture: A Companion to the
     Collected Works*, Oxford: OUP.

Taylor, Gary and Rory Loughnane (2017), 'The Canon and
     Chronology of Shakespeare's Works', in Gary Taylor and Gabriel
     Egan (eds), *The New Oxford Shakespeare Authorship
     Companion*, 417-602, Oxford: OUP.

Taylor, Gary, Terri Bourus, Rory Loughnane, Anna Pruitt and
     Francis X. Connor, eds (2017), *Titus Andronicus*, in Gary Taylor

et al (gen. eds), *The New Oxford Shakespeare*, critical ref. edn, 1.127–213, Oxford: OUP.

Thompson, Ann, ed. (1984), *The Taming of the Shrew*, Cambridge: CUP.

Thompson, Ann and Neil Taylor, eds (2006), *Hamlet*, Arden.

Tumelson, Ronald (2006), 'Ferdinand's Wife and Prospero's Wise', *Shakespeare Survey* 59: 79-90.

TxC (1987), Wells, Stanley and Gary Taylor, eds, *William Shakespeare: A Textual Companion*, Oxford: OUP.

Ullyot, Michael and Adam James Bradley (2018), 'Past Texts, Present Tools, and Future Critics: Toward *Rhetorical Schematics*', in Janelle Jenstad et al (eds), *Shakespeare's Language in New Media: Old Worlds, New Tools*, 144-56, Abingdon: Routledge.

Urkowitz, Steven (1988), 'If I Mistake in Those Foundations Which I Build Upon: Peter Alexander's Textual Analysis of *Henry VI Parts 2 and 3*', *ELR* 18: 230-56.

Vaughan, Virginia and Aldan Vaughan, eds (1999), *The Tempest*, Arden.

Vickers, Brian (2002), *Shakespeare Co-Author*, Oxford: OUP.

Vickers, Brian (2020), 'Infecting the Teller', *TLS* 17 March: 14-15.

Vickers, Brian and Marcus Dahl (2012), '*All's Well That Ends Well*: An Attribution Refuted', *TLS*, 11 May.

Warren, Michael and Gary Taylor, eds (1983), *The Division of the Kingdoms: Shakespeare's Two Versions of King Lear*, Oxford: OUP.

Wayne, Valerie (1998), 'The Sexual Politics of Textual Transmission', in Laurie E. Maguire and Thomas L. Berger (eds), *Textual Formations and Reformations*, 179-210, Newark: University of Delaware Press.

Wayne, Valerie, ed. (2017), *Cymbeline*, Arden.

Wayne, Valerie (2018), 'The Gendered Text and Its Labour', in Valerie Traub (ed.), *The Oxford Handbook of Shakespeare and Embodiment*, 549-68, Oxford: OUP.

Wayne, Valerie, ed. (2020), *Women's Labour and the History of the Book in Early Modern England*, Bloomsbury.

Weis, René, ed. (2012), *Romeo and Juliet*, Arden.

Wells, Stanley and Gary Taylor, gen. eds (1986), *The Oxford Shakespeare: The Complete Works*, Oxford: OUP.

Werstine, Paul (1998), 'Touring and the Construction of Shakespeare Textual Criticism', in Laurie E. Maguire and Thomas L. Berger (eds), *Textual Formations and Reformations*, 45-66, Newark: University of Delaware Press.

Werstine, Paul (2007), 'The Science of Editing', in Andrew Murphy (ed.), *A Concise Companion to Shakespeare and the Text*, 109-27, Malden, MA: Blackwell.

Werstine, Paul (2013), *Early Modern Playhouse Manuscripts and the Editing of Shakespeare*, Cambridge: CUP.

Wiggins, Martin and Catherine Richardson (2013–15), *British Drama: A Catalogue*, 6 vols, Oxford: OUP.

Yachnin, Paul (2003), 'Shakespeare's Problem Plays', in Richard Dutton and Jean E. Howard (eds), *A Companion to Shakespeare's Work: The Poems, Problem Comedies, Late Plays*, 46-68, Oxford: Blackwell.

Yarn, Molly (2020), 'Katharine Lee Bates and Women's Editions of Shakespeare for Students', in Valerie Wayne (ed.), *Women's Labour and the History of the Book in Early Modern England*, 187-203, Bloomsbury.

INDEX